TRACING YOUR
family tree

IN ENGLAND, IRELAND, SCOTLAND AND WALES

Kathy Chater

TRACING YOUR
family tree

IN ENGLAND, IRELAND, SCOTLAND AND WALES

DISCOVER YOUR ROOTS AND EXPLORE YOUR FAMILY'S HISTORY

HERMES
HOUSE

This edition is published by Hermes House

Hermes House is an imprint of Anness Publishing Ltd
Hermes House, 88–89 Blackfriars Road, London SE1 8HA
tel. 020 7401 2077; fax 020 7633 9499
www.hermeshouse.com; www.annesspublishing.com

© Anness Publishing Ltd 2003, 2004, 2005, 2006

A CIP catalogue record for this book is available from the British Library.

Publisher: Joanna Lorenz
Managing Editor: Helen Sudell
Senior Editor: Joanne Rippin
Project Editor: Melanie Hibbert
Editor: Alison Bolus
Designer: Mike Morey
Production Controller: Wendy Lawson

Publisher's note: England's public records were held by the Public Record Office up until
June 2003, when its name was changed to The National Archives. Books and leaflets
published before this date may still refer to the Public Record Office or PRO, in which
case the reader should assume the reference is to The National Archives, or TNA.

For a list of abbreviations and acronyms used in this book, please see p.7.

1 3 5 7 9 10 8 6 4 2

Contents

Introduction 6

First steps 8

How to begin 10
Family photographs 14
A basic family tree 16
Names 20
Research skills 22
Keeping records 24
Interviewing people 26

Back to the early 1800s 28

Certificates after 1837 30
Other indexes at the Family
　Record Centre 34
Censuses 36
The International Genealogical
　Index and other indexes 40
Published material 42
Using the Internet 44
Wills, administrations and
　death duties 48
Inquests 52
Newspapers and periodicals 54

Going back to 1538 56

Record offices, history centres
　and libraries 58
Births, christenings, marriages
　and burials in parish registers 62
Other parish records 66
The poor of the parish 68
Orphans and foundlings 72
Records for other Christian
　denominations 74
Maps 78

**Other countries in the
British Isles** 80

Welsh records 82
Scottish records 84
Irish records 88
Channel Islands records 92
Isle of Man records 94

Working lives 96

Education 98
Apprenticeships 102
Guilds and freemen 104
The professions 106
Other occupations 110
Licences 114
Elections, poll books and
　electoral registers 116
Trade unions and
　friendly societies 118
Bankruptcy and insolvency 120
Physical and mental illness 122

For Crown and Country 126

Members of the armed forces 128
Army records 131
Royal Air Force records 134
The militia, posse comitatis
　and volunteers 136
Royal Navy records 138
Merchant Navy records 142
Other maritime occupations 144
Lifecycle checklist 146

Law and property 148

Researching legal records 150
Church courts 152
Manorial records 154
Crime and punishment 156
Transportation records 162
Equity law: property and money 164

Land ownership and wealth 166
Taxes 172
Customs and excise and
　the Coastguard 174
Rich man, poor man checklist 176

Migrant ancestors 178

Researching migrant ancestors 180
Jewish ancestors 182
French ancestors 184
German and Dutch ancestors 186
Black ancestors 188
Indian ancestors 190
Other overseas ancestors 192
Gypsies and other travellers 194

Emigrants 196

Researching emigrant ancestors 198
India and the Far East 201
North America 204
Canada 210
The Caribbean 212
Australia 214
New Zealand 216
Africa 218
Other British territories 220
British communities overseas 220

Appendices 224

Sources for pre-1538 research 226
Paleography 230
Latin 232
Name changes and
　important dates 234
Heraldry 236
Dates, money and measurements 239
Writing family history 240
Timeline 244
Specialist museums and libraries 248
Directories and ratebooks 249
Books 250
Addresses and websites 252
Picture acknowledgements 253
Index 254

Introduction

In today's increasingly globalized world, there is a desire to know more about ourselves as individuals and where we came from. As a result of this, family history is one of the fastest-growing hobbies.

This book is aimed at those who have British ancestry. There may be many other nations from which our forebears sprang, but, because British people (the English, the Welsh, the Scots, the Irish and the inhabitants of the many offshore islands that make up the United Kingdom) went to all the countries of the world, many of the world's billions of inhabitants have at least a drop of British blood in their veins.

Thirty years of tracing my own family history and working professionally as a television researcher have taught me a great deal about how to find and use information. One of the most important things I have learned is that you don't have to be an expert at everything; instead, you need to be able to find an expert in the relevant field and then tap into his or her expertise. Luckily, the world of genealogy is full of knowledgeable and enthusiastic people who are generous with their help and experience. The recent enthusiasm for the subject has also led to the appearance of a large number of magazines and publications, which provide further help for everyone from the total beginner to the highly experienced.

No single publication can hope to cover everything a family historian might need to

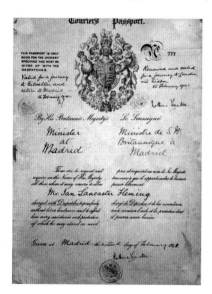

British people have always been great travellers for work, exploration or to settle.

Before the 20th century, this girl would have been lucky to see her second birthday.

The nursing profession has come a long way since it became a job for respectable women.

The children around this table in the early 1950s may have grown up to live and work all over the world.

Members of the armed forces may have brought brides from overseas back home to Britain.

know. The researcher needs to be aware of what the law was at a particular time and how legal changes would be reflected in records produced by the government and private organizations, which is what I have concentrated on here. This will help genealogists find out in the most interesting way how their ancestors contributed to their community and the wider world.

Abbreviations

Genealogy has a host of abbreviations and acronyms. The main ones used in the text are:

BMD = births, marriages and deaths

CMB = christenings, marriages and burials

CRO = County Record Office

DRO = Diocesan Record Office

FFHS = Federation of Family History Societies

FRC = Family Record Centre

GRO = General Register Office

IGI = International Genealogical Index

IHGS = Institute of Heraldic and Genealogical Studies

LDS = Church of Jesus Christ of Latter-day Saints (Mormons)

LMA = London Metropolitan Archives

PCC = Prerogative Court of Canterbury

PCY = Prerogative Court of York

PRO = Public Record Office, now known as The National Archives

PRONI = Public Record Office of Northern Ireland

SRO = Scottish Record Office

SoG = Society of Genealogists

TNA = The National Archives, previously known as the PRO

Many people, like this Italian ice-cream seller, settled in Britain because of political or economic factors.

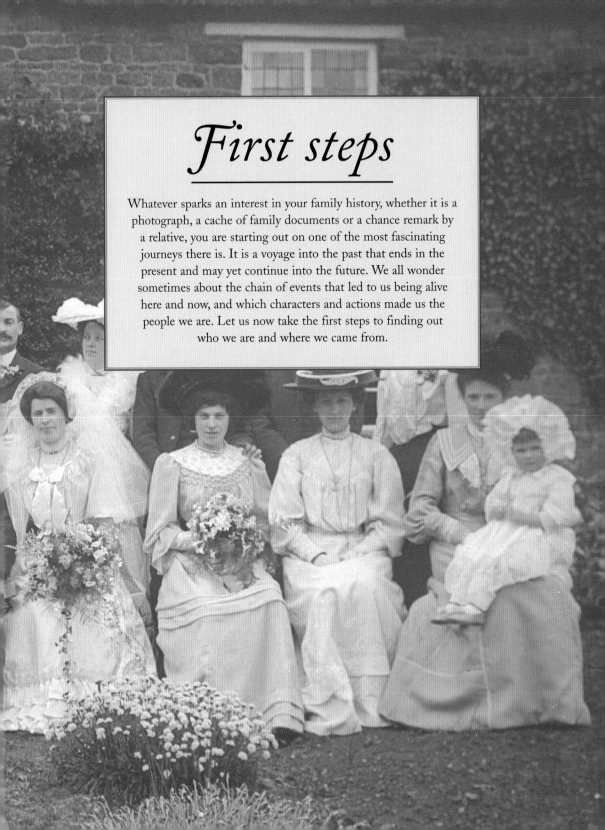

First steps

Whatever sparks an interest in your family history, whether it is a photograph, a cache of family documents or a chance remark by a relative, you are starting out on one of the most fascinating journeys there is. It is a voyage into the past that ends in the present and may yet continue into the future. We all wonder sometimes about the chain of events that led to us being alive here and now, and which characters and actions made us the people we are. Let us now take the first steps to finding out who we are and where we came from.

How to begin

There are several things that can spark off an interest in tracing a family's history. Sorting out possessions after a death, or when selling a family home usually reveals certificates, photographs and other mementos that give tantalizing clues to past joys and sorrows. Often these will be the starting point for a journey back in time.

A great deal of information can be gained from these items, and this, in turn, will give clues to further avenues of research. The first thing to do, therefore, is to sift through what you have found, concentrate on one particular individual, and use this information to create an outline of his or her life. Study these possessions to see if you can glean when and where the person was born, went to school, worked, married, etc. Dates and other information may come from what was

Interpreting the evidence

Among the treasured possessions found in an ancestor's home, you might find some of the following items:

- certificates (birth, marriage, death, adoption, baptism, confirmation)
- photographs and drawings
- home movies
- correspondence (letters and postcards)
- scrapbooks
- diaries
- household and/or business accounts books
- insurance policies
- newspaper cuttings
- family bibles and prayer books
- apprenticeship indentures

- books presented as prizes or inscribed to commemorate a special event
- examination or school-leaving certificates
- identity cards
- ration books (rationing in Britain started in World War II and continued until 1955)
- medals, badges and other objects connected with service in the armed forces
- membership of clubs or organizations such as friendly societies or the Freemasons
- passports
- holiday or travel souvenirs
- retirement presents
- memorial cards
- wills and other legal documents

written or inscribed on the items, but sometimes, especially with pictures (either photographs or movies), this can only be inferred from the content.

RECORDING YOUR FINDINGS

Write down all the information you have found in chronological order. It is a good idea to use a piece of paper divided into two columns. The first column, which should occupy about two-thirds of the page, is where you write the information gained; the other is for a note of its source. On another piece of paper, write down all the questions that are raised.

LEFT Florence Nightingale's birth certificate shows that she was born in the Italian city after which she was named.

LEFT This early
photo was taken
c.1840. The dress
and hairstyle give
clues to the date.

RIGHT A passport
issued in 1921.
Were the couple
going abroad for a
holiday or to work?

BELOW A couple
sign the wedding
register in 1947.

You may find that you recall being told stories relating to him or her. Write these down too (but bear in mind that they may not be accurate).

INVESTIGATING FAMILY MYTHS

Many families have myths and legends about their origins. These usually contain a nugget of truth, but it has probably been distorted over the centuries.

"We came over with William the Conqueror" is a common family myth. Although you will probably find out that your ancestor did not arrive in England from France in 1066 with William the Conqueror, you may discover that you do indeed have French ancestry: perhaps a Huguenot fleeing religious persecution in the 16th or 17th century, or someone escaping from the Reign of Terror that followed the French Revolution in the 18th century. More prosaically, perhaps, your ancestor may prove to be a French sailor who deserted his ship, perhaps smitten by the charms of a British girl.

Other stories, on further research, may prove to be not quite so romantic. Those with Irish ancestry, for example, may be told that their ancestors were heroes transported for political activity. Further research may indicate, however, that the Irish person was in fact transported for a squalid murder or theft, with no glamorous or political circumstances at all.

Another common family myth is illegitimate descent from a noble family. There are very few families who do not have an illegitimate child in their history, but often the story about aristocratic connections is just that – a tale concocted to make a child feel better about his or her fatherless state.

Family history is frequently full of surprises, some pleasant but others less agreeable. When doing research, you have to be prepared for both types.

BELOW This family shot was taken in 1947. Where are all the children now and do they have any useful documents or information?

CHOOSING A NAME TO RESEARCH

It is worth giving some thought to the branch of your family with which you decide to begin your research. Most people begin with their own family surname, but as your first steps into research should be regarded as practising, you should try to make your task as easy as possible. Therefore there are two major factors to consider before deciding which name and which family branch to research: the name and the location.

Name If you have a very common name, such as Smith, Jones or Brown,

you may be setting yourself too hard a task to begin with. An unusual name is far easier to extract from records.

Location London is the location of the major repositories, such as the Family Record Centre (FRC), The National Archives (TNA), the Society of Genealogists' (SoG) library and a number of County Record Offices (CROs) and other archives, so you might think that a London ancestor would be a good starting point. The problem with London, however, is that there are so many places where records relating to your ancestor might be located. Londoners

BELOW If one of your parents had a more unusual name than the other, it will be easier to track down their relatives.

ABOVE A London-dwelling ancestor may well be harder to locate than a town- or village-dwelling relative.

BELOW The exotic background of this picture is a photographer's set, not a clue that the girl was born abroad.

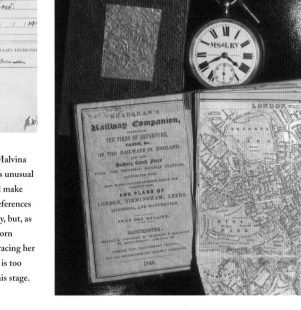

were highly mobile, and a house move of only a few hundred metres (yards) might mean that you have to shuttle between one record office and another. Moving from north to south of the river before 1888 also means changing the CROs and Diocesan Record Offices (DROs) that you will be using (there are at least seven covering different parts of the Greater London area).

If you do not live in London yourself, you will probably spend as much time travelling as you will researching. In addition, you will often find that records in London give much less detail than those elsewhere in Britain. Clerks in the capital were busy and did not know as much about the people who appeared before them as they did in a small neighbourhood.

Tracing ancestors in a smaller city, town or village can be easier. Each county usually has one main record office for all the places in it (although there may be small, local archives). This means that, even if your ancestor moved 32 km (20 miles), as long as he did not cross a county boundary, you will usually find the records in the same place. There are also less voluminous records to search in a small place. Going through the registers of some London parishes can occupy a whole wearisome day, while those in a rural town or village may take only a couple

ABOVE Malvina Brandeis's unusual name will make finding references to her easy, but, as she was born abroad, tracing her ancestors is too hard at this stage.

BELOW Postcards sent home from the front will show where a fiancée was living before marriage.

ABOVE This guard's pocket watch and the railway guide will give clues to an ancestor's job.

of hours. Even names that would be common in a town or city, such as Wood or King, may be rare in a small place, which means that you can be fairly sure that all those of the same name are potentially related.

If you are not doing the research yourself and are planning to hire someone to do it for you, consider how much time all this record searching will take and whether you are prepared to pay for it.

FURTHER HELP

Getting Started in Family History (TNA)
Swinnerton, Iain *Basic Facts about Sources for Family History in the Home* (FFHS)

Family photographs

Photographs of family members not only allow us to debate just who has inherited Great-grandmother's eyes or Uncle Charlie's nose, they also allow us to put faces to the names on official and unofficial documents. There may also be clues in the photographs which will suggest further avenues of research.

COLLECTING PHOTOGRAPHS

Get copies of as many family photographs as you can. Needless to say, if any of them are borrowed, make sure that you return them in good condition. If you need to send them, package them safely and use a secure, insured form of delivery. Ideally, though, they should be returned in person. This has the additional benefit

> ## Interpreting photographs
>
> It is, unfortunately, rare to find that your ancestors have written the date of the photograph, where it was taken and the names of all the people in it on the back (Note that this is a lesson for you to learn about your own snapshots.) Even if you can identify the people, it may be difficult to estimate the date, though clues include:
> - the clothes or uniforms the people were wearing
> - the approximate ages of any children in the picture (children's ages are easier to guess than adults')
> - cars or other methods of transport, such as bicycles or trains
> - shops or other buildings
> - the name of the photographer stamped on the back
> - the type of photographic process used

BELOW This photograph was taken in Northamptonshire around 1900. The grandfather's jacket suggests a countryman.

of giving time in which both you and the owner of the photograph may have thought of other things to discuss.

There are commercial companies that will copy photographs for you. They usually advertise in family history magazines, or you can look for them in local telephone directories. If a member of your family is a good photographer, you can get them photographed directly. They easiest way to do it today, however, is to scan them into your computer.

CLOTHES

People usually dressed up in their best to have their photograph taken. The clothes will therefore be their newest and most fashionable. A book on the history of costume should help you to identify roughly when the photograph was taken. Poor people, however, would not necessarily dress in the height of fashion. Employers often passed on their clothes to their servants, and many people could afford to dress only in second-hand garments.

People dressed in the uniforms of the armed services were often either just joining up or about to go away to war, which might give a clue to the year. As well as estimating the date, you can get a lot of information from the uniform itself. From the style of the uniform, the cap, badges, medals and other insignia you get clues to identify which service they served in, their rank and their regiment, ship or squadron, if you don't already know this from other sources.

Other uniforms can help you to find out what members of your family did. Policemen, postmen, lifeboatmen, bus conductors, hospital nurses and a host of other people all had different uniforms depending on where they worked. Lawyers and judges still wear different styles of wig. You may also find an ancestor wearing the regalia of a Freemason.

Even if your ancestors did not wear the formal uniform of a particular organization, you may get clues about their job from what they wore. It was far easier in the past to tell occupations from clothes than it is today. Many people wore aprons: parlour maids

LEFT A group of nurses pictured where they worked. Unfortunately, the photo is too small to offer any clues about where this might be.

BELOW LEFT Three Air Force pilots in Canada in 1941. The shot's informality shows they were on leave rather than on duty.

usually wore decorative ones, while maids-of-all-work wore much rougher coveralls; butchers' aprons were striped; carpenters' aprons had pockets to hold tools, and woodworkers wore a special side apron with a breastpad to protect their chests. The smocks of farm workers had different motifs and styles depending on what kind of work they did and the area they came from. Fishermen's sweaters also had different motifs, often unique to them, so that bodies washed up after accidents at sea could be identified. All these can be researched through books.

BUILDINGS

If you have a photograph taken outside a shop and the name is visible, you can find out how long it was in business by using street directories. The same applies to pictures taken outside a nursing home, perhaps of a group of nurses that includes your ancestor. If you know in which town it would have been, a street directory will help you to identify the place, and by looking through different years you can find out how long it was in existence there, which will give you dates between which the photograph might have

been taken. Books on transport will also help you to date cars or other vehicles in the photograph.

PHOTOGRAPHERS AND THEIR PHOTOGRAPHS

Street directories will also enable you to locate the photographer who took the picture, if the name is stamped on it. By looking through a succession of years, you can narrow down how long the photographer was in business. The photographic method used can also give clues, but you will need to consult an expert about this.

FURTHER HELP

Pols, Robert *Photography for Family Historians* (FFHS)
Pols, Robert *Looking at Old Photographs* (FFHS)
Pols, Robert *Dating Old Photographs* (FFHS)
Pols, Robert *Family Photographs 1860–1945* (TNA)
Pols, Robert *Understanding Old Photographs* (FFHS)
Swinnerton, I. *Identifying Your World War I Soldier from Badges and Photographs* (FFHS)

A basic family tree

From the very earliest stages of your research, you should find information that, combined with your own family knowledge, can be used to draw up a basic family tree. There are a number of ways in which you can record what is called a pedigree, which is the technical term for an outline showing descent from an ancestor. You will be doing more than simply charting the people from whom you descend – you will be finding out events in their lives to create a family history – but you still need a pedigree as a basis to work from and to refer to.

PREPARING A DROP-LINE CHART

The most common way of drawing up a basic family tree, and the method with which most people are familiar, is the drop-line chart.

Notes
- Keep each generation on the same level.
- Put men/husbands on the left and women/wives on the right.

- Put children in the order of their birth, oldest on the left, not (as was sometimes done in the past) all the boys first and then all the girls.
- Show children descending from the marriage or relationship of two people, not from the father or mother. Legitimate children are

ABOVE A pedigree of King James I, prepared *c.*1605, shows his descent from various Scottish kings and also the god Wodan. Accuracy cannot be relied on.

BELOW A drop-line chart shows descent from a single couple and contains only one family line.

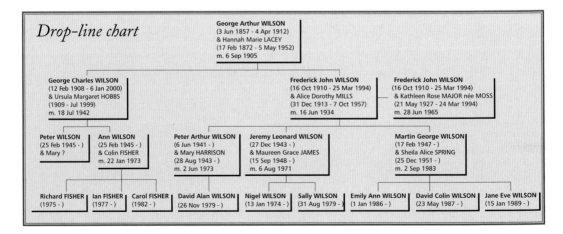

Drop-line chart

George Arthur WILSON
(3 Jun 1857 - 4 Apr 1912)
& Hannah Marie LACEY
(17 Feb 1872 - 5 May 1952)
m. 6 Sep 1905

George Charles WILSON
(12 Feb 1908 - 6 Jan 2000)
& Ursula Margaret HOBBS
(1909 - Jul 1999)
m. 18 Jul 1942

Frederick John WILSON
(16 Oct 1910 - 25 Mar 1994)
& Alice Dorothy MILLS
(31 Dec 1913 - 7 Oct 1957)
m. 16 Jun 1934

Frederick John WILSON
(16 Oct 1910 - 25 Mar 1994)
& Kathleen Rose MAJOR née MOSS
(21 May 1927 - 24 Mar 1994)
m. 28 Jun 1965

Peter WILSON
(25 Feb 1945 -)
& Mary ?

Ann WILSON
(25 Feb 1945 -)
& Colin FISHER
m. 22 Jan 1973

Peter Arthur WILSON
(6 Jun 1941 -)
& Mary HARRISON
(28 Aug 1943 -)
m. 2 Jun 1973

Jeremy Leonard WILSON
(27 Dec 1943 -)
& Maureen Grace JAMES
(15 Sep 1948 -)
m. 6 Aug 1971

Martin George WILSON
(17 Feb 1947 -)
& Sheila Alice SPRING
(25 Dec 1951 -)
m. 2 Sep 1983

Richard FISHER
(1975 -)

Ian FISHER
(1977 -)

Carol FISHER
(1982 -)

David Alan WILSON
(26 Nov 1979 -)

Nigel WILSON
(13 Jan 1974 -)

Sally WILSON
(31 Aug 1979 -)

Emily Ann WILSON
(1 Jan 1986 -)

David Colin WILSON
(23 May 1987 -)

Jane Eve WILSON
(15 Jan 1989 -)

shown by a solid line, illegitimate ones by a broken line.

- Put multiple marriages in order, left to right, and write the number against each one.
- Write the details of the marriage under the mother's name.
- Try not to cross lines of descent. This can be difficult if cousins marry and their descendants also marry, but with careful planning it should be possible.
- Do not include more than one branch of the family in the chart or it will soon become too big and unwieldy to use easily.
- Draw up a different chart for each branch, though this may be impossible where you find that different branches are descended from the same people through relatives marrying each other. When this happens, you may have to break some of these rules to fit it all in, especially if the people who marry are from different generations.

Uncles, aunts and cousins

The drop-line chart method is particularly useful for working out family relationships.

The types of relationship that sometimes give people trouble include great-aunts and great-uncles. In the diagram shown on the right:

- A and B are siblings.
- A is D's aunt/uncle; D is A's niece/nephew.
- A is F's great-aunt/uncle; F is A's great-niece/nephew.
- A is H's great-great-aunt/uncle; H is A's great-great-niece/nephew.

Cousinship is something else that gives people problems, especially when getting into the realm of second/third/fourth, etc., and trying to sort out who is a first/second cousin "removed". The rules, in fact, are very simple:

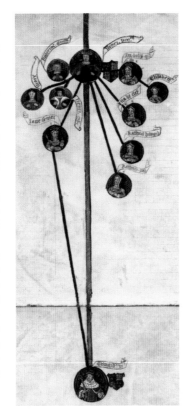

ABOVE A pedigree of Henry VIII, his six wives and their offspring. His son, the future Edward VI, is joined by a thick line.

BELOW Sorting out relationships can be complicated, but this chart should help.

- First cousins have the same set of grandparents.
- Second cousins have the same great-grandparents.
- Third cousins have the same great-great grandparents.

(The quick method is to count the number of "greats" and then add one to get the degree of cousinship.) Cousins are of the same generation, but not necessarily of similar age. When you want to work out the relationship between cousins who are "removed", i.e. who are not of the same generation, you need to go to the generation line on the family tree of the person from the younger generation, and then to move up to the generation of cousinship. In the diagram below, E is the first cousin once removed of D, because E's parent C is D's cousin. E's child G is the first cousin twice removed of D, because G is of the second generation below. G is the second cousin once removed of F, because E is F's second cousin and G is one generation below. Note that cousinship can be removed only upwards, i.e. F is not G's second cousin once removed.

This level of information can seem confusing, but in diagram form can become quite easily discernable.

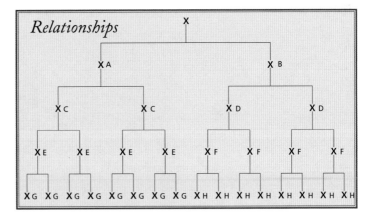

Relationships

CHOOSING ANOTHER METHOD
Alternative formats for beginning to build up a visual representation of your family tree to the drop-line chart include the birth brief, the narrative indented tree and the concentric tree.

Once you have gathered a substantial amount of information about your ancestors, you might want to construct a more elaborate chart for display; there are many decorative charts available, both as printed copy and on CD-rom. The computerized versions are obviously more flexible as you can add or change information as you go.

The birth brief

This is a simple chart that is useful when you are first starting out. The birth brief is a representation of only the direct ancestors of one individual and it usually includes only the last four generations. Brothers, sisters and any second or third marriages are omitted. The format of a birth brief is similar to a drop-line chart, it simply holds less information.

The narrative indented tree

This is the method used for publications such as *Burke's Peerage* or *Debrett's*. It does allow lots of children to be included, but it can be a bit confusing to find your way around. Each generation is assigned a number or letter, and the children of a couple are listed with details of their marriages and, indented, their children. It is important to make sure that every person has a unique number that applies only to him/her, so the tree requires very careful drafting. A lot of information can be packed into less space, so it is worth considering this style when you have done a great deal of research. You also need to be familiar with this type of tree in case the pedigree of any of your relations appears in such books.

RIGHT When you see "of whom presently" (last line) this means that the descent of that person has been written out elsewhere and a new line of descent started for him/her.

BELOW The birth brief shows direct descent and does not include siblings.

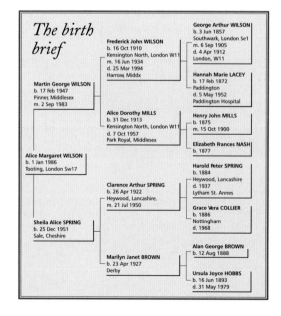

The narrative indented tree

William Williamson b 1840, Rector of Chawleigh Regis, Somerset, m 1868 Harriet Peel (2nd dau of James and Elizabeth Peel of Edinburgh), d 1903 and had issue:

1 William b & d 1869
2 Harriet b 1870 d 1880
3 Thomas b 1871, took holy orders, m 1891 Sophia Ann Bristow, d 1950 and had issue
   a Thomas William b 1891 Fellow of St Chad's College, Cambridge, m 1922 Olive Johnson, d 1949 and had issue
      i Julia Mary b 1923
      ii Ann Elizabeth b 1925 m 1950 Christopher St John Lucas, Esq.
      iii Christine Ann b 1929 m 1949 Percy Arthur Black
   b George Frederick b 1893 m 1918 Ivy Kavanagh and had issue
      i Percival Thomas William b 1925 m 1952 Joyce Lewis
   c Cyril Edward b 1895, sub-lieutenant on HMS Dragon, d 1916
4 George b & d 1872
5 Charles b & d 1872
6 James b 1875, headmaster of Bellingham School, Somerset m 1900 Mary Ann Weston (elder dau of the Hon. Roderick and Lavinia Gascoigne-Hunter), d 1962 and had issue
   a Sarah Catherine b 1902
   b John James b 1904 d 1915
   c Leonard Thomas b 1906 m 1930 Elizabeth Mary James (only dau of Alexander and Aileen McKellan), d 1990 and had issue
      i Marian Mary b 1931
      ii Kenneth Thomas b 1935
   d Ronald Albert b 1909, m 1928 Jessica McDonald and had issue
      i Roderick James b 1928 m. 1955
   e Ethel Rosamund b 1913 m 1933 Professor William Goldblatt
7 John b 1877 <u>of whom presently</u>

The concentric tree

This is useful to show, at a glance, your direct descent from all the different branches of your family. Your details (or those of your children) are placed in the centre. In the next circle appear the father and mother: father at the top and mother at the bottom. The one after is used for the central individual's grandparents, and so on.

The problem with this method is that, because the most distant ancestors appear in the outer sections, where there is more space, annoying gaps can soon open up. However, this kind of chart makes a decorative picture and a good instant reference that

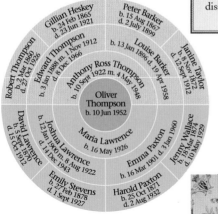

ABOVE The concentric tree puts the most recent generation at the centre. It does not include siblings.

you can hang in your home or give to relatives as a present, but it is best prepared when you have done a good deal of research.

Decorative charts

The other kinds of pictorial and decorative charts that are available to record your family tree are ideal for the culmination of your research, and make perfect special gifts for relatives.

BELOW Not everyone has quite so flourishing a family tree as Queen Victoria. This kind of chart is decorative but not much use in sorting out relationships.

FURTHER HELP

McLaughlin, Eve *Laying Out a Pedigree* (McLaughlin Guides)
Palgrave-Moore, Patrick *How to Record Your Family Tree* (Elvery Dowers Publications)

Names

Researching names can tell us a great deal about our families and their histories. Surnames may reveal where a family originated or what an ancestor did for a living, or it may be a patronymic or nickname. First names, too, can suggest regional links.

UNDERSTANDING NAMING PATTERNS

As you draw up your first family tree, you may notice naming patterns emerging. In the past it was common to call the first child after a parent or grandparent. Second or subsequent names might also be given in honour of a member of the family or to preserve the mother's maiden name. This is how many double-barrelled surnames originated.

Naming children after relatives means that a family might share a small pool of names. For men the most common names were John, William, Henry and Thomas, for women Elizabeth, Mary, Ann/e and Sarah. In the 17th century, biblical names were common, the 18th century brought a fashion for classical names, and in the 19th century Old English names were revived. The name of the current monarch was always a popular choice.

There were also names that had only local popularity. A daughter called Frideswide (sometimes Frideswith), for example, suggests that the family had connections with Oxford, since the cathedral there is built over the remains of an early English saint of that name who founded a convent. Used in the 19th or 20th century, it may suggest that the family were Catholics. Loveday, given originally to

Until the 20th century, it was common to call subsequent children by the same name as a deceased child in order to make sure that the name continued in the family.

both boys and girls but later to girls only, suggests Cornish links, while Marmaduke, which was popular in the north, particularly Yorkshire, was rare in the rest of Britain.

THE HISTORY OF SURNAMES

Before the Middle Ages, people had only one name; it was only in the 13th century that surnames began to be used in England. These names seem to have been developed from four different sources: places, occupations, nicknames and patronymics.

Place names

These can be a large town such as Chester, or a village such as Oulton, which is the name given to four different places in Cumbria, Norfolk, Suffolk and Yorkshire. They may also come from a local landmark, such as Ditchfield, Atwell, or Wood. It is

worth looking up your surname in an atlas or dictionary of place names to see if it comes from a small village.

Occupations

Names such as Smith, Baker, Glover (glove maker) or Fletcher (arrow maker) show that your ancestor played an important part in the economy of his community. A skilled woman among your forebears will have left a surname ending in "-ster", such as Brewster (a female brewer) or Collister (a female collier – a charcoal burner or seller). We call unmarried women "spinsters" because they earned their living by spinning wool – a major source of England's wealth in the Middle Ages. Some of these surnames, such as Faber, meaning a smith, have French or Latin origins. When surnames were introduced, Norman French and Latin were both used by officials.

Nicknames

In these politically correct times it would be unthinkable to call someone Cruikshank (crooked legs), but our ancestors had a much rougher sense of humour. Other names record personal eccentricities, such as Pennyf(e)ather, meaning a miser.

Patronymics

This means a name derived from the name of the person's ancestor or father, such as the son of John being called Johnson, and that of William being called Williamson. Robinson and Wilson preserve pet names for men named Robert or William. Some women are also commemorated in names such as Allison (Alice's son) or Widowson, which may show that an ancestor was illegitimate or posthumous (born after the father died).

Celtic surnames

The Celtic countries (Wales, Scotland and Ireland) adopted surnames much later than England, and they generally used patronymics. In Welsh, "ap" means "son of", but the first vowel disappeared, producing names such as Price (ap Rhys), Pritchard (ap Richard) or Prothero, a variant of Prydderch (ap Rydderch). Such names therefore indicate Welsh origins. A fixed surname here was not common until the 18th century. As an alternative to putting "ap" at the beginning or "son" at the end of the father's name, the Welsh often simply added "s", so names such as Edwards (son of Edward) and Jones (son of John) are common there.

Cornwall, another major Celtic area in England, also tended to use the father's name, though with no prefixes or suffixes. The Cornish also started using a fixed surname much later than the rest of the country. George, for example, did not become a common name until the Hanoverian kings, who started in 1714, long after the majority of surnames in England were formed, so someone with the surname George or John or Thomas should suspect Cornish or Welsh origins.

"Mac" or "Mc" means "son of", so the Macdonalds, the McCraes and the Macmillans have Scottish ancestry, but some of the Mcs, such as McNulty or McMullan, are of Irish origin. (Both the Scots and Irish spoke Gaelic.)

The purely Irish equivalent of the patronymic is "O", as in O'Casey and O'Neill. Sometimes the "O" was dropped, giving just "Casey" or "Neill".

Although patronymics were the most common method of surname formation in the Celtic countries, place names and nicknames were also used.

Uncommon surnames

Although the majority of surnames were, in England at least, fixed by the mid-13th century, and so preserve what was normal in the medieval period, family historians will find many other names in their ancestry that don't appear in the standard reference books. Some may be indications of immigrant ancestry. Others perhaps preserve some long-forgotten incident. The answer may lie in a document somewhere, waiting to be discovered, or it may remain a puzzle for ever.

FURTHER HELP

Cottle, Basil *The Penguin Dictionary of Surnames* (Penguin Books)
Hanks, Patrick and Hodges, Flavia *A Dictionary of First Names* (OUP) (An earlier version of this book, *The Oxford Dictionary of English Christian Names* by E.G.W. Withycombe, is in some ways more useful to the family historian because it includes historical information about the use of names in documents and other sources.)
Mills, A.D. *A Dictionary of English Place Names* (OUP)
Reaney, P.H. and Wilson, R.M. *Dictionary of English Surnames* (OUP)

Younger children often received more fashionable names than their older siblings.

Until very recently, women automatically took their husband's surname on marriage.

Research skills

Try to get into good research habits right from the start of your work. The first rule in genealogy is that you must always work backwards from the known to the unknown; this means starting with yourself. The second rule is that you should never presume that what you have always been told is the truth. There are many stories in the family history world of people who have industriously traced their ancestry back several generations only to find, after getting a birth certificate for some other purpose, that they were in fact adopted but were never told this by their parents. You may also find that it is not only what has been passed down orally that may be wrong. The information given in official records is not always totally accurate, though you should be prepared to take what is written at face value until there is strong evidence against it.

COPING WITH ANY INFORMATION GAPS

The first 100–150 years are often among the hardest to research. Many official records are closed for 100 years in order to protect the privacy of people who could be still alive; gaining access to these records can be difficult or impossible. Most indexes and easily accessible genealogical information date from the mid-19th century. When there is a gap between two pieces of information, beware of making assumptions. For example, you may find a published family tree for someone with the same name as your ancestor in a place where you know your family were living fifty years later. It would be tempting to assume that

someone in the last generation on the published tree is the father or grandfather of your ancestor, but a lot can happen in fifty years – perhaps your forebear moved into a town where a distant relative was already living, or it may just be a coincidence that the two families have the same name.

RECORDING INFORMATION ACCURATELY

When you are copying information, it is vital to distinguish between what is actually there and what you can infer from it. If you cannot read a word or a number, but think that you can guess what it is, record this as a guess, not as a fact. The same applies to abbreviations: don't assume that W. Smith is William Smith – it might be Wilfred or Walter or even Winifred. If you make the firm assumption that it is William, and record this name in your copy of the document, there is a danger that when you come back to this information at a later stage, you will

Following the best research methods will make recording your information easier.

have forgotten that the name was only a guess. As a result of this, your researches may take you up a blind alley, which may not be apparent for a while, wasting your time and effort. The standard way of indicating that this is a supposition is to write the disputed words in square brackets or with a question mark, e.g. W[illiam] Smith of [illegible 5 or 8?] Nelson R[oa]d.

FINDING ANSWERS TO QUESTIONS

In drawing up a family tree, you will probably find that a number of questions are raised. Write them down as they occur to you, or you are likely to forget them. If you have been inspired to compile your family tree by clearing out the contents of a house because elderly people (your parents or other relatives) are moving into a smaller house, you will be able to put your questions to them. If, however, the inspiration was the death of a parent or other relative, then the very person who could have answered your questions is no longer here, and you will have to see if other family members can help you. Get in touch with as many relations as you can, explaining what you are doing.

As you list the questions your research raises, ask yourself where you are likely to find the answers. The rest of this book is concerned with the various different sources, how to contact them, and what information you can expect to find there, but it is worth noting here the various types of sources. Knowing which is the most appropriate one will save you much in the way of time and money.

Telephone directories

If you have a very unusual name, it might be worth writing to everyone with that name in the telephone directory. Directories for the whole country should be available in main libraries. Alternatively, they are obtainable on the Internet, though that is a more complicated procedure.

It is better to write to the contact rather than ring them. How would you feel if a complete stranger suddenly phoned out of the blue and started asking detailed questions about you and your family? Always enclose a stamped, addressed envelope. This is not just a courteous gesture: it also, in an odd way, puts an obligation on the recipient to answer.

Note where the people with your name are living and how many there are in each district. If you plot these on a map, you may see a pattern emerging. The biggest concentration of these people today is likely to be where they were living a few hundred years ago.

The government

Every area of life is regulated in some way by the law. Money and land were, and still are, major concerns of government, and all but the very poorest families will be found in records covering them. Which aspects of your ancestors' lives were covered by legislation, such as paying taxes or rates, that might have generated documentary evidence? Would it have been administered at national or local level?

The Church

Until fairly recently, religion played a major role in everyday life. In Britain, the Church is established, which means that it is part of the government, and it was only during the 20th century that religious belief and attending places of worship stopped

Government records, such as this census, show where individuals were born and give other information, such as ages and occupations, that might help in finding other records.

being part of the majority of people's lives. The Church also had a prominent role in education.

Associations and clubs

Many people belong or belonged to associations connected with their occupation, or to clubs where they shared a hobby or interest with other people. In some cases, membership of a professional association gives the right to work in a particular area, such as freemen of a town or city, or to practise a profession, such as the law.

Charities

Charitable institutions play a large role in some people's lives. Some were run by professional associations, especially for people who had retired from an occupation. Others were set up to help a particular section of society, and distributed sums of money to assist in times of hardship or for specified purposes, such as education.

Was your ancestor eligible for some kind of charitable support, and if so, why would he or she have qualified for

this? Alternatively, your ancestor may have helped with the administration of a charity, in which case, he or she might have been involved in distributing money or other benefits.

Newspapers and periodicals

Britain has had a thriving print industry since the 17th century. Are there events in your ancestors' lives that might have been of public interest? If so where would they be reported?

Some events might be documented in many of the above sources. If your ancestor committed a crime, for example, he or she would have been tried in court, an account of which will appear in government records. If the crime was connected with their profession, they might have been struck off or expelled from an association's membership. A report of the proceedings will probably appear in a newspaper. Other events which might be recorded in print are marriages and births, awards and prizes, even bankruptcy. Obituaries and accounts of funerals can often give an entire life history.

Keeping records

Although you may not have much paper to file yet, a lot will soon accumulate, so setting up an efficient filing system is essential. Most people already have or develop individual methods that best suit them and the records they collect.

STARTING A FILING SYSTEM

A good way to start is to get two large ring binders. The first one will include information you are certain of; the second will include notes you have taken that may be relevant but that you cannot yet link to your family. Divide both into one section per family name you are researching. As your research progresses and the paperwork increases, you may need to give a separate ring binder to each name.

You will also need a master copy of your descent. You could draw your own, but they are available by mail order or in the bookshops of record offices and libraries such as the Society of Genealogists. These are daunting but exciting – the one produced by the Church of Jesus Christ of Latter-day Saints (LDS) has space for 12 generations, which potentially includes over 3,000 ancestors.

CHOOSING A SYSTEM OF IDENTIFICATION

Each ancestor must have a unique number. This can be a single figure (usually already printed on the chart) or you might want to assign each generation a number, usually a Roman numeral, starting with yourself as I1, your parents as II1 (your father) and II2 (your mother), and so on. This will tell you straightaway which generation

When you copy any information from documents, ensure you note where it came from and the archive's reference number.

you are dealing with, but will present problems for your descendants. You also run into difficulties with marriages between cousins, especially those from different generations, which could make a great-grandparent also a great-great-grandparent.

Some professional genealogists use letters instead of numerals. One system, devised by the Surname Index in Sussex, gives each 30-year period from 1380 onwards a letter of the alphabet, starting with A (1380–1409) and finishing with Z (2130–59), which future generations will use. The period of 30 years was chosen because that is the average length of a generation. This system has the advantage of letting you know which period of time you're dealing with, but it presents problems if one of your ancestors had children in two different time periods,

perhaps because he or she married twice. You will have a different problem if an ancestor was born at the beginning of one of these periods and married and had children young. His or her children would then share the same generation letter and possibly even the same name, since it was very common for the eldest child to be named after a parent.

As you file material related to a particular ancestor, you should annotate it with the ancestor's number (or letter) to prevent confusion between family members with the same name. You might also want to give all the children of an ancestor a reference number. To prevent numbers getting out of hand, you could assign the siblings of an ancestor the same number plus a, b, c, d and so on. Your father's brother (your paternal uncle) would become 2a or II1a.

Alternatively, you might prefer to write "William Smith brother of John Smith 2/II 1" on any notes relating to him.

KEEPING FURTHER RECORDS

In addition to the files containing your research results, you will need a notebook. A hardback book is a good idea because it is sturdier and more difficult to lose than single sheets of paper, but you will have to copy the information in order to file it in the right section of your master research file. A more sensible alternative is a block of paper with ring binder holes punched in it: sheets with errors on can just be torn out and disposed of, and once a sheet is completed it can be filed in a ring binder. You should use a separate sheet of paper for each document or source.

Whether you choose to have a separate book in which you list all the sources you have searched, or whether you record this information at the back of your main notebook, is up to you. Making lists of everything you look at is essential to prevent reading the same document more than once. It is also a good idea to have a small copy

Computers are a convenient way to store and manipulate your findings.

Understanding the law

Many countries have legislation covering information that can be stored on computers or in paper files. Check what the position is where you live.

When you copy information, especially from the internet and published books, you also need to be aware of copyright law, especially if you publish your work in either an article or a book.

This might seem unlikely at the beginning of your search, but you should bear this in mind.

When you copy or print out information, always note the source and perhaps put the words you have quoted in inverted commas as a reminder that they are not your own work and therefore may be subject to copyright law or other legislation, such as privacy.

of each separate family tree on an A5 index card in a small ring binder or display book. It needs to give just the dates and places of birth/baptism, marriage and death/burial of each family member (including siblings). It is surprising how often you will be researching one branch of the family when you unexpectedly come across something that could relate to another branch. If you have a basic chart with you, you can refer to it on the spot and open up a whole new avenue of research.

When you get in touch with other people who share your research interests, you will need to decide whether to have a separate file for their correspondence or whether to file their letters with the relevant branch of the family.

USING A COMPUTER

There are a number of software packages for family historians. They are excellent for drawing up charts and so on, but are not a complete substitute for paper-based files. This is mainly because, even if you make backup copies (and you must), you still run the risk of losing all your research through computer or disk failure. Print out your work regularly so that if there is a problem you will lose comparatively little information. Anything you do

lose should be able to be easily reconstructed from your most recent notes.

You can buy or produce on your computer standard forms to help with your record-keeping. They include:

1. Family sheets, which give details of a marriage and all the children of it, including where they were born/baptized, whom they married and when, and the date of their death/burial. Each sheet is numbered, and at the bottom of the entry for each child there is a space in which to write the number of any further sheets relating to them.

2. Individual sheets, which contain details of an individual's life. As well as birth, baptism and parentage; marriage(s); children; death and burial; there is space for where they were living at particular dates, what they were doing, the dates the will (if any) was written and proved and where this information came from, e.g. census returns, street directories or electoral registers.

FURTHER HELP

TNA Family History Starter Pack This contains an introductory booklet, a bibliography and pro forma sheets on which to enter research information. Swinnerton, Iain *Basic Approach to Keeping Family Records* (FFHS)

Interviewing people

Whether you are asking the owners of some mementos about them or trying to find out more from other family members or friends, there are ways of putting questions that will help you to obtain what you need.

GROUP AND INDIVIDUAL INTERVIEWS

Talking to people in a group can be a very good way of getting information, because what one person says may spark off the memories of others. You will need to choose the members of the group carefully, however. One very dominant speaker might not give the others the chance to say much. Alternatively, one shy person in a group of three extroverts may feel too overwhelmed to contribute at all. Group interviews will almost certainly have to be supplemented with individual conversations, since there are frequently pieces of information that people are unwilling to divulge in front of others.

Photographs can help to trigger family memories and may help to fill in some of the gaps in your family tree.

USING OPEN QUESTIONS

Open questions start with the words "Who", "What", "Why", "When", "Where" and "How", and they tend to receive fuller answers than closed questions, which can often be answered with just one word. For example, the closed question "Was your father born in 1920 or 1921?" will probably get one of these dates as the reply. But if you rephrase that as an open question, such as "When was your father born?", you may get a lot more detail: "My father was born in 1920, after the family moved from Nightingale Street. My grandparents already had two kids and they didn't have enough room for a baby as well. Grandad had just been promoted, so they could afford a bigger house." This gives you much more information and prompts other avenues of research that you might otherwise have missed. "Tell me about..." will also get a more detailed reply. You can use closed questions to clarify answers, e.g. "Didn't they have three children then?" "The second one died when he was a baby."

People, especially those from the older generation, may be reluctant to talk about illegitimacy, insanity, suicide or criminal records. They themselves may not have been told the full truth. All this means that you may have to think carefully about how to word the more sensitive questions. When you visit people to interview them, take photographs and other mementos that might prompt memories.

RECORDING THE INTERVIEW

You will need a record of the interview so that you can remember everything that was said. There are three options: a written record, a cassette or a video.

A written record involves making notes as the person talks, but this inevitably breaks your contact with the

Within family groups there are always things that one person will not want the others to know. Such personal secrets must be respected when researching the past.

Asking the right questions

Subjects about which you might want to ask questions include:

- Name: full name and whether the person was known by a different name to the one he or she was officially given.
- Names of other members of the family: father, mother, siblings, as well as more distant relatives with whom they had a particularly close association.
- What the person looked like: height; colouring; size (fat or thin); any physical peculiarities, such as a limp, which might be the result of an accident or illness; dress style; characteristic smell, such as a favourite perfume or aftershave.

- Jobs, including apprenticeship if applicable: what they did and where they did it.
- Hobbies or membership of clubs and associations. These might also reveal special talents.
- Marriage(s) and children, with approximate dates of the end of the marriage, whether by divorce or death. This is where it can get tricky because an ancestor's marriage might never have ended – he or she might simply have gone to live with, and had children by, another person.
- Where the person lived, with approximate dates.
- Holidays and outings: where they went and with whom.

- Religious affiliation, if any, and where they attended church/chapel/temple etc.
- Details of any periods spent in the armed forces: dates; the branch they served with (Army, Navy or Air Force); the regiment, ship or squadron; their service number; whether they volunteered or were called up, either in wartime or for National Service.
- You should also ask if the person you are talking to has any photographs or family papers. If you are allowed to take any documents away with you, you can take copies; alternatively, you will have to ask them to make copies for you.

person, as well as slowing down the interview. The seeming formality of the process – which could be seen as rather like giving a police statement – may also make the interviewee feel inhibited and uncomfortable.

If you decide to tape-record the conversation, take a small recorder, such as the type used for dictation, but don't be tempted to record a conversation without gaining permission first. People can be very self-conscious when what they are saying is being recorded, so make allowances for this.

If you have a camcorder, you might want to use it, but it can make the person too self-conscious to speak or it can encourage them to exaggerate stories and give false information to make a good performance. Camcorders are best used in places connected with the family history. Getting the informant to talk about their memories where they took place is not only a good record to have but it may also help to bring back the past to them.

ASKING THE RIGHT QUESTIONS

The box above has a list of suggested questions to which you might want to add other questions based on family documents or objects. You can design or buy forms to make sure you don't forget anything. Remember to note who gave you the information, their relationship to the person you are inquiring about and when you conducted the interview.

STRUCTURING AN INTERVIEW

Once you have decided on the questions, you need to think about the order in which to ask them. You may also need to gain the interviewee's trust before you start, in case they are worried that you will use their information in a way that might embarrass them or upset other members of the family. Reassure them that you are concerned only with recording the family history accurately and that you will honour any requests for confidentiality.

Begin with simple, factual questions to which they will know the answers. This will give them confidence. Then, when they are more relaxed and start to give more personal information, move on to other matters that might perhaps be more difficult for them to talk about. Go carefully on such issues: just because something happened a long time ago it doesn't mean that it isn't still painful to recall. You can also ask about any of the more uncomfortable subjects mentioned above, but don't force the discussion if the person isn't willing. There may be other people who can tell you this or official records where you can find it out.

FURTHER HELP

Amsden, Peter C. *Basic Approach to Making Contact with Relatives* (FFHS)

McLaughlin, E. *Interviewing Elderly Relatives* (McLaughlin Guide)

Back to the early 1800s

By now you should have a basic family tree and some clues that will help you to move back in time. Most of the information you need at this stage is located in the Family Record Centre in London. It holds birth, marriage, adoption and death certificates from 1837 onwards, and records of some of these events overseas. It also holds copies of census returns, held every year from 1841, and wills proved in the Prerogative Court of Canterbury before 1858. There are also lists of Nonconformist registers deposited in The National Archives.

Certificates after 1837

In 1836 an Act of Parliament was passed to set up the General Register Office (GRO) to record the births, marriages and deaths (BMD) of everyone in England and Wales from 1 July 1837. Before that date, there was no requirement to notify anyone of births and deaths (although churches and other places of worship carried out baptisms and burials). Legal marriages could take place only in Anglican parish churches or be carried out by Jews or the Religious Society of Friends (the Quakers). After 1837, other religious denominations, such as Nonconformists or Roman Catholics, could have their buildings registered to perform marriages.

FINDING BMD CERTIFICATES

Unless you are very lucky and find a complete set of certificates among your family papers, you will need to obtain copies of birth, marriage and (sometimes) death certificates in order to reconstruct your ancestry back to 1837. The GRO compiled quarterly indexes from the returns sent to them from all over the country. Each quarter contains the following months:

March quarter: January, February and March

June quarter: April, May and June

September quarter: July, August and September

December quarter: October, November and December

The indexes list all the births together, all the marriages together and all the deaths. These indexes are now on open shelves in the Family Record Centre (FRC) in London, but there are copies on microfiche in local offices and libraries, and on the Internet.

The entries relate to the date of the actual registration, not of the event itself, so that people who were born,

Not all babies would have been baptized but, after 1837, they should all have a birth certificate.

married or died near the end of one quarter may appear in the index of the next. The registers are stored in Southport, Lancashire, where entries are copied on to blank certificate forms. The researcher has to locate the relevant entry in the index and use the reference number there to place an order. Each certificate must be paid for.

Birth certificates

When researching your ancestry, you must start from the known and work back to the unknown. In certificate terms, this means getting the birth certificate of a child in order to find out the parents' names, especially if you do not know the mother's maiden name, and then using this information to look for the parents' marriage certificate, which will give their fathers' names and occupations. You can then order the birth certificate of each parent, and so find out the mothers' names as well.

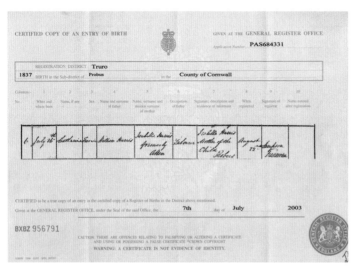

This birth certificate from 1837 will have been relatively easy to find because it was compiled after the setting up of the General Register Office in 1836.

In reality, unfortunately, it never goes as smoothly as this suggests. In the first ten years or so following the introduction of national registration, parents were not obliged to notify the registrar of a child's birth, and if a child was not registered within six months, it could not be included in the records. There seems also to have been some confusion about whether it was necessary to register a child if it had also been baptized. In 1874, fines were introduced for non-notification by the parents, which improved the situation.

This lack of registration, combined with the bureaucracy involved in copying entries as they were passed from level to level in the system, means that a number of events are missing from the indexes, especially in the earlier period. There may be as many as 15 per cent of the births missing for 1837–47, and as many as 1 in 40 marriages missing for 1837–99. There are also the difficulties caused by copying errors and by dealing with illiterate people who did not know how their names were written, and who probably had strong regional accents. Registrars had, in many cases, to guess at the name and how it was spelled.

Marriage certificates

In the days when divorce was practically impossible for poor people, many just left their spouse and set up another family with someone else, claiming to be married to them. Some did marry after the first spouse's death, but others did not, and their children never knew that they were illegitimate.

If either of the parties had connections with Scotland, Ireland or another country, the marriage may have taken place outside England or Wales. There is a link to the Scottish and Irish records at the FRC, which you must pay to access. It is also worth checking the miscellaneous indexes that cover events at sea and all over the world. A reason for marrying abroad was that the parties were related in a way that made their marriage illegal in Britain.

All these factors may account for people not appearing in registers where they are expected to be.

Death certificates

It's comparatively easy to find birth and marriage certificates, since most people had children soon after the marriage, but, since people can die at any time, finding a death certificate can be a much longer job.

SEARCHING THE INDEXES

Researching information calls for patience, diligence, concentration and also imagination.

Be meticulous

Be careful not to miss the reference. It is easy to overlook a name, especially if you have been searching for a long time and are tired. If you are using the books at the FRC, run a sheet of paper down the names to keep your eyes focused on the right place. This also ensures that you do not miss the last one lurking at the bottom of the page. This task is more difficult if you're using microfiche. Take regular breaks.

Leave no gaps

As you work, list all the quarters you have checked, both year and month. It is all too easy, if someone is using the next book that you want to consult, to work on another, planning to go back and then either not do so or forget which one you were going to look at. This can lead to you looking at the same one twice and missing the one that you need.

Try alternative spellings

Ask yourself what the surname in question might have sounded like to the registrar, especially if the informant had a heavy cold or a mild speech impediment, for example Searle/Thurle. Names beginning with an H cause particular problems, because dropping the H is common in many

After 1837 marriages could take place in a register office rather than a church, but most people still preferred a traditional church wedding.

Significant dates in the history of BMD records

1837 1 July Civil registration began in England and Wales.

1866 Death indexes recorded age at death.

1907 Deceased Wife's Sister Marriage Act permitted a man to marry his deceased wife's sister.

1911 September Birth indexes contained mother's maiden name.

1912 Marriage indexes showed name of the second party.

1921 Deceased Brother's Widow Marriage Act permitted a woman to marry her deceased husband's brother.

1926 Adoption of Children Act provided for adoption of children, with the creation of an Adopted Children's Register.

1926 Legitimacy Act allowed for illegitimate children to be re-registered on the subsequent marriage of the parents.

1927 Registration of stillbirths made compulsory (but the register was not put on open access).

1929 It became illegal for anyone under 16 to marry. Previously girls could marry at 12 and boys at 14, although they needed their parents' consent until they were 21.

1931 Marriage between uncle and niece/aunt and nephew allowed.

1947 Short birth certificate introduced. (This does not contain parents' names and so is of no use to the genealogist.)

1949 Register of Births and Deaths in Aircraft listed any births or deaths that took place in aircraft registered in Great Britain or Northern Ireland, wherever they occurred in the world.

1959 Legitimacy Act allowed the children born when one of their parents was married to somebody else to be legitimized when their parents married. The child could be re-registered if it had been previously entered under the woman's husband's name.

1969 Death indexes showed date of birth.

1969 Age of majority reduced from 21 to 18. Parental consent to marriage now needed for people under 18.

1975 Children Act 1975 allowed adopted children to obtain the original information on their birth certificate.

1986 People permitted to marry a stepchild or stepgrandchild, but both parties had to be over 18 and the child must not have been treated as a child of the person's family.

---

local accents, so for Horton try Orton. When handwritten indexes were copied, confusion between M and W could occur, such as Mardell/Wardell. If you look at samples of copperplate handwriting, you will see that confusion between F, J and T was also possible.

Consider alternative first names

Consider whether the person was actually given the name by which he or she was generally known. Children named after a parent might have been known by their second or another name to prevent confusion. Others, for reasons long forgotten, might have been called something completely unrelated to their original name. Alternatively, the parents may not have decided on the child's name until after it was registered.

There was, and still is, no obligation to give a first name, so you need to check at the top of the list of surnames to see if there is a likely registration in the area where the family lived.

Consider illegitimacy

Illegitimate children were given their mother's surname until 1926, when they could be re-registered with the father's name if the parents married after the birth. Also, a couple might not have married until after some, or all, of their children were born.

Broaden your time span

Ages are often inaccurately recorded, so check up to five years on either side of the likely date. If you are relying on the ages given on a marriage certificate to find the person's birth certificate, consider that the ages have been falsified.

Ages at death are especially suspect because the informant may not have known the age and just made a guess.

Consider other districts

The event would have been registered where it took place, not where the family lived. Women might have gone to stay with their mothers or other family members for the birth of a child, and so the birth would have been registered there. Even a hospital just a short distance from home might have been in another registration district.

Narrow the field

If you are researching a fairly common surname, you may find a number of entries, any of which might be the person you are seeking. The staff at both the FRC and the local record office will do some (paid) cross-checking for you. You can ask them to check entries until they find a particular piece of information that matches something you know already, such as the father's first name. Alternatively, you could:

1. Order all the possible certificates; but this can be expensive and may not necessarily help you to decide which one is your ancestor.

2. Look for the birth certificate of a brother or sister about whom you know more (such as exact date or place of birth) or who has a rarer first name.

3. Note the quarters and reference details, then seek out other, more distant, family members in the hope that one of them will know something or have a document that will help.

If none of this works, it can mean going back to the original entry and paying for a search to be made in a local register office.

RESEARCHING BMD CERTIFICATES

Consider carefully whether you need your ancestor's birth certificate. You may find that getting a sibling's would be more useful: you will still get the parents' names from it and you might also get the family's address at the time of a census. These took place every ten years from 1841, so if your ancestor was born in 1846 and had brothers or sisters born in 1841 and 1851, get the older child's certificate (see Censuses for the reason why).

In England and Wales, a time given on a birth certificate means delivery of twins or a multiple birth, so you need to look for another child or children with the same surname and reference number to find out their names. If you want to find out in what order they were born, you will have to order the certificates.

Where you know the surnames of both parties to a marriage, look up the less common one in the index. Note the reference number against the one you think is your ancestor, and then look up the other party's name in the same quarter's index. If the reference

number is the same, you can be fairly sure that you have the right marriage.

Death certificates are not especially useful in constructing family trees. After 1866 the ages at death are given in the indexes. Since this information will give you a starting point to look for a birth certificate, you may not need to obtain the death certificate. If you know that the widow or widower remarried, you can look for their marriage certificate after that date.

Levels of registration
GRO in Somerset House, London
A quarterly index, covering the whole of England and Wales, was drawn up from copies of the certificates sent by the local register offices to Superintendent Registrars.

Superintendent Registrars
In 1834, Poor Law Unions (groups of parishes that banded together to care for those who could not support themselves) were set up, and they became the basis for the new registration system. Each union had a Superintendent

Registrar, who was responsible for a number of local registrars. After checking the entries from the registrars in his district, each Superintendent Registrar sent copies to the General Register office (GRO).

Registrars
At the lowest, local level, the 2,193 registrars recorded births and deaths. Four times a year they sent a copy of these certificates to the district Superintendent Registrar's office.

It is interesting to know when, where and how someone died, but the actual information on a death certificate will rarely help you move back in time.

Other indexes at the Family Record Centre

In addition to the indexes to BMD certificates, the Family Record Centre also has a number of indexes to other events, such as divorce, adoption and some BMD overseas.

DIVORCES

Divorce files for 1858–1958 have been indexed (except for the period 1945–50). The original papers are in The National Archives (TNA), where, unlike the Family Record Centre you will need to get a ticket to carry out research. Before 1858, divorces could be made only through an Act of Parliament. Formal separations and annulments were obtained through the Church courts.

ADOPTIONS

Before 1926, adoptions were arranged informally. After that date, a register of adopted children was set up. The indexes are arranged by the adoptive name, and the certificates do not contain information about birth parents. Adopted people wishing to obtain their original birth certificate should contact the Adoption Section at the FRC to inquire about the procedures.

EVENTS OVERSEAS

In addition to events in England and Wales, the FRC contains copies of a number of records relating to overseas. These came mainly from maritime, military or consular sources. Most are from the 19th century, but some date back to 1627 and some continue until the late 1950s. The originals are in TNA, but there are microfilm copies at the FRC. They are divided between statutory returns (those that had to be made by law) and non-statutory returns (those that were made voluntarily). Researchers must pay the standard certificate fee to get copies of the information from the statutory returns.

From 1627 onwards, miscellaneous notifications of BMD overseas were returned to Britain. These were largely to ensure that, should any dispute arise, the people concerned could prove that they were married, that their children were legitimate, or that someone was dead. Many are BMD of embassy or other government staff or those notified to the local consulate by British people either visiting the country or resident there. These are not limited to British territories, though some of these are included, but cover places in Europe where there were sizeable British communities,

The Family Records Centre, Clerkenwell, London, contains indexes to some BMD overseas as well as in England and Wales.

and countries elsewhere. From 1849, consuls were allowed to carry out marriages and had to make a return of the ceremonies to the GRO in London.

There is a microfilm of a number of certificates (not indexed) to military deaths that took place during and just after World War I (1914–21). They are mainly of soldiers who died not in action but off the battlefield, plus a few civilians.

ARMY BMD

Regimental registers were kept from 1761 and are most likely to contain births in depots in Great Britain. In addition, Army regiments each had their own chaplain, who generally kept a register of the christenings, marriages and burials (CMB) he carried out. Chaplains' returns from 1796 are most likely to contain births overseas.

BMD AT SEA

From 1837, BMD at sea on British ships had to be notified to the GRO. By an Act of 1874, which did not affect the Royal Navy, certificates of births and deaths on Merchant Navy ships and passenger ships travelling to and from British ports had to be sent to the Register General of Shipping and Seamen. From here, they were distributed to the Register Offices in London, Edinburgh and Dublin, depending on the nationality of the people involved (though this wasn't always strictly observed). Certificates concerning foreigners went to the London office. The English Marine Register indexes, covering the Royal Navy, the Merchant Navy and passenger ships from 1837, are at the FRC.

They contain only births and deaths. There are indexes to deaths in the armed forces during and just after the Boer War (1899–1902), World War I (1914–21) and World War II (1939–48). Deaths at sea during the two World Wars were sometimes sent to the GRO but were mainly passed to the Admiralty, which maintained a separate War Deaths register, so consult both.

THE MISCELLANEOUS INDEXES

If you have to visit the FRC and you know that members of your family spent some time abroad, it may be worthwhile checking out the various miscellaneous indexes.

The information in the miscellaneous returns may be found elsewhere, such as the records of the Bishop of London, which are in the Guildhall Library, or the Oriental and India Office Library, which is at the British Library. If you find that the information you want is recorded on a certificate for which a fee is payable, you will have to decide whether you want to save the money by exploring these alternative sources. This is definitely worth considering if you know you will be doing other research in that particular archive.

Copies of the Marine Registers made for merchant ships are accessible, without a fee, at TNA, where there are also indexes. Seamen who died in the course of a voyage had their wages and effects given to the next of

kin or someone nominated in their wills. Records relating to this are at TNA, so if you already know that your ancestor was a merchant seaman, you might prefer to go to TNA rather than the FRC.

Children born at sea were sometimes given the name of the ship on which they were born, so if you trace an ancestor with an odd name that appears to have no family connections, this may be a clue to their birthplace.

ABOVE Deaths of Army personnel who died overseas in wartime are indexed at the FRC but sailors' deaths are more likely to be in Admiralty records at TNA.

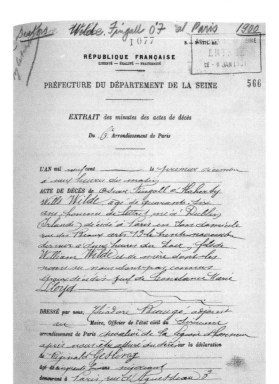

LEFT As a resident in France at the time of his death in 1900, Oscar Wilde's death certificate is in the Miscellaneous Foreign Deaths returns.

FURTHER HELP

Stafford, Georgina *Where to Find Adoption Records: A Guide for Counsellors* (British Agencies for Adoption and Fostering)
Tracing the Birth Parents of Adopted Persons (FFHS)

Censuses

The triggering factor for the first national census in Britain was the need to know whether the population was increasing or decreasing and whether the number of the poor was growing beyond the ability of the country to support them.

A HISTORY OF THE CENSUS
Following some local head counts held at irregular intervals, the nationwide censuses held from 1841 give the family historian a snapshot of the life of their ancestors at ten-yearly intervals.

The first censuses
Although they were not official censuses, there have been head counts of people since the Domesday survey in 1086. Various towns and parishes, such as Poole, Dorset, in 1575 and Ealing in 1522, listed everyone living there, and since those dates many other censuses have been made. Some of them named only the head of the household and added how many people there were in it.

National censuses were first proposed in 1753, but it wasn't until 1800 that legislation to enumerate the entire population of England and Wales was passed. The first census was held on Monday, 10 March 1801, and was carried out by parish officials in England and Wales and schoolmasters in Scotland. Thereafter, a national census was taken every ten years. The next three – in 1811, 1821 and 1831 – were also taken by the same people, but in 1841 the government took over. Only some copies of the first four censuses survive in parish records, but from 1841 there is full coverage of the whole country.

ABOVE Until the last century, a whole family might live in one room, so several, unrelated households may be found in the same house.

BELOW These gypsies have had their census papers brought to them by the police, but many gypsies and other travellers, as well as the homeless sleeping rough, were not recorded in the earlier census returns.

The 1841 census
From 1841, it was decided to seek information about everyone in each house on a particular night (in this case, 6–7 June). The information gathered was broadly similar to previous ones, with the significant addition of the age of each person. Exact ages were required only for children under 16; adults' ages were rounded down to the nearest five years. Thus a person stated to be 30 could have been any age between 30 and 34. People were also required to say whether or not each person had been born in the same county in which they now lived and whether any member of the household was foreign-born. There are, however, omissions from this census: miners on shift were not included, for example, and nor were people on board ships that were in harbour.

The 1851 census
There were several changes in the questions that were asked for this census, which was held on the night of

30–1 March. Instead of asking how many actual houses there were, the government now wanted to know the number of households. More than one household might live in a house, particularly in poor areas, where whole families might live in one room. A line was drawn across the page under each household.

People were also required to state the parish in which they were born. This is what makes this census so useful to the family historian. Those born overseas, however, were required to put only the country, although some did include the place within it. Others put "British citizen", which suggests one of three options: that they were naturalized, had denization or were born in a British colony. For this census, sailors on ships in harbour were included but not, it appears, people on canal barges.

A question about whether a person was deaf, dumb, blind or lunatic was also asked, and researchers are often surprised (and horrified) to find that everyone in their ancestor's family seems to have been disabled in some way, because there is a tick against every option here. Be cautious about this: the column relating to this question was the last on the form, and the ticks are usually just marks made when the numbers were being added up.

Censuses for 1861 and 1871

Held on the nights of 7–8 April and 2–3 April respectively, these asked the same questions as the 1851 census.

The 1881 census

This census, which was held on the night of 3–4 April, is particularly useful to family historians because the entire census for the whole country has been indexed in a project carried

ABOVE Neath Place, London (c.1900), no longer exists. Maps from the 19th century will be needed to find out where it was.

out by the Federation of Family History Societies (FFHS) and the Church of Jesus Christ of Latter-day Saints (LDS). This index exists on both

microfiche and CD-ROM. A separate record was made of those who were lunatic, imbecile or idiot; this replaced the "lunatic" option in the earlier censuses.

The 1891 census

There is no nationwide index for this census, which was held on the night of 5–6 April, so finding ancestors on it depends on knowing where they lived.

The 1901 census

This census, which was held on the night of 31 March–1 April, has been digitized and put on to the Internet at www.census.pro.gov.uk. It can be searched by name to find individuals or by address. A fee is charged for access to the image of the original

RIGHT A 19th-century census map showing the districts of Epping, Chigwell and Harlow, in Essex.

From these you can get what is called the piece number and the folio number. The class mark is the reference number used by the government. The following class marks are used: 1841: class mark HO 107; 1851: class mark HO 107; 1861: class mark RG 9; 1871: class mark RG 10; 1881: class mark RG 11; 1891: class mark RG 12; 1901: class mark RG 13.

The piece number is the individual bundle of documents containing an area's census returns, and the folio number refers to a particular street or, in rural places, locality. Once you have the microfilm or microfiche you need, you can use page numbers given in the FRC reference books to find your ancestor's street, or use an index (if one has been made) to find your ancestor's

census page. Microfiche copies are also available in local record offices, but there is no index with them. Individual family history societies may compile indexes for their area, but if this has not been done you can only search the microfiche copies by address.

RESEARCHING THE CENSUSES

Censuses for the whole country for 1841–1901 are on microfiche or microfilm at the FRC. Microfiche are small sheets of plastic, the size of index cards, and microfilm are rolls of film on to which records have been copied. They both need a special machine on which to view them, and copies can usually be made from them. Some censuses also exist on CD-ROMs, which have to be read on a computer. Sometimes you can print out the information. Some County Record Offices (CROs) and other local offices and libraries have copies for their area too. Many have been indexed by Family History Societies. Check whether this has been done for the area you are interested in. If it has, you can use these indexes and so save yourself a lot of work.

You need to find out where your ancestor was living at the time of a particular census. This information can come from various sources, such as

BMD certificates, trade directories, such as Kelly's, and correspondence. At the FRC there are lists of every place in the country; individual towns and cities with more than 40,000 inhabitants should also have a street index.

ABOVE Tracking down people from a census can be a long task if you do not know the address, as often very few districts were indexed.

RIGHT Trade directories, such as Kelly's, can help you find the address of an individual's workplace, which may help you trace them in the relevant census.

Page 20] The undermentioned Houses are situate within the Boundaries of the

Civil Parish [or Township] of	City or Municipal Borough of	Municipal Ward of	Parliamentary Borough of	Town of	Village or Hamlet, &c., of	Local Board, or [Improvement Commissioners District] of	Ecclesiastical District of
Sheffield	Sheffield	St Georges	Sheffield	Sheffield		Sheffield	St Georges

No. of Schedule	ROAD, STREET, &c., and No. or NAME of HOUSE	HOUSES In-habit-ed	Unin-habited (U.), or Building (B.)	NAME and Surname of each Person	RELATION to Head of Family	CON-DITION	AGE of Males	AGE of Females	Rank, Profession, or OCCUPATION	WHERE BORN	Whether 1. Deaf-and-Dumb 2. Blind 3. Imbecile or Idiot 4. Lunatic
				Ernest B Boyd	Son		3			Yorkshire Sheffield	
				Alice M Do	Daur			1		Do Do	
113	43 Victoria St	1		Ann Moody	Head	Unm		59	Annuitant	Do Heeley	Blind Cataract
				Ruth Moody	Sister	Unm		49	Seamstress	Do Sheffield	
114	45 " "			George H Hodson	Head	Mar	6?		Wine Merchant	Goole	
				Margaret Willshaw	Serv	Unm		22	General Servant	Do Ecclesall	
115	47 " "	1		Joseph Clarke	Head	Mar	5?		Commercial Agent	Wilts Chippenham	
				Eleanor Do	Wife	Mar		48		Yorkshire Sheffield	
				Edmund B Do	Son	Unm	20		Clerk	Do Do	
				William B Do	Son		17		Student of Chemistry	Do Do	
				Elizabeth T Do	Daught			13	Scholar	Do Do	
				Lydia J Do	Daur			10	Scholar	Do Do	
				Beatrice M Do	Daur			5		Do Do	
				Elizabeth Schofield	Serv	Unm		18	General Servant	Do North Anston	
116	49 " "	1		Edward Lipp	Head	Mar	43		Tobacco Manufacturer	Liverpool	
				Sarah Lipp	Wife	Mar		42		Do	
				Mary E Do	Daur			11	Scholar	Yorkshire Sheffield	
				Bridget Gambick	Serv	Unm		40	General Servant	Athy Ireland	
117	50 Victoria St	1		Robert Forbes	Head	Mar	27		Draper	Scotland	
				Jane Forbes	Wife	Mar		26		Scotland	
				John H Do	Son		5		Scholar	Yorkshire Sheffield	
				Abram Do	Son		3			Do Do	
				Elizabeth J Do	Daur			2		Do Do	
				Edmund Do	Son		5/12			Do Do	
				Priscilla Platts	Serv	Unm		19	General Servant	Do Do	
5	Total of Houses..	4		Total of Males and Females..			10	15			

* Draw the pen through such of the words as are inappropriate.

Reference:- PUBLIC RECORD OFFICE RG 10/4677 f75 v

class mark
piece number
folio number
page number

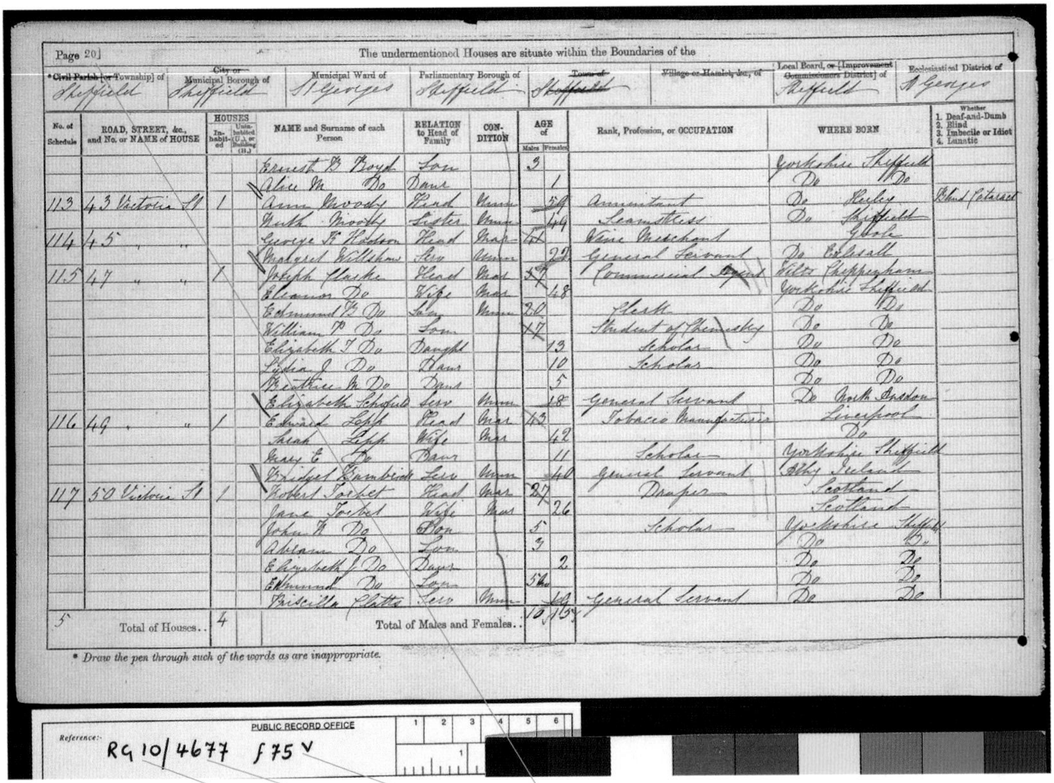

A page from the 1871 census.

actual household. If you know only the town, village or area of a city, it's a matter of working your way through the entire piece.

As the capital city, London is a special case. Local and family historians working on it have created a number of indexes and lists of inhabitants.

To find out where your family was living in a census year, it is sometimes better to get the birth certificate of a sibling born in the year of the census rather than the ancestor. This is where death certificates can also be useful. A death certificate might also give the address at which a family was living in which case you can then locate them in a census. You won't, however, know whether the person died at home or in hospital until you've paid for the certificate.

Although marriage certificates give addresses for both bride and groom, you should not rely on this. For a small fee, couples would leave a suitcase somewhere, usually a lodging house in the parish where they planned to marry, and claim to be resident there, thus saving money by having the banns called in one place rather than in two.

If you can't find your ancestor where you expect him or her to be, consider whether they could have been in the workhouse, in hospital or even in prison. Check these places too. If they were simply paying a visit to friends, and so were away from their house on the night of the census, you are unlucky. Check the streets around your ancestor's residence. Most people had relatives nearby and they may have been spending the night with them.

Once you have found out where those ancestors who lived before the advent of civil registration in 1837 were born, go to the parish records to find out more about them.

FURTHER HELP

Gibson, Jeremy and Creaton, Heather *Lists of Londoners* **(FFHS)**

Gibson, Jeremy and Medlycott, Mervyn *Local Census Listings 1522–1930: Holdings in the British Isles* **(FFHS)**

Using Census Returns **(TNA)**

The International Genealogical Index and other indexes

At this stage, you may have enough information to start linking you and your family to information that is already available and to other people researching the same names. Even if you haven't, this is a section to revisit regularly as your research advances – there's no point in laboriously repeating work that someone else has already done. The growth of interest in genealogy has led to the gathering and dissemination of a huge amount of data. It may not be much use to you at this stage in your research, but the sources are described here to encourage you and to reassure you that soon they can be used to reduce the time-consuming record-searching.

One of the granite vaults in Utah where the Church of Jesus Christ of Latter-day Saints stores records and copies of archive material from around the world.

THE INTERNATIONAL GENEALOGICAL INDEX

The International Genealogical Index (IGI) was set up by the LDS. The Mormons believe that, in order to be reunited with their ancestors in the next world, forebears must be retrospectively baptized into their Church. They have a massive programme of entering data on baptisms and marriages. The majority of entries for the United Kingdom are pre-1837 and come from parish and other Church registers. This enormous database has been placed on the Internet but is also available on CD-ROM, and on microfiche held in record offices and libraries. The IGI is most helpful once you get back before the mid-19th century and civil registration.

Names are arranged by county, with all spelling variants listed together. Within each surname, the entries are put in alphabetical order of first and then subsequent names. Baptisms and marriages are itemized; there are very few burials included.

In some ways the microfiche version of the records is the most useful for the genealogist, since it is easy to get a photocopy from which information can be quickly extracted. You can highlight all the entries before or after a particular date, in a particular place, or all the

Records can be sent from Utah to local Family History Centers around the world.

children of a particular marriage. This is possible, but more laborious, on printouts from the CD-ROM and Internet versions, and the results are less easy to take in since they do not form a coherent visual pattern.

When using the IGI, there are a number of points to bear in mind. First, its purpose is not primarily for family history: it has been compiled

The entrance to the LDS vaults, which are housed within a granite mountain.

for religious reasons, so it does not contain all the information a family historian needs.

Second, there are, inevitably, errors in the data (though this is true of almost all indexes). You must always check the original record, where you may also find additional information. The IGI does not, for example, say whether people getting married were single or widow(er)s of the parish they came from, as opposed to the one where they married. This sort of information will, however, be included in the original record.

Third, although you can, in many cases, compile a rough family tree from the entries on the IGI, not all registers and all dates have been entered. You cannot therefore assume that the John and Mary Smith in a certain village in 1800 are necessarily the ancestors of a John Smith in the same village in 1900. You will need to use other documents before you are able to prove a link.

Finally, the IGI does not include burials, though the word "child" indicates that the person died before the age of eight. This has not been recorded consistently, however, so you cannot always be sure to which entries an early death applies.

The IGI is a finding aid, not a comprehensive record that can be used by itself. With all these reservations, however, it must be said that the IGI is one of the most useful tools a family historian has, so it is worth spending time learning how to use it.

THE ANCESTRAL FILE AND VITAL RECORDS INDEX

In addition to the IGI, the LDS produces the Ancestral File and the Vital Records Index. The Ancestral File contains details of information on CMB from parish and Nonconformist

Using a microfiche reader to search the IGI for family history data.

registers (much of which is also on the IGI) as well as names and addresses of the people who provided the information, generally members of their Church. The Vital Records Index is a database on CD-ROM. It contains lists from records that have been microfilmed.

OTHER INDEXES

There are many other, smaller indexes compiled by Family History Societies and individuals. Some relate to occupations, some are of marriages in a particular area, of criminal records, of inquests, of apprenticeships and so on. They can be recorded on paper, microfiche, microfilm or CD-ROM. Many CROs have copies relating to their areas, and the Society of Genealogists (SoG) library has copies of most of them.

RIGHT GOONS has a website and also publishes material.

FURTHER HELP

Gibson, Jeremy and Hampson, Elizabeth *Specialist Indexes for Family Historians* (FFHS)

THE GUILD OF ONE-NAME STUDIES

An umbrella group of individual societies, the Guild of One-Name Studies (GOONS) consists of members who have an interest in a particular surname. The names vary from the relatively common to the extremely rare.

If you have an unusual name in your ancestry, it is worth getting their directory or logging on to their website (www.one-name.org) to see if one of their members has the same interest as you. Some genealogists also advertise the names they are researching in family history magazines. By getting in touch with them you might save yourself some time-consuming research.

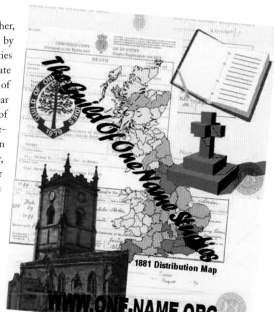

1881 Distribution Map

WWW.ONE-NAME.ORG

Published material

Over the last two decades, a great amount of reference material has been published. The following organizations produce books and booklets on aspects of genealogical records that will help you to find answers to your questions and suggest ways to research information. In addition, there are publishers specializing in books of interest to the family and local historian. Their catalogues are well worth reading for books that may save you doing some research of your own.

THE NATIONAL ARCHIVES

The National Archives (TNA), previously the Public Records Office (PRO), is the repository for govern-

The National Archives is based at Kew, Surrey. TNA, formerly the Public Records Office, produces many useful books and leaflets about the vast number of records it holds.

The SoG's website contains details of its holdings, activities and publications.

ment-produced records. It publishes books and research guides on a variety of subjects, concentrating on the different types of records it holds. Its series on the various branches of the armed services are particularly useful. It also publishes *Ancestors*, a magazine for the family historian. Its website contains both the catalogue of its records and leaflets on topics of genealogical research, including its holdings in that area.

THE SOCIETY OF GENEALOGISTS

The SoG has an extensive library of rare books, transcripts of parish registers and documents, archives of family papers and original research, a series of indexes, a book-ordering service and other facilities for the family historian. It also produces a magazine, the *Genealogist's Magazine*, and book-

lets on topics of interest to the family historian. Its series *My Ancestor Was...* is particularly useful. The library catalogue is included on its website, which also has leaflets about aspects of genealogical research. Non-members of the society can use the library on payment of a fee.

THE INSTITUTE OF HERALDIC AND GENEALOGICAL STUDIES

The IHGS concentrates on courses for family historians and genealogists. It has an extensive library, including a heraldic collection.

THE FEDERATION OF FAMILY HISTORY SOCIETIES

The FFHS has an introductory series of booklets on aspects of genealogical research, including the Basic Facts series. It is worth joining your local FFHS because they hold monthly meetings, usually with a lecture on a specialist topic, and most have a computer section where you can get and swap advice. Members may carry out projects to index or reproduce records. Local history societies also host lectures on aspects of local history, which might contain information of use to a family historian with local ancestors.

THE GIBSON GUIDES

Jeremy Gibson has produced a number of booklets, sometimes with a co-editor, published by the FFHS. They detail, county by county, the holdings of record offices on specific subjects, such as coroners' records, poll books and probate. These are known as Gibson Guides. They enable researchers to plan their work in advance by checking whether a record office holds the documents they need to consult. The introductions also give an overview of the records and the kind of information they contain.

PUBLICATIONS

There are many books and booklets available that not only give information about how to do research, and help to track down surviving records, but also suggest further avenues of research.

Magazines

It is worth subscribing to one or more of the magazines aimed at genealogists. They usually consist of articles on how to research a particular aspect of family history, personal accounts of how a genealogical problem was solved, plus topics of general interest, which build up into a useful body of knowledge. They are especially useful for information on aspects of research that might be too rarely encountered to be included in any of the standard books on genealogy, but which are just what you need to solve a problem.

Specialist publishers

Many companies produce books on genealogy and family history, and one of the larger ones is Phillimore.

Since the 19th century the Harleian Society has been publishing transcripts of registers and pedigrees produced as the result of visitations. Although many of the entries in these transcripts have been entered on the IGI, not all are there, and burials have been excluded from it.

The British Record Society also publishes original records. When an interest in genealogy first began in the 19th century, a number of local societies produced transcripts of registers in their area; most County Record Offices have copies of the ones in their counties, and the SoG has a large collection.

Published books and records

Before going to original records, check if what you plan to look at has been published. In many cases the records are simply transcripts, though in some cases they may have been translated from Latin, but it will save you having

to decipher difficult handwriting. The majority of published registers and records have been indexed, making them simpler to search than the original documents.

Do not buy books (including the ones listed in the "Further help" sections in this book), unless it is the only way you can obtain them. It is always preferable to consult them in a library (or borrow them if you can) before deciding how often you will need to use them.

The same is true of indexes: if you only need to look up one person on a CD-ROM, weigh the cost of purchase against that of travel to a CRO or specialist library. Also, check if the information is on the internet.

FURTHER HELP

British Record Society
www.britishrecordsociety.org.uk
Harleian Society, c/o College of
   Arms, Queen Victoria Street,
   London EC4V 4BT
Phillimore & Co Ltd, Shopwycke
   Hall, Chichester, Sussex PO20
   6BQ www.phillimore.co.uk

If the document you want to see has been published, you may be able to save time and money by getting it through a library, rather than going to a CRO.

Using the internet

Although, in some ways, the internet has made researching family history much easier, the hype around it has raised expectations to an unreasonable level. Although original records are increasingly being digitized and made accessible on it, the majority remain on paper in record offices or have been microfilmed and need to be viewed in an archive or library. What the internet can do, however, is help researchers to locate original documents quickly and conveniently. Most CROs and libraries have a website, and the catalogue of their holdings may be on it. This helps in planning research.

WEBSITES

The websites of organizations of all kinds usually provide a brief history, which will help family historians understand what may be available from its archives and where these are now located. They also give background information that will further your understanding of your ancestors' lives. Many record offices, libraries and museums have on-line fact sheets that you can copy to study at home.

SEARCH ENGINES

A search engine is a way of finding every website that contains the word or words that you enter. They are particularly useful for finding websites on a specific subject, but if you enter just a personal name you will get every site on the web containing that name. If you are researching an individual or a family name, you need to use advanced search techniques. Putting in a common name, such as Johnson, or an ancestor who shares a name with

The internet opens a whole new world of information and allows easy communication with family historians around the globe.

someone famous, such as Elizabeth Taylor, will produce too many irrelevant results. Try adding "family history" – and give dates, places and occupations, and specify the exclusion of certain words, such as "film star".

It is generally agreed that Google is the best search engine, because it arranges the results in order of how frequently they are consulted, but there are many others. If you do not find what you need immediately, it is worth trying searches using two or three search engines. Sometimes, however, you have to accept that the information you need has simply not been researched or put on the web.

In addition to extracting information from the websites of various organizations and individuals (which can contain family histories), there are

also ways of communicating with other researchers. Search engines, such as Google and Yahoo, and genealogical sites, such as RootsWeb, host groups where people sharing the same interests can exchange information.

E-MAIL

This is the most obvious way of writing to someone who shares the same interests as you. Most individuals who have a website on which, for example, they have placed information about their family history will list an e-mail address, which can be used to communicate directly with that person.

MAILING LISTS

All subscribers receive a copy of every communication sent via e-mail. For some of the larger and more general lists, this can be as many as fifty a day, so consider carefully which mailing list or lists you will find most useful. They have specialist interests: a geographical area; an occupation or group of occupations; ancestors from overseas, etc. The lists are managed by a server, but subscription is generally free.

NEWSGROUPS AND MESSAGE BOARDS

These are the electronic equivalent of a notice board and are also dedicated to particular topics. People can simply post messages, asking for information, recommending (or warning against) professional researchers or websites, or writing about a topic they believe to be of interest. Messages on them are not automatically sent to subscribers, so they need to be checked regularly to make sure something of interest is not

Using the internet wisely

- You may need specific software to access certain types of information on the internet. This can often be downloaded from an internet site, but you should get advice about what is necessary if you are not a confident computer user.
- Be focused: it is very easy to spend a long (and potentially expensive) time going through a lot of unrelated records. Formulate questions and strategies for answering them before you start.
- Regard the internet as a giant index. Like all other indexes, it is basically a guide to original documents.
- Treat information on it with caution: anyone can set up their own internet site and put whatever they like on it. A great deal of supposition might be presented as fact. Ask

yourself: how authoritative is this source?
- Be wary about handing over money on the internet. The reputable genealogical sites, which charge for access to their databases and archives, are reliable and generally safe, but buying objects, such as coats of arms, from sites based overseas can be problematic. You have little redress if the goods are not delivered, and giving credit card details on the internet can present problems of security.
- You will find sites offering books that claim to list all of the people with the same surname as you. These are not researched genealogical publications, but are simply lists of usually unrelated people compiled from readily available sources, such as telephone directories. Ignore them.

FURTHER HELP

Christian, Peter *The Genealogist's Internet* (TNA)
Christian, Peter *Web Publishing for Genealogy* (David Hawgood)
Wilson, Richard S. *Publishing Your Family Tree on the Internet* (Writers Digest Books)

PUBLISHING ON THE INTERNET

As well as using the internet to find and communicate with people with the same research interests, you should consider putting your own family tree and history on the web, so that you can be contacted by others.

Unless you are well versed in this area, you will need help with creating your own website. Investigate some existing sites to get an idea of how best to do it. Look at the sites you find easiest to use and let them guide you in organizing your own genealogical information.

missed. Newsgroups have archives of material that has previously appeared, and it is a good idea to check these out.

NETIQUETTE AND FREQUENTLY ASKED QUESTIONS (FAQS)

There are conventions about communicating on the internet, and if you break the rules you may be excluded from group communication sites. Most will, however, have a list of procedures they expect their members to observe. In particular, people get irritated by beginners posing the same basic questions. To avoid this happening, most sites have a list of Frequently Asked Questions (FAQs) that you should consult to see whether your query has already been answered before you ask it yourself.

The IGI is easily accessible to family historians through the LDS website.

Wills, administrations and death duties

I t is often said that you can't take it with you, and wills were made to ensure that a person's possessions went to particular individuals after death. If anybody died intestate (without leaving a will), someone had to be appointed to administer the estate. These administrations (or admons) contain much less information than a will and were usually granted to the next of kin.

WILLS

Most people are familiar with the phrase "last will and testament", which shows the distinction made between land, which cannot be moved, and other goods, which can. The will covers the disposal of estates and property; the testament deals with movable goods, chattels and money.

A history of wills

Until 1858, when a national system was introduced, probate was mainly administered by church courts, but "peculiars" and some manors also had the right to prove wills. During the Commonwealth period (1653–60) a government court handled them.

Nuncupative wills

Before 1838, when nuncupative wills became illegal, a statement of how a person wanted to dispose of his or her possessions could be accepted. They were usually dictated when the person was dying and there wasn't enough time to call in a lawyer or someone experienced in writing a proper will. Although it was witnessed, it was not signed. Such wills usually start with "Memorandum", rather than stating that this is a last will and testament, and are found with the other wills of the court in which they were proved.

Wills before 1858

Before 1858 the proving of wills was done by church courts, which all charged for this service. It has been estimated that in the 19th century only 5 per cent of people's estates went through probate, so the family historian must be prepared not to find a will. When they do exist, however, they can supply a great deal of information.

Wills after 1858

After 1858 the authenticity and validity of wills were proved by the state system on a national basis. The will was taken to the local probate office, which made its own copy and then sent another to the Principal Probate Registry in London, now called the Probate Service of the Principal Registry Family Division. In addition to being the

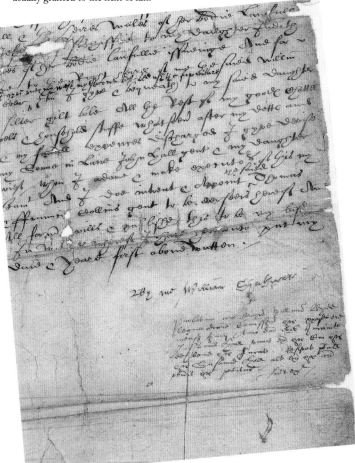

William Shakespeare's will was fairly simple but provides information about family relationships.

probate office for the south-east of Britain, it also deals with wills that present problems from everywhere in the country, and so is a national centre too. The original will was given back to the executor(s) after a note that probate had been granted was added to it. This conferred on the executor(s) the power to administer the estate.

Locating wills

When trying to find a will before 1858, decide how much property was likely to be left, as this should suggest which level of court to start with, but don't assume that a poor person's will would not have been proved in the Prerogative Court of Canterbury (PCC). Check all the courts (see below).

For 1796–1858 the death duty indexes may be a faster way of finding a will than working your way through the various probate courts. These indexes cover all courts before 1811, and after that date each court has its own index. They are especially time-saving if you don't know the exact date on which a will was proved.

Some East India Company (EIC) wills are kept in the Oriental and India Office Library, so those with ancestors living in India, the Far East and other places under the EIC's authority before 1858 might find their wills here.

Indexes to wills for the period 1858–1943 are in the FRC, although the wills themselves are held by the Probate Service. Copies can be obtained by post or a personal search.

If you don't find a will in the area you expect, ask yourself if your ancestor might have died in a "peculiar" (a parish that, for historic reasons, came under the authority of another bishopric or body from the one in which it was geographically located).

Probate could take many years to prove, especially if there were any

The reading of a will might cause dissatisfied family members to challenge its contents through one of the courts that dealt with probate.

difficulties with the will, if it was challenged by the family or if the person lived overseas. In the days before air travel, it could take many months, even years, before the executor(s) might be able to travel to England to prove the will.

If your ancestor was a soldier or sailor, check TNA first. Soldiers and sailors were encouraged to make wills before going overseas, especially in times of war.

Find as many wills as you can for all members of your family, not just your direct ancestors. Married men usually left simple wills, dividing their property between their wives and children. More information may come from the wills of unmarried or childless relations, since they tend to distribute their possessions among a greater number of relatives, and they state the relationship. Maiden aunts are a particularly good source of genealogical information. They may not necessarily have been very rich, but they did like to specify just who would receive a particular piece of jewellery or small sum of money.

If a will isn't listed, see if there is a separate list of administrations. (Sometimes the two are given together; sometimes they are in separate registers.)

The courts you will need to check for wills are listed below.

The archdeaconry courts

These courts were the lowest in the hierarchy and were used by people with property in one archdeaconry. These wills are usually in the CRO but may be in a Diocesan Record Office (DRO).

The diocesan courts

Also called consistory or commissary courts, these came under the jurisdiction of a bishop and were used by people who had property in more than one archdeaconry. These wills are usually in the CRO but may be in a DRO.

The Prerogative Court of York (PCY)

The PCY had jurisdiction north of the River Trent. It covered the dioceses of York, Carlisle, Chester, Durham and the Isle of Man, and wills of people who had property in more than one of these dioceses would have been proved here. These wills are in the Borthwick Institute in York.

The funeral of the Marquis of Bath in 1869. How many of the hundreds of people gathered here were remembered in his will?

The Prerogative Court of Canterbury (PCC)
The PCC was the highest court to prove wills in England and Wales. It was used by those who had property in more than one diocese south of the Trent, or with property in both the PCY and PCC jurisdictions. There was a misapprehension that money invested in the Bank of England counted as property. The bank was sited in the diocese of London, so people who lived elsewhere and had money invested in the bank had their wills proved in the PCC, because they believed that they had property in two dioceses.

The PCC also covered British subjects living abroad in the colonies (including America before the War of Independence, which finished in 1783). During the Commonwealth period (1642–60), all wills were proved in the PCC. Copies of these wills are in the FRC on microfilm, but the originals are stored off site.

All the courts were subject to inhibition from the senior courts. This means that if a bishop were making a

visitation to an archdeaconry, the archdeaconry courts would not be able to carry out their functions, including proving wills. So during the time of the visitation (which usually lasted for a few months), wills would be proved by the diocesan courts.

In addition to these courts, there were "peculiars" (see previous page), which came under the jurisdiction of

someone or some entity other than a court. This might be a manor, a university, the dean and chapter of a cathedral, or the bishop or archdeacon of another diocese.

A sailor's will might be proved in the court connected to the place where he lived in England or Wales; in the archdeaconry or diocesan court of the port in which his ship docked after his death; in the PCC if he died at sea, or in the High Court of the Admiralty.

Of course, wills sometimes created strife in the family, and might have been contested. Any action of this kind will be found in the courts attached to the jurisdiction where they were proved.

Researching wills
To be legal, a will must include one or more executors or executrices (the feminine form of executors). It must also be dated and the signature witnessed by two or more people who must not benefit from the will. If someone dies intestate (without leaving a will), the next of kin can ask for Letters of Administration to be granted so that they can deal with the deceased person's property. These are

---

Digest of will of Sarah Deschamps

PRO PROB 11/995/87
Sarah Deschamps of Maiden Lane, St Paul Covent Garden, widow of Peter Deschamps

To be buried with late husband at Marylebone

To John Deschamps eldest son of my late husband £10

To Francis Deschamps younger son of my late husband £10

To Mrs Susanna Montelln wife of Mr Joseph Montelln

and the daughter of my late husband £10 and my wearing apparel

Remainder to my worthy and most esteemed friend and executrix Mrs Mary Bonouvrier of Maiden Lane

(signed) 15 July 1767

wit: Sam Coates

Mary Hawkes

Proved PCC 12 March 1774

abbreviated to "admon" in records. Also, if the will has not been properly drawn up, for example it was not dated, the next of kin can apply to administer it.

It was, and is still, not necessary to rewrite an entire will in order to vary slightly the bequests within it. The addition of one or more codicils to the will of a member of your family is an interesting source of information about who came into, or fell out of, favour over time.

An inventory – a list of the movable goods of a person – is sometimes attached to a will. This gives clues as to how rich he or she was and also, in the case of men, what their occupation was, since it usually includes his tools.

Be aware that the word "cousin" was used in a much wider sense in the past than it is today. "My cousin Elizabeth" was not necessarily the daughter of an uncle or aunt: she might have been a much more distant relative. All you can tell without further research is that a cousin was a relation of some kind.

If you see that one person, often the eldest son, has been given only a token sum, usually a shilling, don't assume that this is evidence of trouble in the family. He might have already been given a sum of money on marriage or have taken over the family business. Mentioning the person in the will simply showed that he (or occasionally she) had not been forgotten, and so the will could not be challenged on those grounds.

Making a digest of a will

Wills tend to be long and are couched in complicated legal terms, and it is time-consuming and confusing to keep re-reading them to find information. You do need a complete copy of the document for your records, but a digest (a brief summary, in note form, of the contents) is ideal and convenient for everyday use.

Put where the will comes from, with any reference number given to it by the repository. Enter the person's name, occupation and residence, as given in the document. You can omit the standard opening, but note down any special instructions about funeral arrangements, and so on. Then list all the legatees, their relationship to the testator, what they received and any special conditions attached to the bequest. Also note the name(s) of the executor(s) and whether the testator actually signed the will or simply made a mark (which shows how literate he or she was). Write the date the will was written and the witnesses' names. Add the details of when and where it was proved.

ADMINISTRATION

When a will was found to be valid and proved in court, the executor(s) had to sign a bond for a sum of money that would be forfeited if they did not carry out their duties of administering the estate according to the testator's final wishes, as expressed in the will.

If the deceased person had children who were under the age of majority, it was also the executor(s) job to arrange for their ongoing and future education and welfare by entering into tuition and curation bonds, which were pledges to pay a sum of money if these arrangements were not satisfactory. How this was to be done, including the name of any guardian, may have been stipulated in the will. The bonds that were associated with these various duties should be with the other probate records.

Incomplete or non-existent wills required Letters of Administration to be issued before the estate could be administered.

Some places, such as London, had the right to administer the goods of the orphans of freemen through special courts. These records are separate from the probate courts.

DEATH DUTIES

From 1796, various taxes, called collectively "death duties", were payable on estates worth over a certain amount. Initially this was set quite high, but during the 19th century it was progressively lowered, so that a larger proportion of people's estates had to pay duties. The records relating to these and associated matters are held in TNA, with indexes held at the FRC. They are particularly useful in giving the exact amount that an estate was worth. The death duty registers also contain further information, added for many years after the will was proved, such as the dates of death of beneficiaries, which will also help the family historian with research.

Inquests

If a person died in a way that gave rise to suspicions that the death might not have occurred naturally, then an inquest was held. In addition, inquests on all deaths in prison had to be held, even if it was obvious that the person had died from natural causes.

Even if your ancestor was very law-abiding he might have found himself, (or, more rarely, she might have found herself) imprisoned for debt. If he became ill and died while still in prison, an inquest would have been held and the results recorded in the prison inquest records, which makes such records always worth consulting.

ROLE OF THE CORONER

The office of coroner is first mentioned in 1174, though the post itself seems to be much older than that. The coroner had many legal and political responsibilities, but his main function was to look after the Crown's interests, especially in the event of a death. If a person was murdered, the murderer's property was forfeited to the Crown, so the death had to be investigated to see if any property or money could be confiscated. In medieval times the coroner had many duties, but over the centuries his responsibilities were gradually reduced.

OTHER INQUEST ROLES

There are a number of ways in which an ancestor might have been involved in an inquest, and so appear in the records, apart from being either the coroner or the deceased person.

Member of the jury

Once notified of a death that needed investigation, the coroner drew up a list of potential jurors. The parish beadle then visited all the people on the list to call them to serve. Most of the jurymen were respectable tradesmen. Any compensation they received came out of public money, and they were not

A coroner's inquest held at Charing Cross Hospital, London, in 1861. Inquests might also be held at inns, workhouses or prisons.

usually paid for their attendance before the first quarter of the 19th century. Even after this, individual counties had different practices (London did not pay until the end of the century). It was not, therefore, a popular duty, because they would lose business. Sometimes they paid substitutes to attend in their stead or simply pretended not to be at home when the beadle called.

Publican

Until the middle of the 19th century, the majority of inquests were held at a local inn, so, if you have publicans among your ancestors, it is possible that an inquest was held on their premises. Inquests were also held in hospitals and workhouses, which might have involved members of your family in some way.

Doctor

A doctor had to confirm the death and give an opinion about its cause.

Witness

People who had witnessed the death were called to give evidence. These could include members of the dead person's family, neighbours, friends, medical staff at hospitals, workhouse officials, prison workers and even passers-by.

EVIDENCE OF TREASURE-TROVE

The only other major example of the coroner's role in looking after the Crown's financial interests that survives to the present day is the investigation of treasure-trove. If a hoard of gold, silver or bullion is discovered and the owner cannot be identified, then a coroner must hold an inquest to determine whether it was accidentally lost, in which case it becomes the property of the finder, or if it was deliberately hidden, in which case it becomes the property of the Crown. An ancestor's sudden increase in wealth might be due to hard work, an inheritance or gift, criminal activity or the discovery of treasure-trove. The latter is rare but still worth considering. There are papers relating to treasure-trove for 1825–1925 in TNA. Others should be with surviving inquest papers in CROs.

RESEARCHING INQUEST RECORDS

Whenever you go to a record office, check whether it has any surviving inquest papers. If a death took place in the parish where your ancestors were living at a particular time, it is worth checking to see whether a member of your family was involved as a juryman or, if any of them was an innkeeper, as the proprietor of the place where the inquest was held. They might also have given evidence.

When a verdict that resulted in a trial was passed, always follow this up in criminal records. Although the same evidence as was given at the inquest will be repeated, more evidence might have been discovered by the time the trial took place, so the criminal records will give you more information about what happened. You may also find that the trial jury passed a different verdict from that given at the inquest. There were a number of possible verdicts:

- "Visitation of God" (short for "Visitation of God by natural causes") was used for sudden deaths, such as from a heart attack or stroke.
- "Natural causes/natural death" was used to refer to long-standing illnesses such as tuberculosis, or diseases such as smallpox or cholera.
- "Mishap", "casual" or "misfortune" included in a verdict meant that the death was accidental.

- "Murder" and "manslaughter" are self-explanatory.
- "Justifiable homicide" was used when a person, such as a soldier, had grounds to believe that his life was in danger and so killed in self-defence.
- "Want of the necessities of life", which means starvation, shows how hard life could be for the poor.
- "Inclemency of the weather" (what we would call "exposure") might have been the verdict passed on a beggar who died outside on some frosty night or on someone who fell from his horse on his way home and died from the effects of cold.
- "Suicide". If the jury decided that the person had committed suicide, they had to decide whether he or she was sane at the time. People who were "lunatic" (as it was generally called) could be buried with full rites in a churchyard or burial ground. If, however, they were found to be in full possession of their faculties, a verdict of *felo de se* (literally, self-murderer) was passed. Until 1823, a *felo de se* suicide was buried at a crossroads, often with a stake through the body. After 1823, although the person could be buried in a churchyard, the burial had to take place between 9pm and midnight and was without a burial service. Until 1871 the suicide's property was forfeit to the Crown.

Where jurors could not decide why the death occurred, they passed an open verdict, such as "Found dead", or a narrative verdict, such as "Died from a fall".

FURTHER HELP

Gibson, Jeremy and Rogers, Colin *Coroners' Records* (FFHS)

Newspapers and periodicals

Early newspapers were primarily concerned with politics and did not necessarily appear on a regular basis. When something noteworthy happened, enterprising writers and printers would produce a sheet of paper or a small pamphlet describing events and adding editorial comment. The English Civil War, which began in 1641, produced a number of them, some supporting the King, others the Roundheads. Other newspapers, called broadsheets from the size of the paper used, reported sensational events, such as murders. The British Library has a large collection of them, and they are also available on microfilm.

USING NEWSPAPERS FOR RESEARCH

Newspapers, especially local ones, may contain information about ancestors or be used to find out about life in the past.

The *Weekly Telegraph* was one of the many publications aimed at a mass readership.

Early newspapers mainly covered political and commercial matters.

The London Gazette

The *London Gazette* is the Crown's official newspaper, produced by the government since 1665. It lists government appointments and promotions; bankrupts (which other papers, especially *The Times,* reprinted); promotions, medals and other awards made to members of the armed forces, and other miscellaneous notices.

County newspapers

In 1702 the first daily newspaper, the *Daily Courant*, appeared. Other national papers were also founded about this time, and in the mid-18th century county newspapers, usually published weekly, began to appear. These regional publications were aimed at the ruling classes, and much of what they reported concerned the political events in Westminster, and other London news. They also reprinted stories from other counties.

They had, however, some stories of local interest, such as proceedings in criminal courts (for example the quarter sessions or assizes) and inquests. Counties that had a significant sea trade also reported the comings and goings of ships, which might be of interest to those with sea-faring ancestors. Newspapers with an agricultural readership reported farming prices.

Many local newspapers have been at least partially indexed. The standard way to give references is title, date, page, column (*The Times* 27 Feb 1891 4f).

The Times

The Times has been published since 1785 (when it was called the *Universal Daily Register*) and is indexed. Not every single name, however, appears in the index. You might find that something in which your ancestor was involved, such as the opening of a hospital, will appear, but that not all the

A paperboy invites people to "Read all about it!" By the mid-19th century, an increasing number of people could read.

individual people mentioned in the report will be found in the index. In cases such as these, the name of the hospital would be included, so you would need to check all the references to it in the hope that your ancestor was mentioned somewhere. Obituaries have been indexed separately.

In addition to looking up your own ancestors, who might have been involved with a big incident, you can use *The Times* index as a way of finding out when something occurred. The event might be reported at greater length in another national, regional or local paper, to which you can refer later, but you can use *The Times* index to find the exact date.

The introduction of illustrations

Although early broadsheets included woodcuts, they were not the equivalent of photographic representations. They were often standard blocks, of a hanged criminal, for example, which were reused. It wasn't until the mid-19th century that sketches of people and events began to be included. The *Illustrated London News* began in 1842.

From the beginning of the 20th century, technological advances meant that photographs could be used, but the process was expensive and time-consuming, so they were confined to publications with a large national circulation. As technology improved, local newspapers began to use photographs extensively.

Finding old newspapers

The British Library Newspaper Library is the best source of British newspapers and also has a substantial number of overseas publications. A reader's ticket is needed, but one can be issued on the spot on the production of proof of identity. Its catalogue is on-line.

CROs, local history centres and libraries usually have county and local newspapers. Find out in advance which papers they hold and for which dates: some have copies of early newspapers that are missing from the British Library Newspaper Library's collection.

Individual newspapers and periodicals also have their own archives, but they may not be willing to let you search through them.

Press guides, listing newspapers and periodicals, began in 1846. These are useful to find the titles of publications that no longer exist or to track down the kinds of periodicals to which a journalist ancestor might have contributed an article. The British Library Newspaper Library has a complete set of *Willings Press Guide*, and there may be copies in university and other libraries. The British Union Catalogue lists publications (apart from newspapers after 1799) and where copies are available in record offices and libraries.

USING PERIODICALS FOR RESEARCH

Daniel Defoe, now remembered as a novelist, most notably for *Robinson Crusoe*, was for most of his life a prolific journalist, who started the first periodical, called the *Weekly Review*, in 1704. It was followed by the *Tatler* in 1709 and a host of others.

Then, as now, these periodicals were not reporting the news so much as commenting on it for a small circle of like-minded people drawn from the same social background. Similarly, the *Gentleman's Magazine*, which contains BMD notices and obituaries, was a kind of parish magazine for the upper classes. It was published during 1731–1868 and has been indexed. These were the first of a long line of political and social weekly or fortnightly magazines.

FURTHER HELP

Chapman, Colin R. *Using Newspapers and Periodicals* (FFHS)
Ferguson, A. *Directory of Scottish Newspapers* (National Library of Scotland)
Gibson, Jeremy, Langston, Brett and Smith, Brenda W. *Local Newspapers 1750–1920 England and Wales, Channel Islands, Isle of Man. A Select Location List* (FFHS)

The *Methodist Magazine* began in 1798 and was followed by other periodicals aimed at members of religious denominations. Trade journals aimed at people working in particular occupations began with the *Naval Chronicle* in 1799. Later, magazines aimed at leisure interests began to appear.

Published from 1758, the *Annual Review* is a summary of items from the previous year, taken from newspapers and magazines.

The *Illustrated London News* was one of the first publications to include pictures.

Going back to 1538

Now that you have extracted all the material you can from the certificates and other material held at the Family Record Centre and other sources mentioned in chapter 2, it's time to explore the records held at local level. These may date back as far as 1538, which is when parish records began. Here you will find not only ancestors to add to your pedigree, but also more information about their lives. Use this information to flesh out your chart so that you can start to create a true family history.

Record offices, history centres and libraries

All over Britain there is a variety of record offices, local history centres and libraries, which together hold an enormous amount of material. This information was accumulated (in some cases over centuries) without any clearly defined policies, which makes it difficult to know where exactly the material you need is actually held. The following is a rough guide to what you can expect to find in the different types of repository.

IDENTIFYING WHERE TO FIND YOUR INFORMATION

At this early stage in your research, this wide range of repositories might seem very confusing, but, as you work your way through the rest of this book, you will find that the location of each type of record will be given at the relevant point, so you will know where to go. Please note that most record offices and some libraries require users to have a reader's ticket, so find out

before you go what proof of identity you need, as well as any other form of documentation, such as a letter from an official body.

The National Archives (TNA)

This important record centre holds all the records to do with national government. It produces a series of leaflets giving details of its holdings, which you can either get at TNA or copy from its website. It issues its own

The National Archives' building in Kew, Surrey, holds records related to national government matters.

ABOVE AND RIGHT The County Record Office for Lancashire is in Manchester. Its documents and maps relate to the county administration, including parish records.

ticket, and, in order to get one, you need some identification that shows your address. You are also given a tour to find out where all the records are and how they can be ordered, so allow half a day for this preliminary process.

County Record Offices (CRO)

The CROs have various records concerning the local government of a county, including parish registers.

In the 1970s, the counties in Great Britain were reorganized and renamed. In the process, one or two disappeared, others were amalgamated, and some towns came under the aegis of a different county. Despite this reorganization, however, the records of the old counties generally stayed where they were, since moving the accumulated documents of several hundred years was generally not a feasible option. Huntingdonshire, for example, was absorbed into Cambridgeshire, but there is still a record office in Huntingdon covering the ancient county. For records before the 1970s, you need to know where the place you are interested in was situated. The majority of CROs belong to the County Archives

Record Network (CARN), and any participating office will issue a ticket that you can use in all the others.

Diocesan Record Offices (DRO)

A diocese is the area under the jurisdiction of an archbishop or a bishop. Before the mid-19th century, the Church carried out many of the functions later taken over by local and

national government. The DROs hold records concerned with Church administration, particularly wills before 1858. Dioceses did not follow county boundaries, and so you will need to find out where the records you want are: they may have been kept in a separate archive, divided between CROs or deposited in one of the CROs in the diocese.

Staff in record offices will help you to locate material from their resources, but they are not able to do extensive research for you.

records concerned with local administration. They may have copies of census returns after 1841 for their particular area. You may also find copies of local newspapers here.

These centres have a policy of collecting material concerned with their area, so you should find all sorts of non-governmental records here: local businesses, photographs, personal diaries, etc. Most of these will be from the late 19th century onwards, with the majority dating from the 20th century. The centres rarely require a ticket, but it is wise to check in advance.

District Record Offices

Within individual counties there may be District Record Offices, which hold records to do with a fairly large area within the county or a particular town. These can usually be found in the CARN system.

City/town record offices

Individual cities and towns, usually those that originally had borough status, such as York and Colchester, may

have a separate archive, which can include some of the surrounding area. All record offices and most libraries hold maps and photographs. CROs should also have criminal records of one kind or another.

Local history centres

These have clearly defined local boundaries, usually several boroughs, and they hold books on local history, copies of parish registers and other

Local studies libraries

These are usually located in the main library of an individual borough. They hold books and documents related to the borough in which they are located. This may include copies of parish registers and other administrative documents, particularly local council records. There may also be copies of newspapers here. These records will usually date from 1888, when the Local Government Act set

ABOVE LEFT Microfilms/ microfiches of original records may be obtainable in a number of places so you can choose the nearest location.

LEFT The British Library, located at St Pancras in London, holds books, manuscripts and specialist collections useful to the family historian.

Visiting your chosen repositories

While you are looking through your files and notes, ideas about where you might look to find solutions to problems or to get further information will occur to you. Keep a sheet for each record office, history centre and library, and note down each potential avenue of research.

When you have accumulated a few record sheets, it will be time to visit the place in question. Here are a few rules to guide you when using these resources.

- Take pencils with you, since most record offices and libraries forbid the use of ink pens, which might permanently mark their books and papers. Many also forbid the use of erasers.
- Take a transparent plastic bag to hold your notebooks and record sheets, since the majority of

repositories do not allow researchers to take bags into the search rooms.

- Take change for lockers (usually £1 coins) and also for photocopying, microfilm and/or microfiche machines.
- Telephone in advance to find out whether they hold the records you need and to get as much information about what is held.
- Find out how to get there and if there are any places nearby where you can get lunch. Quite a few are isolated, so if you don't want to waste precious time, take your own food.
- Plan on spending at least two days there. Since you will not be able to sort out which information is useful and needs more research and which is irrelevant to your work while you

are actually copying it, you will need to spend some time sorting it all out. This process will give you ideas about what needs to be followed up, so that you can make a list of further work to do.

- When you arrive, spend a little time seeing what research has already been done. Are there name indices? You don't need to follow up references immediately, but you should take a note of what there is.
- While you are there, pick up all the information sheets you can about their holdings as well as any about other sources of information in the area, such as museums. It's worth having a file into which you can put all these sheets for future reference, since you will usually have to return to a record office several times.

up the borough councils. The libraries rarely require a ticket, but you should check about this in advance.

National libraries

These hold material related to their particular specialism, for example the British Library Newspaper Library at Colindale in north London, which has newspapers and magazines dating back to the mid-17th century.

To use the main branch of the British Library at Euston, which holds books and official publications, you will need a reader's ticket. It's quite easy to get one to use for just a day with some form of identification, but for longer periods of research you must also be able to prove that you cannot get the books you need elsewhere, such as your local library. If you want to look at just newspapers, you can get a separate ticket for the Colindale branch.

The British Library's Newspaper Library at Colindale in north London is microfilming its newspapers and magazines.

University libraries

In addition to academic books and material relating to the university itself, a university library may hold private papers that have been deposited there by individual families, particularly benefactors of the university. Most university libraries, like the British Library, will issue a temporary reader's ticket if necessary; others will ask you how long you think you may need for your research, and give you a pass for that period.

FURTHER HELP

Cole, Jean and Church, Rosemary
*In and Around Record Repositories
in Great Britain and Ireland*
(Armstrong Boon Marriott
Publishing)
Short Guides to Records (Series 1
Guides 1–24, Series 2 Guides 25–
48) (The Historical Association)

Births, christenings, marriages and burials in parish registers

Before 1837 and the introduction of civil registration, records of baptisms, marriages and burials were kept by religious denominations. After the Reformation, the Churches of England (also known as the Anglican Church), Wales, Scotland and Ireland replaced the Roman Catholic Church and carried out many jobs for the government as well as fulfilling religious functions. The parish was the smallest unit of Church administration. There were some 10,000 in England and Wales. Larger ones, especially in the countryside, might have townships within them, each having a chapel to serve a section of the parishioners.

A HISTORY OF PARISH REGISTERS

The first legislation requiring parish registers to be kept was passed in 1538 by Henry VIII. Some parish registers from before this date survive, and many are kept in Rome. Unfortunately, most of them don't have any indication on them of where they came from, so this date is the earliest for which the majority of family historians will be able to find records of their ancestors in Britain.

These first registers were usually kept on paper in leather-bound books. The quality of the paper was generally not very good, so over the centuries many registers have disintegrated. Others have been lost or else damaged in some other way.

In 1597, Elizabeth I passed a law requiring parish registers to be kept on vellum or parchment, which are both much more hard-wearing than paper, and for them to be stored in a locked chest. The legislation also required the entries in the old paper volumes to be transferred into the new books. Not everyone copied everything back as far as 1538: most parishes just went back to 1558, the date of Elizabeth's accession.

From 1597 a copy of all register entries had to be made and sent to the bishop of the diocese in which the parish was situated. These are called Bishop's Transcripts (BTs). A few places, such as Lincoln and Canterbury, had already started to do this before this date. Parishes in the three dioceses of Norwich, Canterbury and Worcester returned transcripts to archdeacons as well as bishops.

The "Commonwealth gap"

In 1649, at the end of the English Civil War, the execution of Charles I marked the beginning of a period when Britain was ruled over by a republic known as the Commonwealth. In 1653, Oliver Cromwell became Lord Protector of the Commonwealth. His government did not want the Church of England involved in running the country, so civil servants took over the registration of births and deaths, while Justices of the Peace (JPs) performed marriage ceremonies.

Although the Church of England carried on baptizing, marrying and burying people, the Anglican records

Parish registers were introduced in 1538, but relatively few from that date survive. Fire, flood, enemy action and incompetent parish officials have all taken their toll on later registers.

are less good at this period. This is partly because there was a huge growth in Nonconformist sects and partly because people were afraid that these records might be used against them. This period, which lasted until the restoration of Charles II in 1660, is often known as the "Commonwealth gap", because parish records, the source of so much genealogical information, are patchy for this time.

The Restoration and after

In 1660 the registrars of births and deaths were ejected from their jobs, usually taking their records with them, as a result of which not many have survived. Record-keeping again became the duty of the parish authorities.

Under the Burial in Woollen Acts of 1678 and 1680, which were intended to protect the wool industry, people had to be buried in woollen shrouds or else pay a fine. An affidavit was sworn that a woollen shroud had been used. Some parishes kept separate records of this; others made a note, such as "aff.", next to the burial entry.

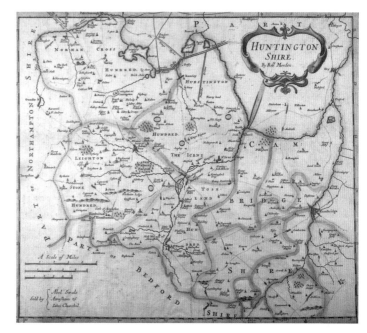

Although Huntingdonshire no longer survives as a separate county, there is a record office in Huntingdon containing parish registers and other material relating to the old county.

Paupers were exempt. These Acts were not repealed until 1813, but by then records of affidavits were rarely kept.

In 1693–1705 and 1783–93, there was a tax on parish register entries, although paupers were again exempt.

The administrative structure of the Church of England

The family historian needs to understand how the Church was organized, because it played such an important part in everyday life.

Province

There were three provinces in Britain: Canterbury and York in England, and Armagh in Ireland. An archbishop headed each one. The Archbishop of Canterbury had precedence over the others.

Diocese

Each province was divided into several dioceses, each headed by a bishop.

Archdeaconry

Dioceses were subdivided into archdeaconries, with an archdeacon in charge.

Rural deanery

Outside cities, each diocese had several rural deaneries (groups of parishes), each presided over by a rural dean.

Parish

The parish was the smallest unit of a diocese, with its own church and clergyman. Within a large and widespread parish there might also be chapels.

The parish church was the focus of people's lives. It was the primary administrative unit.

Gretna Green in Scotland, just over the border from England, was used by couples who did not want to marry in their parish church.

Quakers were regarded as good record keepers and so were allowed to marry in their own places of worship, and record the event.

Regular and irregular marriages

Until the middle of the 18th century, there was no clear definition of how a marriage was made. Most people preferred to marry in church, because then there was proof of the union. Any children the couple subsequently had were then clearly legitimate, and they and the widow could inherit property without having to go to great lengths to prove their rights. In many cases, the church wedding was simply a public announcement of a previous private arrangement. This may account for the number of brides who were pregnant when they married. Sometimes, of course, the man might die before the ceremony could be performed, so a child would appear to be illegitimate, although the parents might have married privately.

If a couple decided to marry in church, they could have banns called in both their parishes for three Sundays before the ceremony, or they could get a licence from an archbishop or bishop, which meant they did not need to have banns called.

There were a number of places and "peculiars", which, for historic reasons, fell outside the local bishop's control, so the minister claimed the right to issue marriage licences. There were many such parishes in London, but the most notorious place was the area around Fleet Prison. For a fee, people could be married here immediately by a clergyman with no questions asked. As well as being a place where people could marry in secret, it seems to have been considered romantic to have a wedding there.

Lord Hardwicke's Marriage Act of 1752

In an attempt to resolve the difficulties caused by all these irregularities, Lord Hardwicke introduced a bill to regularize marriages, which came into effect in 1753. Under this legislation, marriages had to take place on licensed premises, which were limited to churches or chapels, according to the Church of England rites. Jews and Quakers were exempt, but Nonconformists and Roman Catholics had to marry in an Anglican church or chapel. Printed registers to record marriages and a separate book to record the calling of banns were also introduced.

A further Act, passed in 1812, laid down that, from 1813, printed paper registers also had to be used for baptisms and burials.

Marriage licences

Particular sections of the population were likely to prefer marriage licences to having banns called. These were:

- the wealthy
- widows and widowers
- couples where one or both of the parties was under the age of consent and therefore needed the parents' permission
- couples where the bride was very obviously pregnant
- couples where the groom was about to join the armed forces, especially in wartime
- Nonconformists and, after 1753, Roman Catholics

The documents associated with the issuing of a marriage licence consisted of two parts:

- the marriage allegation – a sworn statement by the man or woman that there were no legal impediments to their marriage, giving details of the date and place where they planned to marry.
- the marriage bond – an agreement to pay a sum of money if the couple didn't marry. This was usually sworn by the groom and another man, generally the best man, but it could be a relative of the bride or groom, such as the father.

On receipt of these two signed documents, the licence itself was issued to be given to the minister of the place where the marriage ceremony was to be conducted. The licence itself might be with the parish records, but it is unlikely to have survived. The allegation and the bond, however, will be among the diocesan records, and some have been indexed and/or published.

USING PARISH REGISTERS

If the parish register has not survived, see if there are any Bishop's Transcripts or, in the cases of Norwich, Canterbury and Worcester, Archdeacon's Transcripts. These should be in the CRO along with the parish registers, but in some cases they may be held in the DRO, if this is separate from the CRO.

Look for retrospective baptisms and marriages performed after the restoration of the monarchy in 1660, and baptisms performed after the repeal of taxes on parish register entries in 1705 and 1793. It is not uncommon to find families having two, three or more children baptized together, once the registration was free again. These may appear to be multiple births, although this is rarely so, and twins or triplets are usually stated to be such.

If you are searching for a marriage before 1753 and cannot find it in the most likely parishes, try looking in places where irregular marriages were held, such as the Fleet Prison area. For those in the north of England, it was quicker and cheaper to go over the border to Scotland, where the laws governing marriage were different, so you might consider looking there. Gretna Green was simply the first and most convenient place to marry, but anywhere in Scotland is a possibility. There were also "peculiars" and parishes in rural areas that had a minister who was less scrupulous about carrying out marriages according to Church law, so see if there are any of these in the vicinity of where your ancestors lived.

The parish records were kept by the Church of England, which means that Nonconformists do not appear in them, except for marriages after 1753. If you find that your ancestors were married in the parish church but did not have their children baptized there or were not buried in the churchyard, you can suspect that they were most probably Nonconformists.

Most couples married in the bride's parish, although they might later live in the husband's. The banns book will record the calling of banns in church and should include the parishes of both bride and groom, so you can then look for the marriage in the other parish. Also, check marriage licences in both the Bishop's and the Archdeacon's Transcripts. If neither of these produces a result, look in neighbouring parishes. Sometimes this will take you over the border into the next county (and a different CRO).

After civil registration was introduced in 1837, churches did not stop carrying out baptisms, marriages and burials, so you may find information in parish registers that also appears on certificates, which have to be paid for.

USING DAY BOOKS

Parishes also kept day books, which noted the costs of services and often give additional information. Burial day books are especially useful since they usually include the location of the burial plot, while the amount paid gives an indication of the family's wealth. Relatively few burial day books have survived, but check whether there are any for your ancestor's parish.

FURTHER HELP

Benton, Tony *Irregular Marriage in London before 1754* (SoG 1993)
Herber, Mark *Clandestine Marriages in the Chapel and Rules of the Fleet Prison 1680–1754* (Boutle and King) (3 volumes)
Humphrey-Smith, Cecil *The Phillimore Atlas & Index of Parish Registers* (Phillimore) This book, which includes Scotland, gives county-by-county maps of parishes and also shows which bishopric governed them. Maps of individual counties are also available.

Other parish records

B esides christenings, marriages and burials (CMB) registers, parishes kept many other records containing information about the parish. The various officials had to keep accounts of income from tithes and other sources, such as rates. They also had to account for expenditure. Regular vestry meetings were held to discuss parish business. In addition to this routine work, there may be records from special events, such as the mapping of a parish or the list of communicants at Easter, the holiest day of the Church's year.

The parish had responsibility for keeping the highways in good repair. Rates to pay for this were collected from householders.

THE ROLE OF THE CHURCH

Before the 1888 Local Government Act, the Church of England, in the form of the parish church, was responsible for many of the functions carried out by local councils today. It had both a spiritual role and the responsibility for administering the law at a local level. This involved:

- looking after all those in the parish unable to support themselves because they were unemployed or sick (including those who were not members of the Church)
- caring for orphans
- keeping the highways in good repair

Parish officials included:

- The minister of the church, who usually chaired vestry (parochial officers') meetings.
- The parish clerk (usually also the vestry clerk), who assisted in parish administration and performed minor tasks during church services.
- One or more churchwardens, who were responsible for keeping the church in good repair and reporting on the conduct of minister and parishioners to the bishop. They kept accounts of money collected and spent by the parish on both the church and its services and charity.

- One or more overseers of the poor, who were responsible for collecting the poor rates from householders and spending this money on caring for those unable to work and also for the care and apprenticeship of orphans. They also kept accounts.

- The surveyor of the highways, who kept accounts of collecting and disbursing money for the maintenance of roads, and later on in cities and towns for keeping them properly lit.

- The scavenger, who was responsible for keeping the roads clear of muck and obstructions.

- The constable, or headborough, who was responsible for the maintenance of law and order.

- The beadle, who had miscellaneous parish duties, including informing the parishioners when vestry meetings were held, carrying messages for the other parish officials and assisting the constable.

- The sexton, who dug graves, rang the bells and carried out other small jobs around the church.

With the exception of the minister, these posts were unpaid and therefore not popular. Between 1699 and 1827, anyone who successfully apprehended and prosecuted a criminal who then received a capital conviction, was exempt from serving as a parish official in the parish where the crime took place. These exemptions were known as "Tyburn tickets". They could be transferred to another person, for instance by selling them. A few examples survive, usually found among the parish records.

The income for the parish church came from two main sources: tithes (either "great" or "small") and rates.

Tithes

Each parishioner had to give a tenth of his or her income to the parish church. These tithes paid the minister's salary and provided for the upkeep of the church. They could be in the form of actual goods, such as an animal or part of the harvest, or money. Tithes in the form of goods were usually divided into "great" and "small" tithes. The great tithes were the produce of the land, such as grain or wood, and they were supposed to go to the rector, who was often, in fact, a corporate body. The small tithes comprised everything else, and they went to the minister.

Pressure for commutation (paying a sum of money instead of handing over the goods themselves) grew during the 18th century, resulting in the Tithe Commutation Act of 1836, though this practice had been taking place before it became enshrined in law.

Nonconformists objected greatly to contributing to the Anglican Church, and there were many disputes about non-payment in the Church courts, as well as disputes about under-valuation, about whether minerals that were mined were liable to be tithed, and other issues. An Act of 1891 restricted the payment of tithes to landowners.

Rates

The rates levied on each householder in the parish paid for the non-spiritual duties. The work involved was carried out by a group of (usually) men, who were collectively known as the vestry, after the room of the church in which they generally met. All parishioners were entitled to attend the meeting, and ratepayers were allowed to vote.

USING THE PARISH RECORDS

Ancestors may be found among the parochial officers or those who paid money to the Church or received it, either in payment for carrying out work or to help in times of want. When you visit a CRO, it is worth checking if it has any account books from the parish in which your ancestor lived. Vestry minutes are a good source of information about events in the parish, which might have involved your ancestor.

LEFT Tithes were paid on the produce of the land or labour, sometimes in money and sometimes in the produce itself.

BELOW Tithe barns, like this one in Bradford-on-Avon, were used to store produce for payment in kind.

Lists of the inhabitants of a parish were occasionally made. Some are complete censuses, made before 1801, while others are lists, usually of the male inhabitants, made for a particular purpose, such as assessing tithe payments or church attendance.

Surveys

Parishes occasionally drew up a list of tithe payers, called a terrier, to which a map was sometimes attached, but most useful information comes from the surveys made in the years following the Tithe Commutation Act of 1836. Three copies of the Commissioners' reports were made, with detailed, large-scale maps. One copy remained with the Commissioners, another was deposited in DROs (most are now in CROs) and the third copy went to the parish itself (and may also now be in the CRO). The Tithe Act of 1936 abolished the practice of paying tithes.

> ### FURTHER HELP
>
> Gibson, Jeremy and Medlycott, Mervyn *Local Census Listings 1522–1930: Holdings in the British Isles* (FFHS)

The poor of the parish

The parish's many social obligations included caring for the poor or those unable to look after themselves. Many people who fell on hard times either did not have family close by or had relatives and friends who themselves were too poverty-stricken to be able to help them. The parish played a major role in supporting the unemployed until they could find work, as well as providing for the needs of the physically or mentally ill.

THE POOR LAW BEFORE 1834

The first Poor Law was passed in 1531. It predated the Reformation in Britain by a few years, but it was a sign that the old way of caring for the poor and sick through monasteries, guilds and fraternities was breaking down. The dissolution of the monasteries (1536–40) took away a major source of help and, incidentally, also added to the problems of unemployment. The

Poor and orphaned children were the responsibility of their parish, though some parishes were more generous than others.

government responded by handing over the duties previously carried out by charitable institutions to the local Church of England parish.

Settlement and removal orders

Between 1531 and 1598 a succession of laws to deal with poor people were passed. They were mainly aimed at punishing beggars and also women who had illegitimate children by branding, whipping and/or imprisoning them in houses of correction or poorhouses, where they were given work to do. If there was not enough work locally, JPs could issue them with a licence to beg.

There were also provisions for raising taxes to provide financial assistance for those who were considered genuinely unable to work and for apprenticing poor and orphaned children. The problem with this system was that parishes that were more generous in their interpretation of the laws than others were overwhelmed with applicants for help from outside their locality.

The 1598 Act

To help solve the problem of applicants seeking financial help from the most generous parishes, the 1598 Act was passed. This made provision for beggars to be returned to the place where they were born or to the last parish in which they had lived for a year or more. It was the beginning of the system of settlement, which lasted until World War I. A person's parish of settlement was the one that, in the event of that person becoming dependent on parish relief, had the responsibility for looking after him or her. Gaining settlement somewhere was achieved in a number of ways. The first, and primary, way was by being born there, but others were added by further Acts over the centuries.

Children who lived on the streets might be sent into the Navy.

The 1662 Act

This Act said that a newcomer to a parish could be removed from it within 40 days of their arrival if they did not rent a house worth more than £10 per annum. The person had to go before two JPs, who would determine whether they could remain or whether they would be moved to another parish.

This legislation also decreed that a person leaving a parish to move to another should get a certificate from the original parish to say that, should the person fall on hard times and have to seek relief from the new parish, the old one would pay the costs incurred. These were known as settlement certificates. Relatively few survive, partly because people often did not make the effort to get one.

The 1692 Act

This Act added other ways of gaining settlement in a parish:

- paying rates
- serving a full apprenticeship
- working for a master who himself had settlement there for a year

Legitimate children took their father's parish of settlement, but, if this could not be discovered because he had died or absconded, they took their mother's parish.

The 1697 Act

This Act laid down that newcomers who had a settlement certificate from their previous parish could not be removed until they became chargeable to the parish through losing their employment, or from poverty or illness. It added fines for those who refused to take on pauper apprentices.

The 1782 Act

Other laws relating to the poor were passed, but the next major one was the 1782 Act, which allowed parishes to

The women on this ward in the St James's parish workhouse in London would be required to help pay for their keep by tasks like spinning, sewing or laundry work.

unite in certain circumstances to administer their poor relief jointly under a board of management known as the Guardians of the Poor. Only those physically or mentally incapable of working were to go to the poor-house. The others were to be given outdoor relief (money given to sustain poor people not living in a work-

Dr Barnardo's is the best known of all the charities that took in destitute children.

house), including having low wages supplemented or being hired out for work by the Guardians.

Settlement examinations and removal orders

Determining the parish of settlement of a person without a certificate was complicated. The person would be questioned by two JPs about his or her history: where they were born; whether they had done an apprentice-ship; whether they were married (wives and children took the man's parish of settlement) and where they had lived and for how long. It was, in effect, a potted biography, which provides a great deal of useful genealogical information.

At the end of the examination, the JPs had to decide whether the person should be removed or not. If they decided that he or she belonged to another parish, a removal order was issued. Two copies were made, one for each parish, and these often summarize the information given in the settlement examination. Sometimes the parish of origin accepted that it had

Most elderly widows had no choice but to go into the workhouse. It was a fate they dreaded, both because of the conditions there and the social stigma that it carried.

responsibility for the person, but if it didn't, the matter went to quarter sessions – the legal hearings conducted four times a year. There the matter would be disputed and a final decision arrived at.

Sometimes the parish of settlement would agree to reimburse the new parish rather than have the person returned. Notes relating to this will be entered on the documents or will appear in accounts. They might also be given in the minutes of the workhouse.

If the person (often accompanied by his wife and family or, in the case of a woman, by her children) was removed, the overseer of the poor had to issue a certificate, giving the route by which he or she was to be sent back, often accompanied by the parish constable. Parishes en route may have notes about them.

In general, parishes were not very concerned about young, single men who were capable of earning a living and therefore unlikely to need financial support, as well as being a useful addition to the workforce. They were, however, very quick to investigate any lone women, particularly those who

had children, and also single women, who, they feared, might get pregnant and leave the ratepayers with both mother and child to support.

Bastardy examinations

The various Acts that were concerned with beggars often included provisions for punishing the mothers of illegitimate children, although until the middle of the 18th century, bastardy was, in fact, comparatively rare.

Until 1744 an illegitimate child became the responsibility of the parish where it was born. Some parish officials would go to extreme lengths to avoid an illegitimate child being born within their boundaries, even transporting a woman in labour into a neighbouring parish. They also put pressure on the father to marry the mother, or gave financial inducements to anyone willing to take her on. Details of these practices can appear in all the other sources connected with the administration of the Poor Laws. After 1744 an illegitimate child took its mother's parish of settlement.

Although many settlement cases were sorted out satisfactorily between the two parishes concerned, cases of

illegitimacy usually went to quarter sessions. The aim was to enforce an order making the father pay the costs of raising the child if he would not or could not marry the mother.

EXAMINING THE POOR LAW AFTER 1834

In 1834 the problems of dealing with those who could not, for one reason or another, work or whose income was too small to support themselves and their families, meant that there had to be a major revision of the way in which the system operated. Various Acts of Parliament had permitted particular parishes to band together to care for their poor, but now this system was extended across the whole country. Parishes banded together into what was called a Poor Law Union (these unions formed the basis of registration districts when civil registration was introduced three years later) and built a workhouse into which people would be compelled to live as a condition of receiving help. Outdoor relief was no longer permitted. The aim was to make the experience in the workhouse so unpleasant that only the truly needy would enter.

The workhouse was managed by a Board of Guardians, and, over the years, other functions, such as overseeing civil registration, sanitation and vaccination within the district covered by the union, were added to their duties there. In some places, the board was also given the responsibility for overseeing school attendance and accommodating juvenile offenders. The infirmary attached to the workhouse might also be used to treat non-residents, adding more responsibility.

It was not until 1930 that the workhouses, and with them the Boards of Guardians, were abolished. From this it will be seen that Poor Law Union records can provide a wealth of information about poor and working-class ancestors, especially those who fell on hard times through sickness, either physical or mental.

RESEARCHING RECORDS RELATING TO THE POOR OF THE PARISH

The problems of supporting the unemployed, the poverty-stricken and the long-term sick have never been solved satisfactorily, and, just as today, governments in the past set up an elaborate bureaucracy to define who was and who was not eligible for assistance, how much assistance would be given and how it would be delivered. These policies generated much paperwork that is now of great help to the family historian.

Parish records regarding life in the parish before 1834 will be found in CROs under various headings:

- bastardy examinations
- minutes of the poorhouse/work-house
- quarter sessions
- parish accounts (churchwarden's, overseer's or constable's)
- removal orders
- settlement examinations

After that date, Poor Law Union records can provide detailed information on the poor of the parish.

This cartoon satirizes the effects of the laws on bastardy, whereby parish officials had to pay to support illegitimate children and their mothers.

Orphans and foundlings

Fewer people in the past survived to a great age than do today. Childbirth was a hazard for mother and child, and many people had lost one or both parents by adolescence. Illegitimate children were often abandoned.

ORPHANS

Generally, poor orphans were taken in by another member of the family. If this did not happen, they came under the care of the authorities. Orphans who had inherited land and/or a considerable sum of money needed special arrangements to protect their wealth. In addition, children of a wealthy widow, who might remarry to a man who could defraud the children of their inheritance, were also considered in need of legal protection.

Until 1600, the Crown administered the property of their tenants' orphans through the Court of Wards and had the rights to sell wardships and arrange the children's marriages. If the children did not come under the Crown's protection, it was the responsibility of the Church court where the parent's will was proved to make sure that suitable arrangements were made for their upbringing. Executors of wills had particular responsibilities for the care of orphans.

FOUNDLINGS

In 17th- and 18th-century parish registers of large towns and cities, there are baptism entries relating to abandoned babies and children, usually called foundlings or "dropped" children. Those not lucky enough to be taken in by families were put into the parish workhouse, where most of them died.

The Orphan Boys Asylum in Liverpool was only one of many local homes for children whose parents had died or could not care for them.

Parish officials in cities, where the unhealthy state of the air and water added to the general unhealthiness of the workhouse, often arranged for foundlings to be sent into the countryside to be brought up by families there. They were called "nurse" children. When they were old enough, they returned to the parish, which arranged for them to be apprenticed.

CARE AGENCIES

In addition to two philanthropists, Thomas Coram and Dr Barnardo, church organizations cared for the orphans and foundlings of their parish.

Thomas Coram

A shipbuilder and merchant, Thomas Coram was appalled at the number of babies abandoned in London. He founded an orphanage in Bloomsbury, then in open fields just outside London, called the Foundling Hospital.

It was the first of its kind in Britain and opened in 1747 with many rich and influential patrons.

Babies under the age of two months were admitted. They were baptized and usually given new names, often of illustrious people, which is where some family legends of illegitimate descent from a famous or aristocratic person originate. Then they were sent into the countryside to be raised by paid foster mothers. At the age of four or five they returned to Bloomsbury for their education and apprenticeship.

In 1756, parliament agreed to give financial support to the hospital on condition that any child was admitted. Children were transported from all over the country, as parish officials offloaded their responsibilities on to the Foundling Hospital. More foster parents had to be recruited, and eventually other branches had to be established in various parts of the country.

Parliament stopped its funding completely in 1760, and the hospital swiftly reinstated limits on the number of children that could be accepted. The satellite establishments were wound down as the children in them graduated, and by 1773 they were all closed.

Dr Barnardo

While training as a medical missionary at the London Hospital, Thomas Barnardo was shocked by the poverty he saw around him in the East End. In 1866, he started a charity, Barnardo's, to care for all those children who were orphans or whose parents were too poor to look after them properly. As well as being fed and clothed, the children were educated and taught a trade.

The first home, which was for boys, was established in Stepney, London, in 1870. Three years later, a girls' home opened at Barkingside in Essex. The boys were largely sent into the Army or Navy and the girls into domestic service. In the early 20th century, some children were sent overseas to help to build and maintain the British Empire.

Other agencies

In the early days, churches largely ran orphanages, and did not get involved with arranging adoptions until after World War II. It was believed then that an adopted child should make a completely fresh start, and details of their original parents were withheld. From 1976, however, adopted people have been able to get details of their origins through the Family Record Centre (FRC).

RESEARCHING RECORDS OF ORPHANS AND FOUNDLINGS

Finding an orphan or foundling in your ancestry may lead to a dead end. Records of many orphanages have not survived, and the parents of a foundling may never have been traced.

LEFT The Foundling Hospital in London had many rich and influential supporters.

BELOW LEFT Learning a trade was an important part of life at a Dr Barnardo's Boys' Home.

Poor children

The baptismal records of the Foundling Hospital are in TNA. Babies were frequently renamed, even if their original name was known. There is a copy of each record, along with the rest of the hospital's documents before 1885, in the London Metropolitan Archives (LMA). After 1885, the records remain with the Coram Family establishment and are closed for 110 years, but information may be available to relatives of their foundlings. Parents sometimes left tokens with their children, which could later be used to prove their connection. These were preserved by the Foundling Hospital.

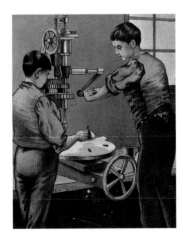

Dr Barnardo took before-and-after photographs of the children he took in and recorded the work of his homes in photographs and (after 1905) on film. The records are unusually complete and are now open to the public.

The records of other, smaller, agencies' records may have been lost or destroyed. They also vary in their attitude to allowing access to them.

Wealthy children

As well as records in the Court of Wards, information about wealthy orphans may be found in church courts, especially if there was a dispute about who should care for them, or if their assets were badly or fraudulently administered.

FURTHER HELP

TNA Legal Records Information 11 Court of Wards and Liveries 1540–1645: Land Inheritance
Stafford, Georgina *Where to Find Adoption Records: A Guide for Counsellors* (British Agencies for Adoption and Fostering)
Tracing the Birth Parents of Adopted Persons (FFHS)
After Care Centre, Barnardo's, Tanners Lane, Barkingside, Ilford, Essex IG6 1QG
www.barnardos.org.uk/
AboutBarnardos/aftercare/index.
html

Records for other Christian denominations

"Nonconformists" is the general term used for the Protestant sects who do not conform to the tenets of the Church of England. They therefore cover a wide range of beliefs and religious practices, from the Methodists, who began as a movement within the Anglican Church, to the Baptists, who do not baptize children, only adults, and the Quakers, who do not practise baptism at all. All their beliefs and practices influence what kind of records were kept.

The other major religion that needs to be considered is Roman Catholicism. Until the 19th century, records of Catholics are sparse because there was much discrimination and, sometimes, persecution. '

A Quaker meeting c.1640. Women were, unusually for the period, allowed to take a prominent role in the movement.

THE REFORMATION

Until the Reformation in the early 16th century, the Roman Catholic Church was the state religion. As the word "reformation" suggests, the aim was originally to change, rather than abolish, the Roman Catholic Church, but while many people were agreed that the faith needed reform, they could not agree on the best way to do it.

The establishment of the Church of England

In 1534, England broke with Rome and established the Church of England. The Roman Catholic Church remained united, but within the Church of England the Protestants (literally those who protested against the tenets and practices of the Roman Catholic Church) divided and subdivided into numerous sects. They ranged from those who retained most

of the Roman Catholic practices to the fundamentalists, who wanted far more radical changes, including purifying the Church of most of its ceremony.

The beginning of Nonconformism

During the reign of Elizabeth I (1558–1603), the fundamentalists became known collectively as the Puritans, although there were many different opinions and religious beliefs among them, and from 1604 groups of believers began to break away from the Church of England.

The Commonwealth (1649–60) brought with it an explosion of political and religious movements as Church of England ministers were stripped of their authority, and religious dissent continued after the Restoration.

Most of these early sects consisted of a few like-minded people meeting in the houses of their members. Many

believed that the Day of Judgement and the end of the world were imminent, so they rarely bothered to keep records. They were also generally persecuted by the government and so were wary of putting anything in writing that might be used against them. As a result, few early records survive.

The authorities became more tolerant of the Nonconformists over the years, however, and, as a result, from the 18th century these sects started to record their membership and activities. As they grew in size and had to move out of their members' houses into dedicated buildings, record-keeping became better.

The role of Roman Catholicism

When the Church of England was established in 1534, not everyone immediately converted to the new religion. In fact, the majority remained

Roman Catholics were regarded with fear and suspicion. Father Garnet was executed following the Gunpowder Plot on 5 November 1605.

Roman Catholics, and became a source of distrust, hatred and fear for many years. Although the brief reign of Mary I (1553–58) reinstated the old faith, from the next queen, Elizabeth I, onwards Anglicanism remained the state religion, though it was not really secure until the mid-17th century.

Until the end of the Napoleonic Wars in 1818, Britain was almost constantly at war with the different European powers, most of which were Roman Catholic. The authorities feared that the Catholics in Britain were a kind of fifth column and might turn traitor, allowing France or Spain or another of their enemies to overthrow the government. They therefore imposed severe penalties on them and particularly on their priests.

Until 1829, Catholicism was effectively illegal in England and Wales, although toleration towards Catholics was gradually growing from around 1700. This, of course, means that relatively few of the surviving records relating to Roman Catholics were created by the Catholics themselves, and much of the information of use to a

family historian is in government sources. (See Appendices for the history of British Catholicism.)

RESEARCHING ANCESTORS FROM OTHER DENOMINATIONS

As the Nonconformists had no official government role, their records tend to be less well kept and well preserved.

The location of Nonconformist records

In 1743, Dr Williams's Library in London invited Nonconformists of all denominations to register births. Some 49,000 were entered before 1837. These records are now held by TNA, with indexes and filmed copies at the FRC. The library also has an index of Nonconformist ministers, with biographical details. Ministers from Nonconformist churches often served in foreign communities.

In 1837, the government asked that surviving registers of Nonconformist churches should be deposited in TNA. The response was good, and a second request brought in even more. Others have been deposited in CROs, but a few remain with their congregations or in private hands. Minute books detailing the church's activities, which might mention individuals, are usually in the archives of the individual sects themselves, or may be in CROs or in other local record offices and libraries.

In addition to sects such as the Methodists, which had substantial followings, there were others that flourished briefly but did not long survive

The Wesley brothers, John and Charles, preaching at Bristol in 1739. They were the founders of Methodism.

the death of a charismatic founder. Their members usually joined other Nonconformist congregations with similar beliefs to their own or drifted back to the Church of England. The 20th century also saw an increasing number of American-based and Caribbean Churches establishing places of worship in towns and cities.

Indications of Nonconformity

If you find a gap in the parish church registers where you would expect your family to be, find out which Nonconformist congregations existed in the area at that time, and check if your ancestors joined one of them.

Anyone returning to or being converted to the Church of England would usually be baptized, especially if they came from a sect that did not practise baptism, such as the Quakers. If you find an adult baptism noted in the parish records, this should suggest looking in Nonconformist or even Jewish records, even if the person's original faith is not mentioned in the records.

Between 1753 and 1837, all marriages had to be carried out in the parish church; only Jews and Quakers were exempt. If you find members of your family getting married in the church but not having their children baptized there, this is a strong indication of Nonconformity or Catholicism. Even before 1753, some Nonconformists couples were married in their local parish church, because it gave incontrovertible proof that they were indeed married.

In the early decades of Nonconformity, very few congregations had their own burial grounds. They would therefore have been buried in the parish churchyard, as long as the local minister did not object because they had not been baptized. If you find

Jews were allowed to perform marriages according to their own rites, both before and after Lord Hardwicke's Marriage Act of 1753.

parish records of burials, but not of baptisms or marriages (before 1753), this is another strong indication of Nonconformity.

In London, an area known as Bunhill Fields was developed as a Nonconformist cemetery in 1665, although the records date from only 1713 and were not very well kept until

after 1786. The cemetery was closed in 1852. The registers were surrendered to the government and are now in TNA, but they have been indexed. The index is on film and copies of it may be in a local library or repository. Those with Nonconformist London ancestors should check these registers for a possible burial date.

FURTHER HELP

Breed, Geoffrey R. *My Ancestors Were Baptists: How Can I Find out More About Them?* (SoG)

Clifford, David J.H. *My Ancestors Were Congregationalists in England and Wales*, with a list of registers (SoG)

Gandy, Michael *Basic Facts about English Nonconformity for Family Historians* (FFHS)

Leary, W. *My Ancestors Were Methodists* (SoG)

Milligan, Edward H. and Thomas, Malcolm J. *My Ancestors Were*

Quakers: How Can I Find out More About Them? (SoG)

Ruston, A. *My Ancestors Were English Presbyterians/Unitarians* (SoG)

Shorney, David *Protestant Nonconformity and Roman Catholicism: A Guide to the Sources in the Public Record Office* (TNA Readers' Guide No. 13)

Steel, D. *Sources for Nonconformist Genealogy and Family History* (Phillimore for the SoG 1973)

Dr Williams's Library, 14 Gordon Square, London WC1H 0AG

The location of Roman Catholic records

There is no central repository for the records of Roman Catholic churches in England. Most are among the Catholic diocese's archives, but they are increasingly being transcribed or published by the Catholic Record Society. A few are in TNA.

Wealthier families sent their children abroad to be educated, and many records relating to the various educational establishments have been published by the Catholic Record Society.

Members of the aristocracy and gentry who were Catholics had servants of the same faith. Information relating to them may be found in the families' private papers and estate records.

During the 18th century, the wills of Catholics were recorded in the Close Rolls held in TNA rather than in church probate courts.

Indications of Roman Catholicism

At various times, the government imposed fines and other penalties on those who did not attend Anglican churches – both Nonconformists and Catholics. These might include forfeiture of land. At other times, people had to swear their allegiance to the Crown. If the oath included the repudiation of Catholicism, most would not take it (though some did with the spiritual equivalent of crossing their fingers). In many places, those who refused to swear were listed.

In London, the presence of diplomats from Roman Catholic countries meant that embassy chapels were permitted. Many also allowed local people to worship there, so if you have Catholic Londoners in your ancestry, check the various legations' registers that survive from the mid-18th century.

Catholic families varied in their attitude to baptisms and marriages in the local parish church. There are occasional references in parish registers to the birth (rather than baptism) of children to Catholic parents, either to establish their right to settlement or because the minister wanted to record it for some reason.

Roman Catholics were not exempt from the law that stated that, between 1753 and 1837, all marriages had to be carried out in the parish church. Even before 1753, some Catholics were married in their local parish church, as well as in a private ceremony by their own rites, because it gave incontrovertible proof and recognition from the state that they were married.

Burials were not necessarily noted in separate registers. There might, however, be notes about the saying of requiem masses, which may give clues to the date of a death.

The anti-Catholic Gordon Riots in 1780 show that prejudice continued for hundreds of years after the Reformation.

FURTHER HELP

Gandy, Michael *Basic Facts About Tracing Your Catholic Ancestry in England* (FFHS)

Gandy, Michael *Catholic Missions and Registers 1700–1880 Vols 1–6* (pub. by the author)

Gandy, Michael *Catholic Family History Vols 1–4* (pub. by the author)

Gibson, Jeremy and Dell, Alan *The Protestation Returns 1641–42 and Other Contemporary Listings* (FFHS)

TNA Domestic Records Information 4: Oath Rolls and Sacrament Certificates After 1660

TNA Domestic Records Information 66: Catholic Recusants

Shorney, David *Protestant Nonconformity and Roman Catholicism: A Guide to the Sources in the Public Record Office* (TNA Readers' Guide No. 13)

Steel, Don and Samuel, Edgar R. *Sources for Roman Catholic and Jewish Genealogy and Family History* (Phillimore for SoG)

Maps

In addition to providing particular information that you might need, such as where ancestors lived, maps give a wonderful idea of what the place looked like. How far did your ancestors have to walk to work, and what was the route they would have taken? Where was the market square? What would they have seen as they looked out of their windows? A detailed map can provide answers to these questions.

UNDERSTANDING THE DIFFERENT MAPS

Maps were produced for different reasons so were not standardized. Comparing maps of the same area will add to your knowledge of where your ancestors lived and worked.

Commercial maps

A variety of commercial map-makers produced maps of cities, towns and counties from Tudor times onwards. They often accompanied directories. Old county maps show roads, rivers and waterways, and so can give you clues about how your ancestors might have moved around. (In the past, rivers were often an easier route to use than bad roads.) From the mid-19th century they will also show railways. The development of towns and the destruction of houses could involve changing street names, which might also lead to the renumbering of houses.

Many maps show parishes, which is useful when planning your research. Our ancestors were highly mobile, so if you don't find your ancestor in the parish you expect, look in neighbouring ones. These sometimes take you over the border into the next county.

Ordnance Survey maps

The first maps created by the government's Board of Ordnance grew out of a need for information to assist the Army. The first published map was of Kent in 1801, produced because of fears of invasion by Napoleon. Thereafter, the rest of the country was mapped, partly for defence reasons but largely to establish parish boundaries and to help make assessment valuations.

Tithe maps

In 1836–70 a series of surveys was made as a result of the Commutation of Tithes Act (1836). Copies of maps made by the government's Tithe Commissioners went to the bishop of the parish's diocese. These are now held in CROs and DROs. The Tithe Commissioners' copies are in TNA, especially if some dispute arose from them either at this time or as a result of later legislation. Unfortunately, many of TNA's holdings were destroyed in World War II. The Tithe Acts did not apply in Scotland or Ireland, so these surveys do not exist for these countries.

Maps deposited at Quarter Sessions

Between the mid-18th and mid-19th centuries, there was a series of local Enclosure Acts, culminating in the

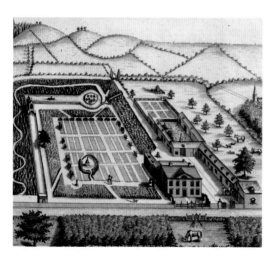

LEFT Estate maps, such as this one from Burbage in Leicestershire c.1780, show what an ancestor living there at the time would have seen every day.

RIGHT This parish map of Cholsey in Berkshire shows individual fields

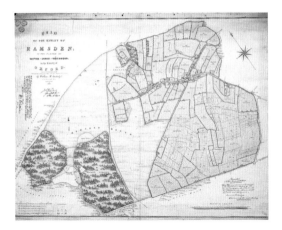

A tithe map of Ramsden, Shipton Under Wychwood, Oxfordshire, compiled in 1838 after the Commutation of Tithes Act in 1836.

Ordnance Survey maps, such as this one of part of Edinburgh, were originally produced for military reasons.

General Enclosure Act of 1845. Maps of the area concerned were deposited with Quarter Sessions. When local authorities wanted to build a turnpike road, a canal, a railway or any similar public amenity, they also had to lodge a map with the Quarter Sessions before they applied to parliament for permission. After 1792, a copy had to be deposited with the Clerk of Parliament. These maps are now in the House of Lords Record Office.

Estate and manorial maps

Landowners and lords of the manor often hired surveyors to make maps of their possessions. This may have been when someone new took over an estate or manor, but might equally have been for other, unknown, reasons. Estate maps are private documents.

Fire insurance maps

Companies involved in fire insurance prepared large-scale maps to assess the risk to properties. These usually include the boundaries of the buildings and details of their construction, including the number of floors. Maps in London date from 1745. One company, Charles E. Goad Ltd, prepared maps for all the fire insurance companies for 1886–1970.

Charles Booth's poverty maps

In 1886–1903, Charles Booth carried out an Inquiry into Life and Labour in London. As part of this inquiry, poverty maps of London were produced, showing the kinds of people and their levels of income in each street.

Charles Booth's papers are held at the London School of Economics. Much of the inquiry he carried out has been published in different editions.

LOCATING MAPS

CROs usually have the best collection of local maps. The British Library and the National Maritime Museum also have extensive map collections. The NMM maps are mainly to do with the sea, of course, which will be of interest to those with sea-faring ancestors.

RESEARCHING MAPS

Note that early maps did not always follow the present-day convention of having north at the top, so you may need a current map to orient yourself.

Many Ordnance Survey maps have been reprinted in facsimile. These can help you to locate your ancestor's residences and any properties he or she owned. Streets were often renamed, and by comparing the names in the past and their location with those of today, you may be able to find the actual house in which your ancestor lived. Also check whether the houses in the street have been renumbered.

Most CROs produce simple outline maps showing the parishes in their county. You can plot occurrences of your family's surnames on it, using one colour for baptisms and another for marriages, plus dates. This may show a pattern of movement over the years that gives you more clues about where your family might have originated.

Welsh records

Wales has effectively been under British rule since medieval times, so the kinds of records found are the same as in England. The exception is land inheritance. By a Welsh tradition called "gavelkind", which ceased with the Act of Union of 1536, a man's property was divided between all his sons, rather than left to the eldest son. This led to people owning smaller and smaller parcels of land, which eventually became uneconomic and had to be sold. Since 1536, inheritance laws in England and Wales have been the same, so the family historian will find the same kinds of records in both countries.

INVESTIGATING BMD AND OTHER RECORDS

BMD certificates began in 1837, and the indexes are in the Family Record Centre (FRC). Other records are much the same as in England.

ABOVE Although Wales has a strong individual identity, in its public record keeping at least it is the same as England.

BELOW Carreg Cennen is one of the many castles built by Edward I of England in his efforts to rule Wales.

Parish records

Following the 1536 Act of Union, the law was the same in both countries, and therefore Welsh parish officials had the same duties and kept the same kinds of records in Wales as their counterparts did in England.

By the mid-19th century, some 80 per cent of the Welsh population was thought to belong to Nonconformist churches, mainly Methodist or Baptist, with a small Catholic community. This means that most of them will not be found in parish registers, apart from those that married between 1753 and 1837. They will, however, appear in other parish records, such as settlement and bastardy examinations, workhouse minutes, etc.

Wills

There are four bishops' dioceses in Wales: Bangor (including Anglesey), St Asaph, Llandaff and St David. Wills not proved in the Prerogative Court of Canterbury (PCC) were mainly proved in the diocesan courts. (The archdeaconry courts were less important for probate matters than in England.) Only in the archdeaconry of Brecon, in the see of St David, was there a consistory court proving wills. There was only one "peculiar" in Wales – the parish of Hawarden, Flintshire – which had the right to prove its own wills. Some Welsh parishes fell within the diocese of Hereford, so the wills of their inhabitants are kept in the Hereford and Worcester County Record Office (CRO).

Only a small number of Welsh families remained Roman Catholic after the Reformation, but their numbers

Understanding Welsh family names

The small number of names shared by a majority of the population meant that many people acquired an extra name to distinguish them from other people with the same name in the same locality. This might be a mother's name, making hyphenated or double names quite common in Wales, or it might be a geographical location or an occupation, such as Jones of Mostyn or Jones the Baker. This helps the researcher to distinguish between individuals in records, but can become confusing with the next generation, since a child would not necessarily inherit the extra name but might acquire one of his or her own instead. This practice of using patronymics rather than fixed surnames did not fully die out until the advent of civil registration in 1837.

were swelled in the 19th century when many Irish Catholics came to the industrialized parts of Wales.

INTERPRETING THE LAW

Although Wales had its own legal system before the Act of Union in 1536, since that date the law has been the same as it is in England.

The Poor Laws

It seems that in Tudor times the Poor Laws operated only in Monmouthshire, and in many of the more sparsely populated parishes poor rates were not collected until 1755. The poverty stricken in many places therefore relied on charity and the support of landowners rather than parish relief. The Napoleonic Wars from the end of the 18th century led to an increase in the collection of rates.

Assize courts

From 1542 to its abolition in 1830, the Court of Great Session sat twice a year in each of the Welsh counties, with the exception of Monmouthshire, which was excluded from 1689. From 1831 there were two circuits, North and South Wales, and from 1945 Wales and Chester.

LOCATING RECORDS RELATING TO WELSH ANCESTORS

Since England and Wales have the same government, many of the official records relating to Wales are found in The National Archives (TNA).

Those searching for Welsh ancestry will find the National Library of Wales (NLW) is also a good starting point. Although the Welsh counties do have individual CROs, the NLW has copies of parish registers as well as diocesan records, court papers, newspapers and other material covering all the counties collected together in one place. Documents relating to manors, estates and other property in Wales may be here or in TNA.

RESEARCHING WELSH ANCESTORS

The ancient Palatinate of Cheshire, whose records are in TNA, included the old Welsh county of Flintshire, so it is possible you may find some relatives recorded there.

The area around the border between Wales and England is known as the Welsh Marches, and if your ancestors lived here, it is probably worth checking for missing ancestors in the records of the neighbouring English counties.

The Welsh courts went on returning coroners' inquests to the assize circuits well into the first part of the 19th century, long after the English courts ceased to do so. These records, which are in TNA, are therefore worth consulting for the genealogical information they might contain.

Just as in England, Welsh counties have their own CROs, in which are held the wills of their inhabitants.

FURTHER HELP

Hamilton-Edwards, Gerald
In Search of Welsh Ancestry
(Phillimore)
National Library of Wales,
Aberystwyth, Ceredigion SY23
3BU www.llgc.org.uk/. A reader's
ticket is necessary to use the
library. It is one of the copyright
libraries in the British Isles, so
publishers should have deposited
a copy of all new books there.
Rowlands, John and Rowlands,
Sheila *Welsh Family History:
A Guide to Research* (FFHS)
Rowlands, John and Rowlands,
Sheila *Second Stages in
Researching Welsh Ancestry*
(FFHS)

Scottish records

Before the Act of Union in 1707, Scotland had a separate parliament from England and Wales. After nearly 300 years, its own parliament was restored in 1999. Scotland had, and still has, a different legal system to the rest of Britain, which affects the types of records that are kept.

INVESTIGATING BMD AND OTHER RECORDS

Civil registration was introduced in 1855. Scottish certificates contain the same information as those south of the border, but with a few major, and useful, additions regarding BMD.

Birth certificates

On a child's birth certificate, the date and place of the parents' marriage is entered. This was dropped between 1856 and 1860. In the first year of registration (1855) only, the ages and birthplaces of both parents and details of their other children (if any) are recorded. All birth certificates also include the time of the child's birth, not just (as in England and Wales) if it was a multiple birth. For those genealogists who are interested in astrology, this presents an opportunity to have a full birth chart drawn up. There is an index of adopted children from 1930, though this does not contain the names of natural parents, and one of stillbirths from 1939, though the latter is not on open access.

Marriage certificates

The names of both parties' fathers and mothers (with maiden names) are included on marriage certificates. They also, until 1922, state whether

New Register House in Edinburgh, designed by Robert Adam, holds BMD records and parish registers for Scotland.

the bride and groom were related and what the relationship was. In Scotland, a legal marriage could be contracted by agreement before witnesses or a sheriff, and the certificate will show whether the couple were married in church (the officiating minister would have signed the certificate) or by agreement. Certificates drawn up in 1855 only will also give details of previous marriages, any children and the birthplaces of both parties. There is a register of divorces from 1984.

Death certificates

In addition to the information given on death certificates in England and Wales, these contain the names of the deceased's father and mother (including her maiden name). In 1855, certificates also noted the deceased's birthplace and how long he or she had been resident in the place where they died, plus the names of spouses (including maiden names) and children, with their ages. For 1855–1861, details of the burial place and undertaker were noted.

Parish registers

When civil registration began in Scotland, the parish registers of the Church of Scotland parishes were called in. These are known as the Old Parochial Registers. Although some began in 1558, registers were generally not kept until about 1750 in the Highlands. Most were indexed by the original compilers, but in a variety of sometimes confusing and unhelpful ways. The Church of Jesus Christ of Latter-

---

Understanding Scottish family names

Before the 20th century, the Scots had a fairly standard pattern of naming children, which may give clues to the names of grandparents:

- eldest son was named after the paternal grandfather
- 2nd son was named after the maternal grandfather
- 3rd son was named after the father
- eldest daughter was named after the maternal grandmother
- 2nd daughter was named after the paternal grandmother
- 3rd daughter was named after the mother

It was also quite common to create girls' names by adding "-a" or "-ina" to a man's name, e.g. Jacoba, Jamesina, which in some cases seems to have been done when there weren't enough sons in the family to commemorate the male relatives.

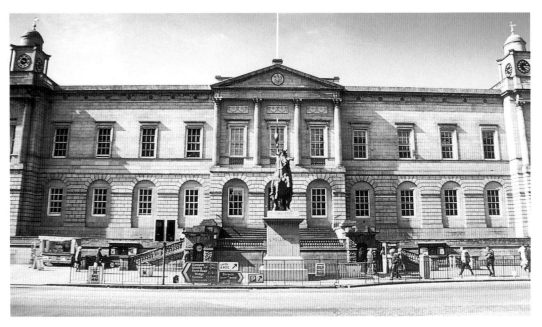

The National Archives of Scotland in Edinburgh, formerly the Scottish Records Office, holds a wealth of material on Scottish ancestors.

day Saints (LDS) has produced a better index of baptisms and marriages on CD-ROM and the internet. Many have also been published by the Scottish Record Society. Some do not include the actual details of a service but do, in the case of marriage, include notice of the intention to marry.

The registers contain relatively few burial records, but might have a note about the hiring of the mort cloth – a cloth to cover a body. They do, however, usually give the names of godparents in the entry for a baptism.

Many Scots were Nonconformists, mainly Presbyterian. There was also a strong Catholic presence in Scotland, particularly among those of Irish origin who migrated in the 19th century.

Testamentary records

The inheritance of land and buildings in Scotland was according to laid-down rules, not the owner's personal whim. This meant that only movable property could be left at death, with the details recorded in a document called the testament.

Before 1823, Scotland was divided into areas called commissariots, which were roughly the equivalent of a bishop's diocese, where testaments were proved. The Commissariot of Edinburgh had both local and national jurisdiction, as well as over those Scots who died overseas. Most testaments have been indexed. If heirs were under the age of majority, the commissary courts could appoint guardians of their interests, called tutors. Even though rules on inheritance were clear-cut, there could be disputes about the provisions of a testament, which would be heard in the court in which the wills were proved.

If someone died intestate, a testament dative, including an inventory of the deceased's possessions, was drawn up. A notice, called an edict, might be nailed to the church door requesting anyone who had an interest in the deceased's goods to attend a commissary court hearing. These notices appear in commissary court records, to which other documents relative to the matter should be attached.

Sheriff's Courts took over the administration of testaments in 1823 and continued to do so until 1876, when a national system was instituted.

Armorial bearings

The Lord Lyon King of Arms has jurisdiction over all matters relating to armorial bearings, and the records of the Lyon Court contain much information about pedigrees. Ancient heraldic material is often worth researching, as it is not only the wealthy and nobility who are entitled to bear and apply for arms.

The interior of the impressive dome of the National Archives of Scotland.

Service of Heirs and Register of Sasines

The Service of Heirs relates to the inheritance of property other than land and generally states the relationship of the person who inherited it to the deceased. The Register of Sasines relates to the inheritance of land and dates from 1617.

These are the major differences to be found between family records in England and Wales and those in Scotland. Other information relating to

family history, such as apprenticeships, freemen, criminal and civil proceedings, will be found in the equivalent Scottish records.

INTERPRETING THE LAW

Scotland has a separate legal system from the rest of the UK. The differences of most interest to genealogists relate to wills and inheritance of property, but other areas, like family law, will need to be considered and investigated when doing research.

The Poor Laws

Before 1845, the Scottish Poor Laws were administered by parish officials, and references to relief may be found in the minutes of Kirk Sessions. After 1845, Parochial Boards were set up in each parish. Lists of people receiving assistance in their homes and those who had entered the poorhouse were compiled. Some children, invalids and lunatics were placed in private homes to be cared for, and the board made reports on them.

Courts

The lowest level of criminal courts is the Sheriff's Court (which also had jurisdiction over some civil matters). Appeals from here went to the High Court of Justiciary (the highest criminal court in Scotland), which dealt with serious crimes. The statements of witnesses, called precognitions, are held in the records of the Lord Advocate's Department, but there might be copies of some with the papers of the Sheriff's Court. There are few surviving precognitions before 1812.

In some places, a particular person held a franchise from the Crown that gave him jurisdiction over both civil and criminal matters in a specified area.

Before the Act of Union in 1707, which led to its abolition in the following year, the Scottish Privy Council dealt with criminal cases, generally among the higher echelons of society. The Admiralty Court, abolished in 1830, had jurisdiction over the high seas and harbours.

Fatal accident inquiries

Scotland did not have a system to investigate suspicious deaths. Any that resulted in legal action will be found in the criminal courts, but there were no investigations into deaths through, for example, suicide or misadventure.

From 1848 there are records in the Lord Advocate's department of inquiries into accidents, and after 1895 Sheriff's Courts had, by law, to conduct inquiries into fatal accidents.

LOCATING RECORDS RELATING TO SCOTTISH ANCESTORS

The genealogist tracing Scottish ancestry has a great advantage over those doing research elsewhere in the British Isles, because BMD certificates after 1855, census returns, and parish registers before 1855 of the Church of Scotland are all kept in the same record office at New Register House in Edinburgh. The records of the Lord Lyon King of Arms are also located here.

Other registers of Nonconformist and Roman Catholic churches are stored next door in the National Archives of Scotland (NAS). It also contains testamentary records (not wills) and minutes of Kirk Sessions, which contain information about illegitimacy, irregular marriages, claims for poor relief and the like. It is also the major repository for local and national government records, including law courts and business archives. The Scottish Archives Network has a database of wills covering 1500–1875.

FURTHER HELP

Ferguson, Joan P. S. *Scottish Family Histories* (National Library of Scotland): a compilation of printed books, pamphlets and articles, and where they are found, about individual Scottish families.
General Register Office (Scotland), New Register House, Edinburgh EH1 3YT www.gro-scotland.gov.uk/
National Archives of Scotland, HM General Register House, 2 Princes Street, Edinburgh EH1 3YY www.nas.gov.uk/: has information leaflets about its holdings, which are also available on-line.
Scottish Association of Family History Societies www.safhs.org.uk
Sinclair, Cecil *Tracing Your Scottish Ancestors in the Scottish Record Office* (National Library of Scotland)

Most, but not all, of the records of the courts dealing with testaments have been deposited in the National Archives of Scotland. From 1876 an annual calender of testaments was compiled, and this is also in the NAS.

The miscellaneous indexes at the NAS contain a Marine Register of births from 1855, listing the births of children on British-registered vessels if the father was Scottish. There are also registers of BMD in foreign countries during 1860–1965; in the High Commissioner's Returns of BMD from 1964; in Air Registers of Births and Deaths from 1948; in Service Records from 1881; in Consular Returns of BMD from 1914 and in Foreign Marriages from 1947.

After 1707, the armed forces covered the whole of the British Isles, so records relating to Scottish soldiers, sailors and airmen will be found in The National Archives of England.

Despite being housed in a historic building, the National Archives of Scotland has modern facilities and a vast collection of records.

Irish records

The family historian researching Irish ancestry faces a number of problems. The first is that the majority of the population was Roman Catholic, and their registers did not begin until late in the 18th century. The second is the relatively few number of surnames shared by most of the population. The third is that the Irish Public Record Office, housed in Four Courts, Dublin, was destroyed by protestors against British rule in 1922. Very few of the contents, which included about half the Church of Ireland parish registers, census returns, wills and other government records, survived.

Four Courts, Dublin, was bombarded during the 1922 uprising, and many records were destroyed.

INVESTIGATING BMD AND OTHER RECORDS

After 1922, BMD records are complete but, as the country was then divided into two, these and other records are in different places.

Civil registration

Civil registration of all BMD began in Ireland in 1864, but non-Catholic marriages were registered only from 1845 onwards. The partition of Ireland has meant duplication of material between the two General Register Offices. Records up to 1922 are held in the General Register Office (GRO) in Dublin. After that date, it holds copies of records in Northern Ireland. The GRO (Northern Ireland), in Belfast, is a separate register office. It holds BMD records for Northern Ireland from 1922 onwards and copies of indexes to pre-1922 events. There are also Marine, Consular, and Foreign Marriage Registers of BMD relating to Irish people at sea or overseas in

both offices. After 1922, laws on registration of events such as stillbirth, adoption and illegitimate children were different in Eire and Northern Ireland.

Parish registers

The Church of Ireland served a small percentage of the population, mainly the Protestant middle and upper classes. As mentioned above, about half their registers from before 1870 had been deposited in the Dublin Public Record Office and were destroyed. However, others had remained in their own churches; some transcripts of these had been made before the registers were surrendered, and others had already been published. The surviving material, in addition to parish accounts and other documents, are scattered among various locations. The records of parishes that no longer exist, for example, have been deposited in the library of the Representative Church Body.

Between 1915 and 1922, proof of age in order to claim benefits might be extracted from Church of Ireland parish registers, and the forms to do this, which contain parents' names, are preserved in the National Archives.

Unlike the Church of Ireland, the Roman Catholic Church did not have a role in local government, and so it did not need to keep registers in the same way. Most baptisms and marriages took place in the priest's home or in the home of the family. Catholic registers did not begin until the middle of the 18th century in towns and the 19th century in rural areas. Most original registers remain with their churches, but the majority has been copied on to films, which are held in the National Library. Some burials of Catholics took place in Church of Ireland burial grounds, depending on the attitude of the minister.

Other denominations, such as the Nonconformists (Baptists, Congregationalists, Huguenots, Lutherans,

Methodists, Moravians, Presbyterians and Quakers) and Jews, kept their own records. Although all the original registers of the Huguenot churches were destroyed in 1922, they had already been published. Other records are deposited in various archives or remain with their congregations, but many have also been copied.

Wills

Between 1536 and 1858, wills were proved in Church of Ireland ecclesiastical courts. The senior court was the Prerogative Court of Armagh, which had jurisdiction over all the commissary courts (there were no archdeaconry courts in Ireland) but was inferior to the PCC. People with property in both Ireland and England would therefore have had their wills proved in the PCC, and those records are in the Family Record Centre in London.

After 1858, the proving of wills was taken over by the government. Transcript copies of wills proved in local registries were passed to Dublin, where an annual index was made. The original wills, before and after 1858, were deposited at Four Courts, and so destroyed in 1922, but the indexes, which give some useful information, have survived and so have the post-1858 transcript copies from the registries outside Dublin.

Between 1858 and 1876, the Principal Probate Registry in London had an additional section at the end of its indexes, which included some Irish probate records dealing with people who owned property in both Ireland and England.

INTERPRETING THE LAW
Ireland had its own parliament, but all of its activities had to be approved by the British government. Although the majority of the population was Roman Catholic, laws were passed at various times to penalize them and prevent them from holding office of any kind. This discrimination finally ended in 1829, although some provisions had been repealed at different times before that date.

Land records
The paucity of registers and the destruction of many documents mean that much information about Irish family history will come from records relating to land tenure. Most land in Ireland was owned by a relatively small number of people and let out on leases. Private estate papers may contain information about tenants. Because they are private papers, they may be with the original owners or in a number of repositories in Ireland or mainland Britain. During the famine years, many landowners abandoned their properties and left Ireland.

Registry of Deeds
The Registry of Deeds was set up in 1708, primarily to stop Catholics acquiring land. A variety of documents, including wills, land transfer documents, mortgages, marriage settlement letters and share sales, are included in these records. They mainly relate to upper-class Anglo-Irish families, and so are not typical of the average inhabitant. Registration was not compulsory, so not every transaction will be here.

As the laws on Catholics were relaxed towards the end of the 18th century, more people were able to lease or own land. The records are in the Registry of Deeds, in Dublin, where there is an index containing abstracts of the documents.

Ejectment books
Before a landlord could eject tenants from his property, he had to obtain a court judgement, and ejectment books summarizing these cases provide much information of use to genealogists, especially those whose ancestors emigrated. Not all have survived (there seem to be none, for example, from Northern Ireland), but they are worth checking out.

The famine of the 1840s created a huge increase in ejectments, but this was not entirely a case of hard-hearted

The Irish potato famine led to widespread poverty and eviction.

landlords throwing out starving people. The landlords had to pay rates on their land, and, in order to help the increasing number of poor, the amounts rose. Those with land-owning ancestors may find their problems reflected in ejectment books.

The Incumbered Estate Court

From 1849, if bankruptcy resulted, the landlords' estates were disposed of in the Incumbered Estate Court, which dealt with the auction of lands. This was renamed the Landed Estates Court in 1858. In 1877, it became part of the Chancery Division of the High Court in Ireland. Here it was called the Land Judges' Court, and continued until 1880. Records are in the National Archives of Ireland. Much valuable information, including maps, is given in the sales catalogues (called rentals) produced when landowners had to sell, these are in the National Archives, the National Library or the Public Record Office of Northern Ireland (PRONI).

Other sources

Ireland possesses records giving the same kinds of genealogical information as the rest of the British Isles, such as courts, apprenticeships, freemen, commercial and trade directories, and so on. Newspapers and magazines, especially the *Hibernian*, will provide additional facts, but it is mainly the well-to-do and criminal classes that are recorded in them.

Tithe Plotment Books

Compiled in the 1820s and 1830s, Tithe Plotment Books cover landowners and primary tenants in parishes. The LDS has filmed these records, so they are available through their Family History Centres and in a number of record offices.

BELOW After eviction, an Irish peasant would have little with which to start again.

Griffith's Primary Valuation

Information about landowners and occupiers in the mid-19th century was issued in stages for 1848–1864. This publication's official title is *General Valuation of Rateable Property*, but it is generally known as Griffith's Primary Valuation, after the commissioner who was responsible for carrying it out. The surveys largely took place after the Irish famine, and so are valuable for allowing the family historian to see who survived or remained in Ireland. Almost every head of a household is listed in these surveys.

Land Commission

The 1881 Land Act set up the Land Commission, which originally determined fair rents. Its work developed into helping tenants purchase their property. These records are currently in the Irish National Archives, but public access to them is restricted. A summary of the Commission's documents is held in the National Library.

LOCATING RECORDS RELATING TO IRISH ANCESTORS

Listing where in Ireland your ancestors were before and after 1922 will make locating records easier.

Census returns

A few records of censuses before 1901 survived the 1922 destruction: there are fragments from 1821, 1831, 1841 and 1851. The pre-1851 censuses in Ireland contained more information than their English or Scottish equivalents. In addition to the original records, there are some forms relating to information from searches made in the census records, which were used by elderly people to prove their ages in order to claim old age pensions after 1908. The 1901 and 1911 censuses survived and are open to researchers, but you do need to know where your ancestors were living in those years.

Heritage Centres

The increasing growth of interest in family history led to the setting up of Genealogical Indexing Centres, also called Heritage Centres, around Ireland. These centres index and computerize church registers and other records in their area. The public is not allowed access to the databases, but information from them is provided for a fee. They are useful if you know at least the county from which your ancestors came.

Service records

Records for the Irish branches of the armed services are in TNA.

Education records

Charter schools began in 1731, and by the beginning of the 19th century there were a variety of private, Church and "hedge" schools in Ireland. Hedge schools, which dated from medieval times, educated children in Gaelic, which was the first language of most Irish people until the 19th century. They declined for a number of reasons: the growth of state-run education, which was in English; the recognition that, in order to succeed professionally, people needed to speak English; and the emigration of many of the poorer Irish citizens.

The National Board of Education (Ireland) began state-run schools in 1831. Information from school logbooks, where they survive, can substitute for the destroyed censuses. Although the schools were non-denominational, their records include a note of the children's religions. When and why children left the school is also entered, and this may give useful information about families who emigrated.

IRA forces fought a bitter struggle with the British in the streets of Dublin in 1922.

Records of university graduates from Ireland's main universities have been published. Although Roman Catholics were officially barred from universities until 1793, some seem to have received a university education before this date and are noted as "RC" in the registers.

FURTHER HELP

General Register Office, Joyce House, 8–11 Lombard Street East, Dublin 2, Eire www.groireland.ie
General Register Office (Northern Ireland), Oxford House, 49–55 Chichester Street, Belfast BT1 4HL www.groni.gov.uk
Mac Conghail, Maire and Gorry, Paul *Tracing Irish Ancestors* (Harper Collins)
National Archives of Ireland, Bishop Street, Dublin 8, Eire www.nationalarchives.ie
Public Record Office of Northern Ireland, 66 Balmoral Avenue, Belfast BT9 6NY www.proni.nics.gov.uk
Representative Church Body, www.ireland.anglican.org

RESEARCHING IRISH ANCESTORS

The destruction in 1922 of Four Courts in Dublin, which contained centralized records, means that it is essential to find out where in Ireland your ancestors originated. If they emigrated to England, Wales Scotland, or overseas, this may come from census returns (although many people simply entered "Ireland" on the return) and settlement examinations. Those who entered the armed services will also have their birthplace entered in records. It is worth remembering that the Republic of Ireland was neutral during World War II.

When civil registration was introduced in 1864, a fine was payable if a birth was not registered within three months, so poor people might have adjusted the date of a child's birth to avoid a penalty. Roman Catholics would, however, have had the child baptized within a few days of birth, either at the priest's house or their own home, so it is worth cross-referencing the civil and church records if you can.

Channel Islands records

The Channel Islands came under British rule with the accession of William the Conqueror in 1066, and they retained both a system of law very different from that of England, especially in respect of land inheritance, and a form of French as the inhabitants' first language. As a result, the majority of earlier records are in French.

Many of the islands' inhabitants were involved in the fishing industry. Their proximity to the West Country in England, where fishing was also a major industry, means that there was a fair amount of interchange between the two places.

A number of Huguenots emigrated from France to the Channel Islands, and refugees from the French Revolution also settled there. Although the islands have their own dialect, the language was similar enough for them to have integrated easily.

During the French and Napoleonic Wars, the islands were heavily garrisoned to keep them out of French

LEFT The castle above Gorey Harbour in Jersey was built to defend the island from seaborne invasion.

BELOW LEFT The French failed to gain control of the Channel Islands in the late 18th century.

hands. A number of soldiers and sailors married local women. A local militia was also raised, and many of its records are in TNA.

During World War II, the Channel Islands were occupied by the Germans. There are a number of books on this period.

Guernsey

Civil registration of births, deaths and non-Anglican marriages began in 1840, but all marriages did not have to be registered until 1919.

During the 19th century, accounts of strangers, or etrangers, were kept, which included passenger lists. These will be found among the constable's records in each parish.

The island's Archives Office, the Greffe, contains the registers of BMD and wills from 1841. It also contains the records of St Peter Port's Hospital, which was built in 1741 and served both as a place to treat the sick and a workhouse. The records cover 1741-1900. Records for the prison, known as the House of Separation, also survive.

Jersey

Civil registration of BMD began in 1842. Before that date, information was recorded in parish registers. Jersey has separate archives for civil registration from 1842 (which are in the Superintendent Registrar's) and other records (in the Judicial Greffe).

Before 1602, matters concerning land were arranged verbally in front of witnesses, generally after church services. The Land Registry was then set up to document transactions. On the death of a landowner, his estate would be divided between his children, with the eldest son receiving the largest

share. Wills of Realty, relating to land and buildings, date from 1851 and are deposited at the Land Registry, while Wills of Personality, covering money and movable goods, are in the Probate Registry. Both have been filmed by the LDS. Legal courts covered inheritance, crime, civil cases, small debts and bankruptcy.

Refugees from the French Revolution in 1789 came to Jersey. They established a Roman Catholic congregation, which was later joined by an influx of Irish immigrants. Many of these left for America from the 1870s, when there were financial problems and the work dried up in the Channel Islands. A chapel was built in 1825 and two other churches in 1867 and 1877. The surviving registers of all three have been transcribed and deposited in the Channel Islands Family History Society's archives and the Société Jersiaise. There is an index.

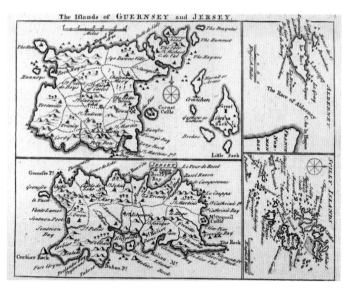

The Channel Islands and the Isles of Scilly are just some of the UK's many offshore islands.

FURTHER HELP

Channel Islands Family History Society, PO Box 507, St Helier, Jersey, CI JE4 5TN and on the Channel Islands Pages site at http://user.itl.net/~glen/index.html

H.M. Greffier, Royal Court House, St Peter Port, Guernsey, CI GY 2PB

Judicial Greffe, Morier House, Halkett Place, St Helier, Jersey, CI JE1 1DD

Société Guernesiaise, Family History Section, PO Box 314, Candie, St Peter Port, Guernsey CI GY1 3TG
www.societe.org.gg/

Société Jersiaise, Lord Coutanche Library, 7 Pier Road, St Helier, Jersey, CI JE2 4XW
www.societejersiaise.org

Superintendent Registrar, 10 Royal Square, St Helier, Jersey, CI [need postcode]
www.judicialgreffe.je

Alderney

The civil registration of births and deaths dates from 1850, and marriages from 1886.

Many of Alderney's earlier records seem to have been destroyed during the German occupation in World War I. Those that have survived (apart from censuses) have been copied by a local volunteer. Enquiries are routed through the Greffe in Guernsey.

Sark

The island of Sark was uninhabited until 1563, when the Seigneur of St Ouen in Jersey moved there with his family and a number of followers to prevent it being taken over by the French. They were joined by other people from Guernsey and Jersey and a few from the English mainland. A small Huguenot community established itself there in 1570.

The island still has a feudal system of land tenure. Inheritance laws are very strict, so relatively few people made wills. The records of Sark are accessed through the Greffe in Guernsey. Civil registration of deaths began in 1915, marriages in 1919 and births in 1925.

RECORDS RELATING TO ANCESTORS FROM THE CHANNEL ISLANDS

Although there are copies locally, TNA holds census returns. It also has some records of BMD notified to the British authorities between 1831 and 1958. The Bouillon Papers contain information about refugees from the French Revolution who went to Jersey. The Chelsea and Greenwich Hospitals' records contain information about retired soldiers and sailors living in the Channel Islands and receiving a pension from them. A particularly useful source is the Association Oath Rolls of 1696 for Guernsey and Jersey, since they constitute a virtual census of the adult male population of the islands at that date. There are also documents relating to the rental of Crown lands in Alderney for 1832–1961.

Isle of Man records

The Isle of Man was ruled by Norsemen from the 10th century, until the King of Norway sold it to Scotland in 1266. In 1341, it came under English control, but the feudal system of land and property laws remained in force until 1867. Tenants paid for land owned by their lords by handing over part of the produce of their holding and by doing work for the landowner.

The Isle of Man is self-governing and levies its own taxes. Its legislative body, the Tynwald, is divided into an upper and a lower house. Otherwise, the Isle of Man came under English rule, so the administrative system of parishes is the same. It forms the diocese of the Bishop of Sodor and Man.

Manx, a form of Gaelic, was spoken on the island until the 18th century, but legal and official documents were written in English. This language gradually took over, hastened by the

ABOVE The Isle of Man's ancient Scandanavian heritage is celebrated at the annual Viking Festival.

BELOW Viking ship-burials are no longer practised, only recreated at festivals commemorating the Isle of Man's past.

introduction in 1872 of free elementary schools, where the teaching was in English. The last mother-tongue speakers died in the 1940s.

INVESTIGATING BMD
Civil registration of births and deaths began in 1878 and of marriages in 1884. From 1849 there are some certificates of Nonconformists' marriages, obtained by those who did not wish to be married in a parish church. Wills were proved in ecclesiastical courts until 1884, when a system of civil probate was instituted.

LOOKING FOR MORE SOURCES
As elsewhere in the United Kingdom, property records and local newspapers are a vital source of information about Manx ancestry.

Property records
The Isle of Man's feudal system of land tenure means that land records are essentially the same as manorial records. They are recorded in books called Libri (from the Latin for books): Libri Assedationis contain rent rolls, while Libri Vastarum contain details of admissions of landowners to property and the fines and rents they paid.

Composition Books contain descriptions of individual holdings and fines paid on them. They were no longer kept after 1704, when some of the more feudal rights of the lord were removed, though some remained.

Newspapers
Local newspapers started around the beginning of the 19th century. Before then, the *Cumberland Pacquet* carried

some Manx news. Copies are held in the Heritage Library, as well as in the British Library Newspaper Library at Colindale in London.

LOCATING RECORDS RELATING TO ANCESTORS FROM THE ISLE OF MAN

The National Archives holds records of the Isle of Man's government and government employees, armed services, and assize records. It also has documents relating to land rented from the Crown for 1832–1954 and pensions paid to ex-servicemen living there. It may also hold wills of inhabitants proved in the PCC before 1858.

The Manx National Heritage Library is the equivalent of the CRO and holds copies of the surviving church registers, which are all indexed on the International Genealogical Index (IGI), as well as copies of the census returns (the originals are in TNA, with filmed copies at the FRC). The 1881 census is recorded on the

CD-ROMs produced by the LDS. The Heritage Library also holds copies of wills before 1910 and property records, including a large collection of deeds between the late 17th century and 1910, which were enrolled with the local courts. Wills proved after 1916 are in the Registry, as are deeds after 1910.

ABOVE **Germans in a camp at Douglas during World War I. These internees were kept occupied by making brooms.**

When plans to destroy the majority of Merchant Navy crew lists held at the Registry of Shipping and Seamen were announced, due to lack of space, the Heritage Library managed to save those relating to Manx ports, and these have now been indexed. In addition to Manxmen, there are many sailors from Ireland and Scotland in these records.

During the two World Wars, there were internment camps on the Isle of Man holding German and Italian men. The records are in TNA.

LEFT **Mooragh camp, an internment camp set up during World War II, is now a public park.**

FURTHER HELP

A good site for the history and
records of the Isle of Man is on
www.ee.surrey.ac.uk/Contrib/
manx/famhist/genealgy
General Registry, Finch Road,
Douglas, Isle of Man
www.gov.im/infocentre
Isle of Man Family History Society
www.isle-of-man.com/
interest/genealogy/fhs
Manx National Heritage, Douglas,
Isle of Man IM1 3LY
www.gov.im/mnh
Narasimham, Janet *The Manx
Family Tree: A Guide to Records in
the Isle of Man* (Isle of Man
Family History Society)

Education

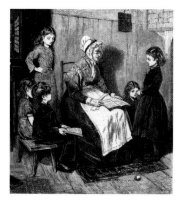

Before the 20th century, relatively few people needed to be able to read and write, since there were plenty of jobs that did not need literacy or numeracy. Indeed, many of the upper classes resisted plans to educate the poor, fearing that teaching them these skills would make them dissatisfied with their lives and lead to social unrest.

PRIMARY AND SECONDARY EDUCATION

Education was, until comparatively recently, not seen as the responsibility of the state. It was up to individuals to arrange for their children's education, and there were a variety of different ways to deliver it.

Early schools

There was a strongly defined hierarchy to the education provided for children in the past. Grammar schools, many of which were founded in the 16th century under Edward VI, and public schools, such as Eton, had originally been intended for poor children but were quickly taken over by the rich. The better-off sections of society employed tutors or governesses for their children. Among the middle and lower classes, it was mothers who were expected to teach their children to read and write. The children of tradesmen also learned account-keeping, either from their parents or from someone paid to teach them.

There were, in addition, a variety of schools, most of which were established as charitable foundations by either an individual or a religious organization, such as the Society for Promoting Christian Knowledge. Many

had distinctive uniforms, such as the blue coats and yellow stockings of Christ's Hospital in London. Cathedrals also had (and still have) schools for choristers, who were, until the end of the 20th century, always male. Nonconformists also established schools to educate their children. What all schools had in common was that they based their education on religious faith.

There were a few occupational schools before the 19th century. Most of these, such as Christ's Hospital in

London, were connected with the sea. Although most pupils at this establishment had a general education, the boys in the mathematical school were specifically prepared for their apprenticeship to sea captains.

Schools in the 19th century

Dame schools, usually run by a single woman, started from the 1830s. The standard of teaching was variable: some were little more than child-minding services so that mothers could work, but others did provide a basic education, mainly in reading and, for girls, sewing. It was not until the beginning of the 19th century that proposals for a national system of education were made. The first was in 1802, but the government was reluctant to get involved until 1870, when the Education Act obliged local authorities to provide education, which was made compulsory.

Schools to educate children and young people who had committed petty crimes or who were deemed

ABOVE LEFT Dame schools provided a basic education for those whose parents could afford a few pence a week.

LEFT Sunday schools, set up by churches, were another source of education for poor children.

likely to get into trouble were started around the beginning of the 19th century. In addition, Magdelen Hospitals, which attempted to reform prostitutes, often educated the women they took in, many of whom were very young, then tried to place them as servants.

Other establishments, known as reformatories, Certified Industrial Schools or Day Industrial Schools, educated children and trained them in a skill that would help them to obtain employment. In 1933, they were renamed Approved Schools.

Schools in the 20th century

The 20th century brought various changes in education, but these largely built on the work done in the 19th century. The major difference was the 1944 Education Act, which made primary and secondary education free to all, and set up grammar, technical and

After 1887, delinquents could be sent to special schools instead of being imprisoned.

secondary modern schools for children over 11. Comprehensive schools, from the 1970s, no longer divided children according to academic ability.

The place of girls

Most education was given to boys, because they were expected to earn a living, in order to support their families, when they grew up. Girls' education was considered to be of secondary importance. Small private schools, some of which took boarders, taught girls accomplishments designed to help them attract a husband. These were set up from the late 18th century and taught reading and writing; some history and geography; a little fashionable French and/or German; and a musical instrument, usually the piano. During the 19th century, the number of these schools increased, but it wasn't until the end of the century that a few with academic ambitions for girls were started. The number increased throughout the 20th century as the need for women to earn a living, both before and after marriage, was recognized.

Significant dates in the history of primary and secondary education

1780 Sunday School Movement began.

1802 Act for the Education of Apprentices stated that apprentices should have at least an hour a week's religious instruction on Sunday. They were to be examined by the parish minister.

1810 Ragged Schools, free to very poor children and orphans, began. They encouraged practical skills and expected their pupils to earn money from a very early age by cleaning shoes or running errands.

1811 National Society for the Promotion and Education of the Poor founded with the aim of providing a school in every parish.

1814 British and Foreign Schools Society founded to provide schools with a Nonconformist ethos.

1833 The government awarded a grant of £20,000 to introduce denominational schools. In 1839, inspectors were appointed to ensure that the money was being properly spent. The grant was increased in 1850, 1858 and 1861, when pupil teachers were introduced. These were bright pupils who were paid to work and train as teachers for five years, getting a certificate for each year successfully completed.

1857 Industrial Schools set up to educate delinquents in a trade. They were also called reformatories.

1861 Payment by results introduced. Schools received 4s for each pupil who attended and 2s 8d for each subject passed by each child in the annual examinations. This led to a national syllabus.

1870 Education Act made education compulsory for children under 10. It was free to the poor, but others paid a small weekly fee.

1893 School leaving age raised to 11.

1899 School leaving age raised to 12.

1902 Local Education Authorities (LEAs) replaced the old School Boards and received increased powers.

1908 Borstals for delinquent children replaced reformatories.

1944 Education Act created grammar, technical and secondary modern schools. The 11-plus examination was introduced to decide which type of school each child should attend.

1947 School leaving age raised to 15.

1974 School leaving age raised to 16.

Locating school records

From 1862, all schools had to keep logbooks, and references to individual pupils can be found in them. You may also find admission books and attendance registers, which were begun in order to record the number of pupils. Some local authorities gave awards for good attendance.

The managers of the school (later known as the governors) kept minute books, which may also have survived. These deal largely with administrative matters and should include information about children punished for bad behaviour. School magazines and ex-pupils associations' newsletters may provide further useful information.

Some school records remain with the schools themselves; others have been deposited in County Record Offices (CROs), and those for Church schools may be located through the denomination's archives. Dr Williams's Library holds information on some Nonconformist schools. Many of the registers of the early grammar, charity and more up-market schools, such as Wellington and Haileybury, have also been published.

Researching school records

The following points should help you in your research:

- In census returns, school children were noted as "scholars".
- If your ancestors lived in a large town or city, you may find directories useful to locate the nearest school to their home, then find the records.
- As well as the child's date of birth, father's name, address and previous school, admission books usually record the date and reason a child left, if this was before the school-leaving age. This could give clues to when your ancestors moved house.
- Events in schools are usually well reported in local newspapers from the end of the 19th century.
- Many schools have honours boards, which list pupils who went on to higher or further education, and Rolls of Honour, which list ex-pupils and teachers who died while serving in the World Wars.

TERTIARY EDUCATION

Before the 19th century, any form of higher education at universities was the preserve of the wealthy or the very clever, who managed to get scholarships, although this would only be with considerable support from a teacher or patron. Most universities and some colleges have published lists of their graduates.

Universities

Until 1836, there were only two universities in England: Oxford and Cambridge. Scotland had four: St Andrews, Glasgow, Edinburgh and Aberdeen, and there was one, Trinity College, Dublin, in Ireland. These all had their origins before 1600. Those people who could not accept the tenets of the established Church, such as Nonconformists, Roman Catholics, Jews and others, were barred from these universities. If your ancestors were not members of the Church of England, they are unlikely to have gone to the established universities, so you need to look elsewhere for records of their tertiary education.

Catholic tertiary education

Catholics often sent their children to the Continent for both secondary and tertiary education. Some lists of

St Paul's School in London had an imposing classroom where boys received a classical education.

The great respect for education in Scotland meant that Glasgow University was one of four founded here before 1600.

Significant dates in the history of tertiary education

The list of institutions included here is not exhaustive: many large hospitals trained doctors and nurses, for example. Also, all the many denominational colleges are excluded.

1167 Oxford University founded.
1209 Cambridge University founded.
1411 St Andrews in Scotland founded.
1451 University of Glasgow founded.
1495 University of Aberdeen founded.
1583 University of Edinburgh founded.
1593 Trinity College, Dublin founded.

1663 First Dissenting Academy founded.
1799 Royal Military College Sandhurst set up to train Army officers.
1804 East India Company started two establishments – one for its army, the other for its civil servants.
1820s Mechanics Institutes and Working Men's Institutes started to hold classes in the evenings for men. Most were on technical subjects to help them progress at work, but there were also lectures on cultural matters.
1844 Royal Agricultural College, Cirencester, founded.
1855 The Jews' College (later

renamed the London School of Jewish Studies) founded to train Orthodox rabbis. It is now part of the University of London.
1869 Girton College for women founded. It moved to Cambridge University in 1873.
1879 Lady Margaret Hall and Somerville, the first two women's colleges of Oxford University, founded.
1889 Technical Instruction Act made provision for the establishment of part-time and evening classes to provide technical and occupational qualifications.
1903 Founding of the Workers Educational Association.

Catholics who graduated overseas have been published by the Catholic Record Society.

Nonconformist tertiary education

A few Dissenting Academies were established after the mid-17th century, and from the 18th century more and more Nonconformists founded their own denominational colleges and academies. Most were started to train clergymen, but others existed to provide a university-level education for those who, for religious reasons, could not go to the established universities. London University started out by awarding degrees gained through a number of colleges and institutions, such as the Inns of Court and medical schools, which later joined together under its aegis.

The admittance of women

Towards the end of the 19th century, women began the fight to enter higher education, and colleges for them were founded within universities.

Teacher training colleges

Pupil teachers in elementary (now primary) schools started work at about 14. Some were apprentices, but most were simply children in the school who showed an interest in and aptitude for teaching.

The first teacher training college for primary teachers was started in Glasgow in 1837. From the early 1900s, Local Education Authorities set up day training colleges, and universities established departments of education, which catered for both primary and secondary school teachers.

Alternative further education

Before the advent of grants for tertiary education, most working-class people could not attend university. Even if a child was able to get a scholarship, poor families depended on their children's income, and so needed them to work. The answer was night school. Most taught commercial practical skills that would improve the students' job opportunities, but the Workers Educational Associations aimed to provide classes in a variety of subjects for those who had not been able to pursue their education while younger.

FURTHER HELP

British & Foreign Schools Archives Centre, West London Institute of Higher Education, Borough Road, Isleworth, Middlesex TW7 5DU
Catholic Education Council, 41 Cromwell Road, London SW7 2DJ
Chapman, Colin R. Basic Facts *About Using Education Records* (FFHS)
Dr Williams's Library, 14 Gordon Square, London WC1H 0AG

Methodist Church Division of Education & Youth, 2 Chester House, Pages Lane, London N10 1PZ
Ragged School Union (now incorporated into the Shaftesbury Society), 10–20 Kingston Road, London SW19 1JZ
www.shaftesburysociety.org.uk
Minutes of both organizations have now been issued on microfilm.

Apprenticeships

The majority of children started work between the ages of 12 and 14. Many went into domestic service (before World War I this was how most people began their working lives), but others were apprenticed to learn a trade.

APPRENTICESHIPS BEFORE THE 19TH CENTURY

In 1563, the Statute of Artificers laid down that no one could practise a certain occupation without serving at least seven years as an apprentice and

until reaching the age of 24. In 1768, this was reduced to 21, and the statute remained in force until 1814, although by that time enforcement of it had become rather lax. The 1563 legislation also applied only to occupations then in existence. As other trades started, the requirement that practitioners should serve an apprenticeship in full was not enforced in many cases.

If the master could not complete the full term of training, arrangements were usually made to find another master to complete the apprenticeship. This was known as "turning over".

There were three distinct kinds of apprenticeship:

- voluntary apprenticeship, where the child was placed by its parents
- Poor Law apprenticeship, where parish authorities placed a child in the master's care
- apprenticeship to a guild or livery company of a town or city

Voluntary apprenticeship

This was a private arrangement, usually made by parents on behalf of their child. They paid someone a fee to

BELOW Apprenticeship indentures included strict conditions about how the apprentice should behave.

cover the cost of tuition as well as the apprentice's keep while he or she was learning. Both parties signed a legal document called an indenture, which had two parts. One part was kept by the parents and the other by the master.

If children were apprenticed to their father, mother or another relative, there was only a token fee.

Between 1710 and 1808, apprenticeship premiums over 1s were taxed. The records, which actually finish in 1811, are in The National Archives (TNA). Until around 1752 they contain the parents' or guardian's names. There are indexes up to 1774 to both masters and apprentices in TNA, the Guildhall Library and the Society of Genealogists' library. Poor Law apprenticeships were exempt, so will not appear here, nor will the apprenticeship of a child to a father.

Poor Law apprenticeship

It was the responsibility of the overseer of the poor for each parish to provide for orphans and those children whose parents were too impoverished to care for them. The 1601 Poor Relief Act allowed parish officers, with the consent of Justices of the Peace (JPs), to bind a child under the age of 14 to a master (either a man or woman). This was not a proper apprenticeship, and was called an "apprenticeship binding". Often these hapless children were simply used as unpaid labour rather than being taught a skill.

In 1696, it became compulsory to take apprentices in this way, and masters were selected in rotation or chosen by ballot. Apprenticeship bindings lasted until 1834. Since 1662, serving a full term of apprenticeship had given settlement rights in a parish, and so officials tried to find masters outside their own parish, in order to evade potential responsibility for the apprentice and any dependants. Records relating to Poor Law apprentices will be found in parish records in the CRO. The SoG has a large collection of original indentures made between 1641 and 1888, including many Poor Law apprenticeships.

There were also local charities that paid for the apprenticeship of poor children, although as time went on better-off parents sometimes managed to get their sons and daughters placed in good trades through this route. These records will be found in the CRO.

Guild apprenticeship

Members of guilds were responsible for teaching apprentices their various trades and crafts. Completing a guild apprenticeship brought all kinds of privileges, so a high premium could be charged for taking one. A record of these premiums appear in TNA's tax records, as well as in the records of the guilds themselves, which are usually in the CRO.

Guild records will also contain information about disputes over apprenticeships and the turning over of an apprentice from one master to another. Sometimes this was due to the inability of a master to continue in business, but in other cases children simply proved to have no aptitude for or interest in a craft, and so started again in a different trade or skill.

Quarter sessions papers contain many examples of apprentices petitioning to be released from their indentures because their master was either not teaching them his or her craft or ill-treating them. Some apprentices did not go to the trouble of legal proceedings: they just ran away, and advertisements for their return may be found in local newspapers. Anyone employing such a runaway was liable to prosecution. Newspapers may also contain reports of legal proceedings. Masters also went to law to cancel the indenture of an unsatisfactory apprentice.

APPRENTICESHIPS IN THE 19TH AND 20TH CENTURIES

The strict controls exercised over apprentices started to loosen in the mid-18th century. Many people did not complete their full term but still practised a trade.

In the 19th century, with the growth of large companies, apprentices were increasingly taken on by businesses, such as shipbuilders, gas companies, and motor manufacturers.

Surviving records of indentures from the 19th and 20th centuries will be found either in company archives (many deposited with CROs) or among private family papers.

RESEARCHING APPRENTICESHIP RECORDS

Completing an apprenticeship was one of the ways after 1662 in which to gain settlement in a parish, and so settlement examinations will always say whether an apprenticeship was started and if it was completed, and will give the name and parish of the master.

The dates of the beginning and end of an apprenticeship will give clues to the person's age: the standard term was seven years, ending at the age of 21 (or 24 in the 16th and 17th centuries).

Directories and advertisements in newspapers may help to locate where an ancestor served as an apprentice.

FURTHER HELP

TNA Domestic Records Information 80 *Apprenticeship Records as Sources for Genealogy* Some guild records, including apprenticeships, have been published.

Guilds and freemen

The guilds of cities and towns began in the Middle Ages. They were originally made up of reputable merchants, tradesmen and craftsmen who organized themselves into groups to maintain occupational standards and agree prices. They also arranged many welfare services for their members, such as insurance, burial clubs and financial support for widows and orphans of members.

Someone who had successfully completed an apprenticeship to a member of one of the guilds became a freeman, which usually gave the right to vote in local elections.

BECOMING A FREEMAN

At the end of his or her guild apprenticeship, the aspiring guild member produced an example of the skills that had been learned. This was often a miniature article, such as a piece of furniture, and was called the "masterpiece". If this masterpiece was considered satisfactory, the person paid a fee to be enrolled into the guild as a freeman and could practise his or, much more rarely, her trade.

Most men then became journeymen. This name is not connected to the fact that they travelled around, which they often did, but comes from the fact that they were paid by the day. (It comes from the French word *journée*.) They worked on a casual basis until they had the means to set up their own businesses, hire other workers and take on their own apprentices. The more prudent ones waited until they found somewhere that needed their skills before settling down and starting a family.

There were three other ways of becoming a freeman:

- by redemption or fine, i.e. paying to join a guild or livery company when you had not completed an apprenticeship in its trade or craft
- by patrimony, if your father was a freeman at the time of your birth. In some places, therefore, the freedom of a guild or borough could be inherited and passed down through the generations, although this usually applied only to eldest sons. This inherited freedom still operates in some of the ancient boroughs,

so you may find that you or your eldest son are entitled to become a freeman.

- by marrying a freeman's widow or daughter (this was only practised in some guilds)

These different methods meant that a man might have a different trade from that of the guild he entered.

If someone was expelled from a guild, he would not be allowed to trade within the radius of the city or town. This is where the expression "sent to Coventry" may have originated.

Freemen had certain rights granted to them by the city or town:

- to take apprentices
- to trade
- to vote for officials such as the Mayor and Aldermen, and also in national elections.

In addition, freemen were responsible for local government functions, such as the running of schools and care of the poor, as well as the administration of both civil and criminal law within their borough, including inquests. Many guilds supported local charities and educational establishments.

The guilds and livery companies of the City of London have their own crests (from left to right: the Mercers, Merchant Tailors, Grocers and Ironmongers), which may appear on heirlooms and provide the family historian with clues about an ancestor's membership.

CITY OF LONDON GUILDS

Outside London there was usually a single guild to which all traders and craftsmen belonged, whatever their business. In the City of London, however, there were different livery companies and guilds, which originally had their basis in specific occupations. (The livery companies are chartered companies that originated from the craft guilds.) There are 102 companies, of which 77 are ancient and 25 modern. Before about 1700, people tended to belong to the same company as their trade. From 1750, the other methods of gaining the freedom of the City became more common. The cost of apprenticeship to a citizen of London meant that skilled people who could not afford to become a freeman tended to live in the parishes around the Square Mile.

CITY OF LONDON BROKERS

Commodity brokers who wanted to trade in the City of London had to be freemen (until 1856) and be licensed by the City authorities (until 1886), although some evaded being licensed from the 19th century onwards. They were issued with a medal to prove their credentials. The numbers of Jews and other aliens were strictly limited. Between 1738 and 1830, Jews were not admitted to the freedom of the City, but twelve were allowed to become brokers.

KING'S/QUEEN'S FREEMEN

Between 1784 and 1873, discharged servicemen and their wives and children had the right to trade in any town in the British Isles. They were called King's/Queen's Freemen, and received a certificate. Relatively few seem to have taken advantage of this, because, from the beginning of the 19th century, strict control started to decline. Fewer and fewer men chose to pay the

The Stock Exchange was set up in 1760 by a group of men thrown out of the Royal Exchange for rowdy behaviour. By Victorian times, it was a respectable place to work.

costs of guild membership, especially if they had done their apprenticeship in a city or town but decided to set up in business elsewhere, so King's/Queen's Freemen had no special advantages.

HONORARY FREEMEN

City and borough councils could grant someone who had done their community some special service the title of honorary freeman.

RESEARCHING GUILD RECORDS

Electoral registers and poll books before about 1835 will list those who had the right to vote in local and national elections. They usually state how the individual was qualified to vote, including if they were freemen. If your City of London ancestor was a grocer, he may not have joined the Grocers' Company. The variety of ways of becoming a freeman means that he could also have belonged to any of the other companies. Wills usually state whether a person was a member of a City of London livery company.

The archives of most of the City of

London's livery companies and guilds are in the Guildhall Library, but a few remain with the companies themselves. There is a complete list of freemen between 1681 and 1915, which includes the guild to which they belonged. City of London apprenticeship records are in the process of being published. The guild records of many provincial cities and boroughs have been published, at least up to 1800.

> **FURTHER HELP**
>
> Aldous, Vivienne E. *My Ancestors Were Freemen of the City of London* (SoG)
> CLRO *City Freedom Archives* (CLRO Research Guide No. 1)
> CLRO *Sworn Brokers' Archives* (CLRO Research Guide No. 2)
> GL *City Livery Companies and Related Organisations* (Guildhall Library Research Guide No. 3)
> GL *Searching for Members or Those Apprenticed to Members of the City of London Livery Companies at Guildhall Library*
> Ward, Harry *Freemen in England* (self-published)

The professions

The British practice of leaving land and money to the eldest son meant that the other children had to make their own way in the world. Within the upper classes, there was sometimes enough money in the family to ensure that younger sons didn't have to do anything so vulgar as work, and the lower middle classes had businesses or trades to pass on to their sons, but there were many families where profitable occupations had to be found for their sons. (The daughters were expected to marry well.) Some purchased commissions as Army officers or went into the Navy; others became clergymen, lawyers or perhaps doctors but not, until the late 19th century, surgeons, who were not held in such high respect.

THE CHURCH

Clergymen of the Church of England usually went to university, then, having obtained their degree, were appointed to a parish, either as the incumbent or as a curate. Many parishes, or livings, were in the gift of the bishop of a diocese or an individual, such as a lord of the manor. In the 18th century, it was common for a clergyman to have more than one living: he would pay a curate to look after the parishioners of the less glamorous parish, or parishes, and live elsewhere.

There were often complaints about clergymen neglecting their duties or committing other sins; these are found in the records of the Church courts in either the DRO or CRO. From 1792, all clergymen and preachers had to be licensed by the bishop, who also issued licences for a number of other matters,

George Whitefield, one of the founders of Methodism, joined the society while at Oxford in 1735 before it broke away from the Church of England.

such as holding more than one living, or engaging in a trade. Not all clergymen became the incumbent of a parish: some became chaplains, others missionaries. Information about chaplains will be found among surviving papers of the organizations they served. There were a number of missionary societies linked to different denominations. Since they depended on subscriptions and voluntary contributions, they usually produced annual reports, which contain information about individuals' activities.

The Clergy List, published from 1841, lists the names of all the Anglican clergy and gives details of their livings, including when they were appointed, how much each living was worth per annum and who was the patron. From 1858 this list was taken over by a man called Crockford, and it continues as Crockford's Clerical Directory to the present day. There are other sources of information: most dioceses issued publications listing the personnel in them, and DROs and CROs may hold ordination papers for individual clergy, containing letters of recommendation, references and other useful documents.

Nonconformist clergy

After the restoration of Charles II in 1660, Nonconformist clergy faced official persecution. From 1672, they had to be licensed, but it was not until the 1689 Toleration Act that they and their congregations had complete freedom of worship.

Nonconformist clergy tended to come from a lower social class than Anglican clergy, and, as they did not have parish tithes to support them, they depended on what their congregation could give them and what they could earn themselves. Most, therefore, had another occupation. Surviving records will be found in the denomination's archives. From the mid-19th century, most produced both magazines and directories, which contain obituaries and other biographical material on ministers.

Researching clerical records

Look first at the lists of Oxbridge alumni, which contain biographical details. From there, you can go on to the records of the organizations or places where your ancestor(s) worked.

If your ancestor isn't an Oxbridge graduate, look at the records of Nonconformist colleges in the 19th century, or records of licences.

THE LAW

There was, and still is, a distinction between solicitors (known as attorneys until 1875) and barristers. Only the latter could appear in court to plead for their clients. Attorneys conducted legal business, such as drawing up marriage settlements and wills or dealing with property matters. Some also dealt with other estate business, such

as collecting rents, and were involved with manorial courts. Attorneys could also carry out their clients' business in those courts to which they were admitted to practise.

Qualifying for the law

People wanting to become barristers mainly went to university, either Oxford or Cambridge, and then to the Inns of Court in London, where they had to remain for a certain period of time before qualifying. An examination was introduced in 1853. Those wanting to become solicitors might also go to university, but the majority were apprenticed. The period of apprenticeship was fixed at five years in 1728.

Researching legal records

Most of the admission registers of the Inns of Court have been published. Surviving records that have not appeared in print are still with the individual Inns, apart from those of Clement's Inn, which are held by TNA. It's also worth checking the registers of the chapels attached to the inns: barristers were sometimes married or had children baptized there.

TNA holds records of attorneys admitted to the various courts: Common Pleas, King's/Queen's Bench,

FURTHER HELP

TNA Domestic Records Information 36 *Lawyers: Records of Attorneys and Solicitors*

Exchequer, Equity, Chancery, Bankruptcy, the Palatinate Courts, High Court of Admiralty and the Prerogative Court of Canterbury. Lawyers practising in the last two courts were called "proctors". An oath had to be sworn before they could be admitted, which effectively disbarred Catholics from practising in these courts before 1791. Judges also had to take an oath.

The Law List, containing attorneys, was published from 1780, and the Law Society was founded in 1828. The society also holds records relating to their members dating back, in some cases, to 1790. Between 1710 and 1811 there was a tax on apprenticeship premiums, so attorneys will appear in these records too.

Some lawyers, of course, completed their training but did not practise, so if you find an ancestor in the records of the Inns of Court or apprenticeship records, don't assume that he necessarily became a lawyer. An education in the law was regarded as good preparation for life.

LEFT Judges' wigs and gowns date from the late 17th century, when they were everyday wear.

Calling in a doctor was expensive, and before the mid-19th century he had few effective remedies for illness.

Apothecaries dispensed medicines and offered advice to those too poor to pay for a doctor.

MEDICINE

Since the medical profession deals with life and death, it has, for obvious reasons, been strictly regulated. Before the 19th century, when there were considerable advances in both medical science and public health, the profession was not highly specialized. Women were largely responsible for their families' wellbeing and any nursing that needed to be done. Calling in a doctor might be expensive and, in many cases, there was little that he could do. Some of the drugs in common use, like mercury, might be almost as harmful to the patient as the diseases they were meant to cure. Many people relied on folk medicine, like wrapping an old sock or stocking around the neck to cure a sore throat, or went to people who had a reputation for herbal medicines (but no formal qualification or licence).

Physicians and surgeons

From medieval times, there was a sharp distinction between physicians and surgeons. Before anaesthetics made invasive surgery possible, only minor operations, blood letting and amputations could be carried out, and their familiarity with razors meant that barbers carried out these operations. In London, surgeons belonged to the same company as barbers until 1745, when a separate Company of Surgeons was established. Training was by apprenticeship.

Surgery was considered only one step up from butchery, so the men who went into this branch of medicine were (and still are) called "Mr", rather than "Doctor". Medical men who went to sea were almost invariably surgeons: the ability to carry out amputations was vital in battle. The Royal College of Surgeons was founded in 1801.

Physicians treated all illnesses not requiring surgery: indeed, some prided themselves on not touching their patients at all. Before the late 18th century, they were apprenticed, but increasingly went to university, especially in Scotland. Lists of university graduates have been published. From 1512, all medical men practising in London had to be licensed by the Bishop of London.

Apothecaries

Apothecaries, who dispensed drugs and medicines, and chemists and druggists, who made them, came into the medical profession through apprenticeship. Both doctors and surgeons might also have training as apothecaries. From 1815, they had to be licensed by the Society of Apothecaries, whose records are in the Guildhall Library.

Dentists

In early years, dentistry consisted of little more than extracting teeth. Any strong person could set himself, or more rarely herself, up as a tooth-puller. The first dental hospital, which also carried out training, was founded in London in 1858.

Nurses and midwives

Women have been involved in caring for the sick since before records began. From medieval times, many orders of nuns were involved in this work. After the dissolution of the monasteries, a few hospitals remained, and women worked in them, but they were rarely those who had gone into nursing because of a religious vocation. Most were elderly widows, for whom the alternative was starvation, and they were paid a pittance for their work. Workhouses and parish infirmaries usually employed a matron and occasionally other women, often one of the paupers in the workhouse, to care for the sick.

Hospitals were very unhygienic and dangerous places to stay in, so most people preferred to be cared for at home and might hire nurses to look after them there, especially after childbirth. There was no recognized training for nurses, and those who undertook such work had the unwelcome reputation of being drunken, slovenly and incompetent.

Florence Nightingale transformed both the image and the training of nurses. After her experiences in Scutari during the Crimean War, she came back to Britain determined to make nursing a skilled and respectable profession. The first training school for nurses was set up at St Thomas's Hospital in London in 1860. State registration of nurses began in 1919.

Researching records of medical practitioners

Since 1845, an annual directory of practitioners has been published as the *British Medical Directory*, and this is the best starting point for the family historian. Dentists were included from 1886. Local and trade directories list medical practitioners before and after these dates. Records of apprenticeships can be found in TNA for 1710–1811.

FURTHER HELP

History of Nursing Society, Royal College of Nursing www.rcn.org.ik/learning/archives
Magg, Christopher *Sources for the History of Nursing in Great Britain* (Kings Fund Project Paper No. 46)
The Wellcome Insitute for the History of Medicine www.wellcome.ac.uk

Before the mid-18th century, physicians, surgeons and midwives had to be licensed by the bishop of their diocese, because they might have to baptize a newborn child in danger of dying. Records will be found in Diocesan Record Offices (DROs) or CROs.

The United Kingdom Central Council for Nursing, Midwifery and Health Visiting (UKCC) holds a list of registered practitioners, but this has only their date of registration. To go further, you need to know in which hospital your ancestor trained. Photographs may help, as hospitals had their own, distinctive uniforms. Records relating to military and naval nurses will be in TNA.

ABOVE Until the 20th century, most women gave birth at home.

RIGHT Florence Nightingale's efforts made the nursing profession respectable.

The introduction of the penny post meant that even the less well off could keep in touch with their families.

FIREFIGHTERS

Early firefighters were either employees of the fire insurance companies or volunteers. The insurance companies employed firemen and porters (the latter carried out the salvage operation after a fire). Records relating to fire brigades are usually deposited in the CROs.

AWARDS FOR BRAVERY

Many of those in the above-mentioned uniformed services behaved heroically in the course of their duties and might have received recognition of this. There are various awards for particular services.

Ordinary people were also given awards for bravery. There are a number of organizations that might have issued some token, such as a medal or certificate. One of the main bodies involved in this is the Royal Humane Society, which was established in 1774, originally as a way of encouraging people to bring drowned bodies to two doctors who were interested in

researching resuscitation techniques. It grew into a charity that both employed rescuers stationed at places, such as rivers and lakes, where drowning was a danger, and gave awards for bravery. Some of its records date back to its founding, and it has a list of awards made from 1823 onwards. These have not been indexed, so the date of the event, which would have been covered in newspapers, is necessary to get further information.

THE POST OFFICE

In 1636, Charles I allowed the general public to use the royal mail services, and the Post Office was born. In 1840 the practice of requiring the sender, rather than the recipient, of a letter or package to pay began. An adhesive stamp, the first being the Penny Black, showed that the sum had been paid.

Although most of its records were destroyed in the Great Fire of London in 1666, the Post Office's archives include some records dating back to 1636. From 1719, many Post Office employees received pensions, and their application forms are indexed. In addition to information about employees'

appointments and careers, there are copies of union publications, company newsletters and magazines, and an extensive collection of photographs and artwork. Records relating to telegraph and telephone services are now with British Telecommunications, and these include telephone directories dating from 1880.

RAILWAYS

Originally the railway system in Britain consisted of individual private companies. In 1947, the whole railway system was nationalized, and the vast majority of surviving records of all the different companies were deposited in TNA or the Scottish Record Office (SRO), though a few may be in CROs. There are many books available on aspects of the railways and their history.

OTHER COMPANY ARCHIVES

Histories of many individual companies have been written and published, but they usually mention only the higher echelons of employees. Archives may have been deposited in CROs, while others remain with the company. Many large organizations,

The vast amount of waste produced in cities needed an army of refuse collectors and cleaners, many of whom were women.

including department stores and hotels, have their own archives. Among their records may be personnel details and company newsletters, which usually mention people's retirements and carry obituaries.

RESEARCHING ANCESTORS INVOLVED IN A PARTICULAR OCCUPATION

There are a large number of occupational indexes. Some are in the possession of individuals who have, through a personal interest, set them up; others are attached to specialist museums. Local historians may also have set up an index of everyone in their area of study, which will include the occupations of all the people there. It is quite difficult to find out where all these indexes are located, as many people have compiled them mainly for their own interest.

The title and further information about companies, particular occupations and directories of those engaged in them can be found by typing an occupation into the search engine of the British Library's on line catalogue. The book can then be ordered through your local library's service or, if this is impossible, read at the British Library or the nearest library that holds a copy, which your library should be able to discover for you.

If the occupation was a skilled trade that generally required a period of apprenticeship, or needed some kind of licence to practise the trade, there will be a variety of sources you can check with.

It is worth remembering that every trade or occupation has its own association and specialist magazine. Some professional societies, including the livery companies, date from medieval times, but from the 19th century onwards trade associations for other

Working for a railway company was regarded as a prestigious job and brought a pension, which meant a secure old age.

occupations were set up. Records of members may still be with the relevant association; if not, the association should be able to tell you where they are now deposited.

Many of the skills learned by people in the past no longer exist or have been replaced by machines. If you find that a reference to your ancestor's occupation is something you don't understand, and a dictionary does not contain it, look at a book such as the *Book of Trades or Library of Useful Arts* (pub. 1811–18 and reprinted by Wiltshire Family History Society), which describes pre-19th-century occupations, or Colin Waters' *A Dictionary of Old Trades, Occupations and Titles.*

FURTHER HELP

BT Group Archives, Third Floor, Holborn Telephone Exchange, 268–270 High Holborn, London WC1V 7EE www.btplc.com/ Corporateinformation/BTArchives/ Appointment needed.

The Directory of British Associations (CRD Research) and other similar directories publish all those in existence today and usually give the date of foundation.

Harvey, C. *Business Records at The National Archives* (TNA)

Hawkings, David T. *Railway Ancestors: A guide to the staff records of the railway companies of England and Wales 1822–1947* (Alan Sutton Publishing)

Heritage Services, The Post Office, Freeling House, Phoenix Place,

London WC1X 0DL www.consignia.com/heritage/ has information sheets about genealogical research. A reader's ticket and an appointment are not necessary, but proof of identity is required.

Jewell, Andrew *Crafts, Trades and Industries: A book List for Local Historians* (National Council Social Service 1964)

National Railway Museum, Library Archive, Leemans Road, York YO26 4XJ www.nrm.org.uk

Raymond, Stuart *Occupational Sources for Genealogists: A Bibliography* (FFHS)

Torrance, D. Richard *Scottish Trades and Professions: A Selected Bibliography* (Scottish Association of Family History Societies)

Licences

A number of occupations required the practitioner to have a licence. Sometimes it was a matter of ensuring competence, as in the case of gamekeepers. In other instances, such as printers, it was to ensure that laws were not broken.

LEFT Anyone selling alcohol needed a licence, which could be withdrawn if customers became too rowdy.

VICTUALLERS

There can be very few families who do not have someone connected with the manufacture or sale of alcohol in their ancestry. (In some places, every third house was licensed to brew or sell alcohol, in the times when water was too dangerous to drink.) The Crown also made money by selling licences to import and sell wine and spirits.

Different regulations applied to alehouses, taverns and inns. An alehouse was usually a small establishment where ale, beer or sometimes cider was made on the premises and sold to customers. Often this was a single person working from his or her own home. Taverns, which were in towns, boroughs or cities, offered wine as well as ale and might also have sold spirits. Inns sold alcoholic drinks and had rooms where travellers could stay.

The first law regulating the sale of alcohol was passed in 1553. Licences to sell alcohol had to be granted by JPs, which remains the case today. People who wanted to provide entertainment as well as sell alcohol on their premises needed a licence from 1752, and if they also wanted to hire out horses they had to get a separate licence from 1784.

In 1828, the laws were revised and different types of licences to sell beer, wine and spirits on and off premises

were granted. From 1830, those selling only beer and cider could get a licence from the local excise office rather than in court.

Locating records of alcohol-related licences

The National Archives holds records relating to licences to sell wine in the 16th and 17th centuries, and some licences for this period are also found in quarter sessions held in CROs. From the 18th century, matters to do with licences - both the granting of them and cases involving illegal sales - were dealt with at petty and quarter sessions. Recent records relating to licences may still be with the magistrates' courts that granted them.

GAMEKEEPERS

Between 1710 and the middle of the 20th century, the men who looked after the game birds on a country estate were supposed to be registered at the local quarter sessions, though it seems that this was not always observed. Court records may also contain legal proceedings relating to

poachers apprehended by gamekeepers. Estate records mentioning gamekeepers may remain with the owner or may have been deposited in CROs or other repositories. Local directories may also list gamekeepers in their area.

COACHMEN AND DRIVERS

Coachmen in general did not have to have a licence or be registered anywhere, but hackney coachmen, the taxi-drivers of the 19th and early 20th century, did have to be licensed. Records of these licences, which do not include the licences themselves, are in TNA. Sometimes hackney coachmen gave the number of their licence in census returns.

London taxi-drivers are now licensed by the Public Carriage Office, but records of individual cabbies are destroyed six years after their death or

FURTHER HELP

Gibson, Jeremy and Hunter, Judith *Victuallers' Licences: Records for Family and Local Historians* (FFHS)

retirement. Other local authorities generally license taxi-drivers in their own area, and the survival of records depends on their policies.

From 1903, drivers of motor vehicles, including motorcycles, had to have a licence issued by the local authorities, so surviving records will be in CROs.

PAWNBROKERS AND CHIMNEYSWEEPS

From 1786, pawnbrokers in all parts of the country had to have annual revenue licences. Records before the Pawnbrokers' Act of 1872 are sparse, but after this date there are some records in CROs, since the licence was dependent on a certificate granted by a magistrate. Chimney sweeps were given similar certificates after 1875.

TRAVELLING SALESPEOPLE

Itinerant sellers of goods had to be licensed by a magistrate from 1698 to 1772. They had to wear a badge showing that they were licensed, and so were sometimes called "badgers". These records will be in the CRO, and there are also lists of licences granted in TNA among the Exchequer records. There was a fine line between sellers of some goods, such as matches, and beggars. From 1531, beggars had to be licensed by JPs or mayors.

DROVERS

Before railways and motorized transport, the only way to get cattle and other animals, such as sheep, pigs and even geese, to market was to drive them there. Most, of course, went to the nearest market town, but others were taken much longer distances to cities, especially London. The men engaged in this trade were known as drovers, and they, like other itinerants, were licensed.

BARGEES AND RIVER SAILORS

Boats had always been used to transport goods around Britain's coastline and along the navigable rivers inland. The first canals were constructed in the late 18th century by private companies. There were no common agreements between them about the width and depth of these waterways, so barges could be used only on particular canals, which was restrictive.

Between 1795 and 1871, owners of barges had to be licensed. Records of christenings, marriages and burials (CMBs) of bargees, river sailors and their families should be found in the parishes along the route of canals. Some families actually lived on their barges, while others had a home on land instead.

The 1861 census uniquely required additional details about ships in port to be included, and, since this would include river and canal boats delivering or collecting goods to or from ports, respectively, it is a useful source of information. There is an index to ships' names in TNA. In 1877, an Act required registers of canal boats to be kept, and those that survive are usually in CROs.

PRINTERS AND PUBLISHERS

The government has always worried about what is published, especially if it criticizes them, but also if it contains material defined as seditious, blasphemous or obscene. Since 1834, all printed material has had to contain the name and address of the printer. Between 1799 and 1869, the owners of printing presses had to be licensed.

GUN OWNERS

Not surprisingly, a strict eye was kept on those who owned guns (a situation that has not changed today), and the manufacturers of guns were also carefully regulated. Initially most gunsmiths worked in and around the City of London and belonged to one of the livery companies there. After the Civil War, the Midlands, especially Birmingham, became another centre of arms manufacture. The government was a major customer, and employed some gunsmiths through the Board of Ordnance, whose records are in TNA. The arms they made had to be tested in proof houses, which still exist. The one in Whitechapel, East London, dates back to 1675.

Before the growth of railways and motor vehicles, the waterways were an important form of transport. Barge owners needed a licence.

Elections, poll books and electoral registers

Until the 20th century, the majority of people did not have the vote, which usually depended on owning property as a qualification.

PARLIAMENTARY ELECTIONS

Before the 19th century, Members of Parliament were returned for three types of constituency: counties, boroughs (burghs in Scotland) and the universities of Oxford and Cambridge.

County MPs

The franchise was largely based on property qualifications. Before 1832, the vote was restricted to those who possessed land or a house worth 40s or more in annual rent.

Borough franchises

Only those towns that had an ancient charter were boroughs. This is why many of the northern and Midlands towns that grew out of the Industrial Revolution had no individual MPs but were included in the county elections until after the 1832 Reform Act.

Only a small section of the population could vote, and they cast their ballots in public until 1872. Allegations of bribery and vote-rigging were common.

The vote in these boroughs depended on local customs. In some, all freemen had the franchise but in others, it was only those who were resident there that qualified. In some boroughs, ratepayers could vote. The lists of people entitled to vote in boroughs are called burgess or freemen's rolls.

The City of London

All the Acts that gradually eroded the rights of freemen in boroughs to elect their own MPs and officials have always excluded the City of London, where a system of government, relatively unchanged since medieval times, still operates.

The right to vote

Until the 20th century, the majority of people did not have the right to vote. At various times, certain people were not allowed to vote in parliamentary elections:

- women (until 1918, and even then there were certain restrictions)
- peers of the realm (though peeresses could vote between 1918 and 1963)
- those under 21

- lunatics
- sentenced criminals in prison
- aliens who had not been naturalized
- those in receipt of public alms, i.e. those receiving outdoor relief (money given to poor people not living in a workhouse) or those living in parish workhouses
- anyone convicted of bribery at an election
- those not included in an

electoral register (after 1832, when they were introduced)

Certain occupational groups were also excluded:

- serving policemen (before 1887)
- postmasters (until 1918)
- customs and excise men (until 1918)

Conscientious objectors in World War I were also forbidden to vote in the 1918 and 1923 parliamentary elections.

Significant dates in the history of the franchise in England and Wales

1429 All men over the age of 21 who held land or property with a rental value of 40s or more per annum in a county, and were resident there, could vote in county elections.

1774 Men no longer needed to be resident in the county where their property was situated in order to vote.

1832 Reform Act revised constituencies and extended the county franchise to tenants of land worth between £2 and £5 per annum (p.a.); to those paying more than £50 p.a. in rent; and to those with a long lease on land worth more than £10 p.a. All the varied qualifications in the borough franchises were standardized to those who had property with a ratable value of more than £10 p.a. All voters had to have paid their rates and taxes. This Act also introduced electoral registers.

1867 Representation of the People Act gave the vote to all men paying £10 or more p.a. for housing in towns (but not in rural areas), reduced the property value in counties to £5 and extended the franchise to all men paying £50 or more per year in rent for a building or land. The right afforded to Oxford and Cambridge to elect their own MP was extended to the University of London.

1869 Municipal Franchise Act gave unmarried women who paid rates the right to vote for certain local officials.

1870 Electoral rights of unmarried women ratepayers extended to school boards.

1872 Secret ballot introduced.

1888 County Electors Act allowed women with property qualifications to elect county councillors.

1894 Married women allowed to vote for local officials on the same basis as unmarried women.

1918 Women over 30 allowed to vote in national elections if either a householder or married to a householder.

1928 All men and women over the age of 21 given the vote.

1971 Age of majority (and therefore the right to vote) reduced from 21 to 18.

University seats

Oxford and Cambridge returned two MPs each. They were elected by the universities' legislative assemblies.

POLL BOOKS

In 1696, the sheriff of a county was given responsibility for compiling a list of all those who voted in a county election and for whom they cast their vote. This was to be made available to anyone who wanted to consult it. In 1843, a similar Act was passed relating to borough elections, but, unfortunately, most of these manuscript documents have been destroyed.

The poll was not secret before 1872, and poll books were published. They often include an account of the electoral campaign, though they are not always completely accurate. There is also no standard format. People who were not able to vote, for example those whose religion meant that they could not take the oath of allegiance, might or might not be listed. The candidate's political party might not be recorded, so you will have to look at a parliamentary history book to find out whether he was a Whig or a Tory. It is a good idea for family historians to investigate the policies of the individuals for whom their ancestors voted.

Researching poll books and electoral registers

These usually state individuals' addresses, occupations and qualifications for voting, which will give you further avenues to explore.

After 1774, when voters no longer had to be resident in the counties where they had property, land tax records were often used to prove their qualifications. Copies made of these might be found among quarter sessions records in CROs.

If you find that your ancestor appears in one poll book or electoral register but not the one before, don't automatically assume that he had only recently moved into the county. Check the date to see whether the franchise qualifications had changed in that time, as new legislation might have brought him into the electorate. In a borough, for example, he might have only recently become a freeman, either by completing his apprenticeship or by one of the other ways of gaining entry to a guild.

FURTHER HELP

Gibson, Jeremy and Rogers, Colin *Poll Books c.1696–1872: A Directory to Holdings in Great Britain* [FFHS]

Gibson, Jeremy and Rogers, Colin *Electoral Registers Since 1832 and Burgess Rolls: A Directory to Holdings in Great Britain* [FFHS]

In addition, there are a number of books about individual boroughs, counties and elections, which are listed in the Gibson Guides.

Trade unions and friendly societies

The government has always been highly suspicious of working men gathering together. At the end of the 18th century, the ruling class was afraid of revolution – a fear that the French Revolution largely confirmed – and it is true that many of the "corresponding societies" set up at about that time, ostensibly for social reasons and to discuss current affairs, did want changes in society. The two types of organization had much in common, especially in the early days: trade unions concentrated on pay and working conditions, while friendly societies concerned themselves with benefits for the unemployed and sick.

Another kind of revolution, the Industrial Revolution, began in this period, and changed the way people had previously worked. The scope for exploitation was now much greater, and workers realized the benefits of concerted action. The government responded with a series of laws against "combinations" – both trade unions and friendly societies.

TRADE UNIONS

From the mid-19th century, the government began to accept the right of people to form unions to negotiate with employers. Some unions were highly specialized, while others had a more general membership.

Throughout the 19th and 20th centuries, the number of unions grew. In many industries, membership became mandatory – the so-called "closed shop". Those who refused to join or who were rejected or expelled could not work in a particular company or occupation. This situation lasted until

the last quarter of the 20th century, so if you have ancestors in certain occupations, they will have been members of the relevant union. The Trades Union Congress (TUC), founded in 1920, is an association to which the majority of individual unions belong. Unions were an important factor in the founding, growth and development of the Labour Party.

Researching trade union records

The TUC Library Collections holds books and documents relating to the trade union movement. These largely relate to its history, but active and prominent members of unions may also appear in them. Its own archive holds records relating to the development of the TUC itself. Individual unions' records may still be with the

ABOVE Members of the Ancient Order of Foresters carry tools of agricultural trades.

LEFT Women were expected to support their menfolk when they went on strike.

union itself or may have been deposited in a separate archive, often within a university.

FRIENDLY SOCIETIES

Before the 20th century, illness and unemployment meant penury for not only the average working man but also his family. The workhouse was a grim experience, and, although there were charities to help, not everyone qualified for their assistance. To avoid the threat of the workhouse, groups of people would get together and pay into a fund designed to assist any of their number in financial trouble. Such benevolent and fraternal associations did, however, run the risk of being seen as a cover for political subversion. In 1793, the Friendly Societies Act regularized their position by requiring such clubs to draw up a set of rules and get themselves approved by local JPs, but this did not prevent official suspicion of their activities.

The major friendly societies were the Ancient Order of Foresters and the Independent Order of Oddfellows, but there were a number of other, smaller, ones. Individual branches were called "courts" in the Foresters and "lodges" in the Oddfellows, and, at the beginning, their members usually met at a local inn. Each member, who had to live within walking distance of the inn, received a certificate, which may survive in family papers. The courts or lodges retained the services of a medical man to provide treatment for its members. Those who were ill received sick pay, and a lump sum was paid to their families on death. As the trade union movement gathered strength, the membership of friendly societies declined.

Initially the Oddfellows met in public houses, but, during the mid-19th century, as the temperance move-

By the 20th century, the trade unions had become a powerful political force, as well as supporting their members in times of unemployment.

ment grew, lodges began to build their own halls to keep their members away from the demon drink. The Oddfellows had a system whereby members could be issued with a document to allow them to stay overnight in any Oddfellows Hall. This was of great use to members looking for work. Emigrants took the principles of the society overseas, and Oddfellows lodges were founded in America and the Commonwealth. The American soci-

ety (which split from the British organization in 1834) founded lodges in many European countries.

Researching friendly society records

Surviving records may be with local branches, in record offices or with the individual societies' archives. There were also annual published accounts, which often included the names of officials and of members who had left or died in the preceding year.

FURTHER HELP

Foresters Heritage Trust, Ancient Order of Foresters, College Place, Southampton SO15 2FE

Independent Order of Odd Fellows, Oddfellows House, 40 Fountain Street, Manchester M2 2AB www.oddfellowsco.uk/

Logan, Roger *An Introduction to Friendly Society Records* (FFHS)

People's History Museum (formerly the National Museum of Labour History), 103 Princess Street, Manchester www.nmlhweb.org/ houses the Labour History Archive and Study Centre (LHASC), which has records

relating to working-class political organizations from the early 19th century onwards.

The Labour Party and the Communist Party of Great Britain site at www.a2a.pro.gov.uk has an index of archives.

TUC Archive, Modern Records Centre, University of Warwick Library, Coventry CV4 7AL http://modernrecords.warwick.ac.uk

TUC Library Collections, Learning Centre North Campus, London Metropolitan University, 236 Holloway Road, London N7 6PP www.unl.ac.uk/library/tuc/

Bankruptcy and insolvency

There is a distinction between someone who was bankrupt and someone who was simply an insolvent debtor. Before 1868, bankruptcy, which wipes out the debts and allows the person to begin trading again, was available only to people who owed more than a specified amount of money. Anyone owing less than that sum was an insolvent debtor and continued to be liable to repay debts.

BANKRUPTCY

Between 1571 and 1841, bankruptcy was possible only if a trader owed more than £100. This was a comparatively large sum at a time when the average income was about £1 a week. After 1842, the sum was reduced to £50, and after that the figure was amended from time to time. It was not until 1862 that all insolvent debtors were liable to bankruptcy proceedings. Until 1844, only individuals or partners in a business could be made bankrupt: companies could not.

Before 1832, creditors wanting to have a person declared bankrupt, so that they had some hope of recovering at least part of their debts, applied to the Lord Chancellor for a commission of bankruptcy to handle the sale of assets and distribution of the resulting proceeds. In 1832, the Court of Bankruptcy was set up so that creditors could go directly to it.

Outside London there were district bankruptcy courts, which functioned between 1842 and 1869. Thereafter matters were dealt with by the county courts, which might transfer cases to the London Court of Bankruptcy, which became part of the Supreme

The entrance to the Fleet prison was a chilling sight to those whose business careers ended in debt: many might never be released.

Court as the High Court of Justice in Bankruptcy in 1883. This court might transfer cases to and from county courts. Since 1869, there have been various other changes about how bankruptcy is administered, which affect where records will be found. It's a complicated area.

People who owed money to the Crown between 1314 and 1947 might have their property and goods valued by a county sheriff and jury. This valuation was called an Extent of Debt.

Sometimes, of course, bankrupts had committed a crime, such as fraud, or refused to pay, even though they had the means to do so, and they would be imprisoned for this rather than the fact of owing money.

INSOLVENCY

Those who owed less than the amount in force were insolvent debtors and so could not apply for bankruptcy, which would allow them to start again. The only redress their creditors had was to apply to the courts to have them put in prison until the debt was paid. This seems self-defeating – a person in prison was not able to work and therefore was even less likely to be able to repay debts - but the situation continued until 1869, when imprisonment for debt ended. The position of these prisoners was not helped by the fact that warders charged them for superior lodgings, food and bedding, so they incurred further debts. Some spent the rest of their lives in gaol. The only consolation was that wives and children could usually join them there.

Outside London, debtors were held in local prisons. In London, they might be found in a number of places. Those imprisoned for small debts were usually held in the Palace Court. The better-off went to the King's/Queen's Bench Prison or Fleet Prison. Others went to the Marshalsea or Newgate, where they had separate quarters from the criminals. There were other, less well-known, prisons, such as Giltspur Street Compter, Poultry Compter and Whitecross Street in the City of London. Prisoners had to submit a petition to be discharged to the relevant court.

LEFT Some prisons allowed wives and children to join the husbands who had been imprisoned for debt.

RESEARCHING BANKRUPTCY RECORDS

Notices of proceedings against bankrupts in England were published in the *London Gazette*; in Scotland, where such notices were called sequestrations, the details appeared in the *Edinburgh Gazette. The Times* also published information about them, often giving details of the cases. Information on cases in county courts might be published in local papers, either by the courts themselves or as reports of proceedings.

County court records will include cases of people being imprisoned for debt and will mention if a person was later released, implying that the debt had been paid in full. There may also be lists of people imprisoned for debt among prison papers. These records will be found in CROs.

There was supposed to be an inquest on everyone who died in prison, so there may be records or reports in newspapers of inquests if your ancestor died while they were imprisoned for debt.

Records held in TNA relate to:
- proceedings in the national courts
- official bankruptcy
- Extent of Debt valuations
- petitions for discharge (1813–69) made to the Commissioners of Bankrupts (before 1832) or the Court of Bankruptcy (after 1832) for the release of insolvent debtors
- a register of petitions for protection against bankruptcy (from 1854)

The SoG has two directories of bankrupts, 1774–86 and 1820–43, and TNA holds copies of them.

FURTHER HELP

TNA Legal Records Information 5
Bankrupts and Insolvent Debtors: 1710–1869
TNA Legal Records Information 6
Bankruptcy Records After 1869

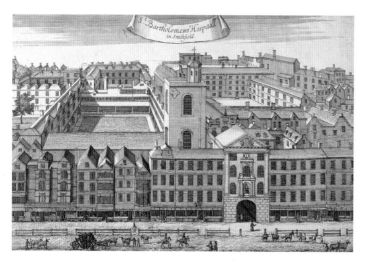

St Bartholomew's Hospital in Smithfield, London, has records dating back to medieval times and still treats patients today.

Researching hospital records

Both TNA and the Wellcome Insitute for the History of Medicine have databases on the internet that contain details of where surviving records of hospitals are held. Most have been deposited with CROs but some remain with the original hospital.

Hospital records on individual patients are closed for 100 years. Workhouse infirmaries, however, come under a different ruling, and their records are closed for only 65 years. Although access to these records may be allowed under certain conditions, it is generally not given for genealogical research.

Individual patient files that are more than 100 years old have generally not survived. What the family historian might find, however, are the names of patients who were admitted to a hospital and on whose authority they were admitted. There are rarely specific details of their illnesses.

Hospitals linked to a religious foundation, such as St Bartholomew's Hospital in London, might have their own baptismal registers, which often contain adult baptisms carried out on patients thought to be in danger of death.

In addition to information about patients, hospital records contain information about the medical staff, such as training and promotion, as well as details of those who supported the hospitals through subscriptions.

THE CARE OF THE MENTALLY ILL

Beliefs in the causes of mental illness went through as many fashions in the past as they do today. The distinctions between mental handicap, temporary insanity and psychosis - a long-term and incurable mental state - were well understood, but before the 19th century there was little public provision for the care of the insane.

Private and public treatment

Mentally handicapped children from better-off families might be cared for privately. For the disturbed, or temporarily insane, there were a number of "mad doctors" who had their own theories about the causes and treatment of insanity. They ran private institutions of various sizes, but care in them was expensive. Finally, for those who were a danger to themselves or others, incarceration on a warrant from two JPs was the only remedy.

The Hospital of St Mary of Bethlehem, in London, known as "Bethlem" (hence "bedlam"), is the best known of the lunatic asylums, where the violently deranged were detained. One of these asylums – the York Asylum – had a very brutal regime, and William Tuke (a Quaker merchant) was so shocked by this that he set up the York Retreat in 1796, which pioneered more gentle treatment, based on modifying behaviour, than was available in most mental hospitals.

Unfortunately, most people could not pay to have their mentally handicapped or ill relatives looked after, and so they had to join all the other unfortunates in the parish workhouse.

The government took an increasing interest in the treatment of the mentally ill from the early part of the 19th century. In 1808, permission for counties to set up asylums for lunatic paupers was granted, but it was not until 1845 that this was made compulsory. Some county asylums were converted prisons that had been used in the Napoleonic Wars.

Commissions of Lunacy

When a wealthy person was unable to function properly, from the mental point of view, the state became involved to protect his or her interests. From medieval times, the assets of a lunatic became the property of the Crown, but by the last part of the 18th century a procedure was established whereby the next of kin of someone mentally afflicted could petition the Chancery Court to have the person declared a lunatic and appoint trustees to administer his or her estate. There were, of course, abuses of the system: families might try to get someone committed to an asylum in order to take control of their money and possessions. Visitors in lunacy were appointed by the court to visit each "chancery lunatic" every year and to write a report on the person.

In 1842, this system was put on a statutory basis, and the Chancery Commission in Lunacy was established. This department was renamed the Masters in Lunacy in 1845. Their inquiries, called Commissions of Lunacy, were occasionally reported in newspapers, but the names of those involved were not always given, since, by the 19th century, mental instability had become a social stigma extending to the whole family.

Criminal lunatics

Although it was always recognized that many people who committed murder were not responsible for their actions, it was not until 1800 that legal provision was made for the care of the criminally insane. In 1840, an Act was passed that allowed all criminal lunatics to be put into an asylum rather than a prison.

Locating mental health records

Some mental hospitals retain their records; other records have been deposited in the usual repositories: CROs, denominational archives and specialist libraries.

TNA holds some asylum registers and returns (surveys) of lunatics in workhouses and asylums (1834-1909), as well as some records relating to naval lunatics. It has a database of the location of the records of county lunatic asylums, and a copy of an unpublished thesis containing TNA sources that can be consulted there.

Researching mental health records

From 1851, census returns have a column to note whether a person was deaf, dumb, blind or lunatic, but after 1871 there was a separate record of those who were lunatic, imbecile or idiot. When you are using census returns, it is always worth checking the parish workhouse, prisons, hospitals and asylums in the area where your ancestors lived to see whether a member of the family might be there. Unfortunately, in the earlier censuses, hospital patients' full names may not be given, simply their initials.

Distinctions were made between the different types of mental state:

- a *lunatic* had periods of sanity
- an *imbecile* was someone who had, later in life, become demented
- an *idiot* was mentally handicapped from birth
- a *moron* had a mental age of 8–12 years
- a *cretin* had mental retardation caused by thyroid deficiency

These words have, over the years, lost their medical connotations and simply become terms of abuse, but they were originally used as fairly precise definitions. They will help you to understand exactly how members of your family were afflicted.

Many lunatic asylums have been closed, but those that remain as mental hospitals tend to be on the same sites as their original incarnations. Most have, unsurprisingly, changed their names. Directories and maps will help you to find out what they are called today. Many, however, have been converted to another use, often divided up into luxury apartments.

The workhouse was often the only place where the poor, whether they were physically or mentally ill, could find shelter.

FURTHER HELP

Faithfull, Pamela *Basic Facts About Lunatics in England and Wales for Family Historians* (FFHS)
TNA *Lunacy and the State*
TNA *Domestic Records Information 104 Lunatic Asylums*

For Crown and Country

There can be very few people who do not have an ancestor who was a member of the armed forces. It has been estimated that during the whole of recorded history there have been only a few years when there was no warfare anywhere in the world. As a major power, Britain was almost constantly at war with European nations until the mid-19th century and needed military personnel to defend and maintain its empire during the following one hundred years. The two World Wars in the 20th century also involved thousands of servicemen and women, from Britain, from the Commonwealth and from the United States. Did your ancestors serve? Were they rewarded with a medal, perhaps for bravery? Did they die in the service of their country, or did they survive to draw a pension and tell their children stories of their experiences?

Members of the armed forces

The creation and maintenance of the British Empire needed considerable numbers of armed personnel. They were also called on to keep order at home before the advent of police forces from the mid-19th century.

SERVICEMEN AND WOMEN

To research service personnel, you need to think about what could have happened to a serviceman or woman. Every stage of his, or her, career would have generated records. The National Archives (TNA) has detailed leaflets giving the class marks of surviving records for the three branches of the services of all the events listed below, and more:

- joining up, either on a voluntary basis or through conscription
- training
- transferring from one unit to another
- wages
- commissions and promotion
- being awarded a medal or other distinction
- being taken prisoner
- dying in battle or while serving
- deserting
- getting court-martialled
- being discharged from the service
- pensions for those who survived
- widows', children's and dependants' pensions
- war memorials and graves

There was always a sharp distinction between officers and other ranks, and their records are generally kept separately. Promotions of officers were published in the *London Gazette*, and lists of officers in the three services were published as the Army List, the Navy List and the Air Force List. The

Recruiting Sergeants at Westminster in 1877 wait for potential recruits. Their aim was to enlist all who were able to serve.

family historian must do more research work to find out about those lower down the hierarchy.

In addition to the soldiers, sailors and airmen, the armed forces needed support staff, and you may find your ancestors among them. They could be medical personnel, chaplains, spies or government employees of the Board of Ordnance, which was responsible for weapons, ammunition and stores. This division employed craftsmen, such as carpenters or smiths. Unfortunately, there are no records specifically relating to the craftsmen and others who supplied goods to the forces (though their names may appear in account books), because they were not directly employed by the government.

The East India Company had its own army and naval officers until 1858, when the company was wound up, so if you don't find a military or naval ancestor in the regular forces, consider searching the East India Company records.

Any bookshop will reveal that military, naval and airforce history are subjects of enduring interest, and the family historian will find a great deal of background information in them. Some are, of course, academic tomes on the causes and tactics of a war, but others are more concerned with the individuals involved in campaigns and battles. One or more of these books may even include some research concerning your ancestor.

CONSCIENTIOUS OBJECTORS

In both World Wars, those who were opposed to fighting on moral, political or religious grounds, such as Quakers or Jehovah's Witnesses, had to go before a Military Service Tribunal to explain their reasons. Other people, who claimed that they were medically unfit or that their work was too valuable to stop, had to attend tribunals that were held locally. Special Tribunals were held for medical practitioners (including dentists) or vets who wanted to avoid conscription on the basis of their profession. There was also an Appeals Tribunal in almost every county for people who wanted to appeal against the local tribunal's decision. Some conscientious objectors were imprisoned and some were court-martialled.

Unfortunately, most of the government papers relating to World War I tribunals were destroyed in 1921, so TNA has only a few records relating to conscientious objectors. The minute book of the Central Tribunal, which dealt with appeals from the Special Tribunals, was kept, and the records of the Middlesex Appeals Tribunal and the Lothian and Peebles Local Tribunal were retained as samples. Not all other local tribunal records were destroyed, and those that did survive are now stored in either County Record Offices (CROs) or local record offices.

Some people avoided conscription in other ways – by fleeing to Ireland, by bribing officials or by taking drugs to make them appear medically unfit – and a few files relating to these people can be found in TNA.

LEFT Temporary grave markers were made of wood until more permanent memorials could be erected.

BELOW World War I soldiers rest in the trenches.

COMMONWEALTH WAR GRAVES COMMISSION

Founded in 1917 as the Imperial War Graves Commission, this organization aims to care for the graves of members of the armed forces who died on or as a result of active service, and to commemorate those who have no known grave or who died as a result of enemy action. It maintains cemeteries all over the world and publishes lists of the dead buried there. Casualty lists were also published at the time in local newspapers and recorded on war memorials erected to commemorate those who died.

PRISONERS OF WAR

In earlier times, the majority of defeated enemies were usually put to death or enslaved. People of higher rank, however, might be ransomed.

By the mid-18th century, most captives were released after a period of imprisonment. TNA holds some lists of British POWs held in France and French POWs held in Britain during the French Revolution (1789–93) and Napoleonic Wars (1793–1815). The other 19th-century wars for which there are records relating to POWs in

TNA are the Crimean War (1853–55) and the Boer War (1899–1902).

There are very few records in TNA relating to POWs from either of the World Wars: some records were destroyed by bombs, others, unfortunately, were destroyed as a result of official policy, and other records were passed to the International Committee of the Red Cross for safekeeping. The TNA leaflets listed on the following page give information about the records it holds.

INTERNMENT OF CIVILIANS DURING THE WORLD WARS

There was a great fear that nationals of countries against which Britain and her allies were fighting might be used as spies and saboteurs. Germans in World War I were rounded up (in some cases for their own protection) and interned in various places in Britain and Ireland. There was also a camp on the Isle of Man, which was used again in World War II for Germans and Austrians, many of whom

Wars, campaigns and military actions involving British forces from 1538

1587–1603	War against Spain	1838–42	1st Afghan War	1914–18	World War I
1642–46	English Civil War	1839	Opium War	1919–21	Ireland
1652–54	1st Anglo-Dutch War		(against China)	1936–39	Palestine
1665–67	2nd Anglo-Dutch War	1843–48	1st Maori War	1939–45	World War II
1702–13	War of the Spanish		(in New Zealand)	1945–48	Campaign in Palestine
	Succession	1845–46	1st Sikh War	1946–47	Withdrawal from India
1739–42	War of Jenkins' Ear	1846	Maori insurrection	1948–60	Malayan Emergency
1740–48	War of the Austrian	1846–47	War against the Bantu	1950–53	Korean War
	Succession		(in South Africa)	1952–60	Mau-Mau Revolt
1753–63	Seven Years' War	1848–49	2nd Sikh War		(in Kenya)
1755–63	French and Indian War	1852–53	2nd Anglo-Burmese	1955–59	Campaign in Cyprus
	(in North America)		War	1956	Suez
1775–83	War of American	1853–56	Crimean War	1956–63	Northern Ireland
	Independence	1856–60	Anglo-Chinese War	1962	Brunei
1775–82	War with Marathas	1857–58	Indian Mutiny	1963–66	Borneo
	(in India)	1873–74	1st Ashanti War	1964–67	Aden
1779–83	Siege of Gibraltar	1875	3rd Anglo-Burmese	1969–	Northern Ireland
1793–1802	French Revolutionary		War	1982	Falklands Campaign
	War	1878–80	2nd Afghan War		
1803–15	Napoleonic Wars	1879	Zulu War		British forces have been, and still
1808–14	Peninsular War	1880–81	1st Boer War		are, involved as peace-keepers in a
1812–15	War in America	1882	Occupation of Egypt		number of places around the world.
1824–26	1st Anglo-Burmese	1896	2nd Ashanti War		The more recent the conflict, the
	War	1899–1902	2nd Boer War		easier it is to trace individuals.

were refugees, and Italians, most of whom had arrived as economic migrants during the 1930s. The Manx Museum contains many records relating to those internees who were held on the Isle of Man.

Other camps were set up elsewhere in the British Isles, and a number of internees were sent to Canada and Australia. The initial panic had died down by 1941, and most of those held in camps were gradually released. British territories overseas also interned foreign nationals during World War II.

INTERNATIONAL COMMITTEE OF THE RED CROSS

Very few records about internees are held in TNA, as the British government passed information to the International Committee of the Red Cross in Geneva. This organization has compiled records of prisoners of war and internees from all nations during both World Wars. Researchers cannot consult these, but the Red Cross will supply information in response to written requests and the payment of a fee. At TNA there is also a list of internees' names and an index to World War II internees.

FURTHER HELP

Commonwealth War Graves Commission, 2 Marlow Road, Maidenhead, Berkshire SL6 7DX. The Debt of Honour Register, listing those killed and where they are buried (if known) during the two World Wars, is available on CD-ROM and on the website www.cwgc.org

TNA Military Records Information 12 *British Prisoners of War c.1760–1919*

TNA Military Records Information 16 *First World War: Conscientious Objectors*

TNA Military Records Information

26 *Intelligence Records in the TNA*

TNA Military Records Information 27 *Prisoners of War and Displaced Persons 1939–1953*

TNA Military Records Information 29 *Prisoners of War in British Hands, 1698–1919*

TNA Military Records Information 55 *Military Nurses and Nursing Services*

TNA Military Records Information 66 *Records of the Board of Ordnance*

TNA Military Records Information 74 *Records of Women's Services: First World War*

Army records

Before 1660, there was no standing army: soldiers were recruited as the need arose. Each regiment was generally known by the name of the colonel who commanded it, until the early 18th century, when they acquired more permanent names. Since then, the Army has been reorganized several times, and regiments have been renamed and amalgamated. There are histories of the Army and individual regiments that will help researchers.

FOREIGN SOLDIERS

Men from many different nationalities joined the Army, but, in addition, there were regiments composed of foreign soldiers commanded by white British officers. The most famous is the brigade of Gurkhas, originally formed in 1815, which comprises soldiers recruited from Nepal in North

ABOVE Cavalry troops took part in battles until World War I.

BELOW Armies depend on men willing to die for their country's cause.

> ## The structure of the Army
> Brigade
> Battalion/regiment
> Company
> Platoon/troop
>
> Cavalry are mounted troops
> Infantry are foot soldiers

India. Others were the West Africa Regiments, raised from 1800, and the West Indian Regiments, from 1795. The latter had their origins in the Carolina Black Corps established in America during the War of Independence. On the independence of their various countries, the West African and West Indian regiments ceased to be part of the British Army.

ABOVE Women and children were among the "camp followers" who went on military campaigns with the army.

131

WOMEN IN THE ARMY

Women didn't officially join the Army until 1949, when the Women's Royal Army Corps (WRAC) was formed, although there had been a few women's units in World War I. As long as there were soldiers, however, there were women, including wives, accompanying them. They were called camp followers, and they did the laundry, nursed casualties and provided other services. This was semi-acknowledged: the Army kept records of births of children to serving soldiers whose wives were attached to the regiment while on a campaign. Surviving registers from 1761 are in TNA and have been indexed.

RECRUITMENT AND TRAINING

Until 1871, commissioned officers were almost exclusively drawn from the upper classes or wealthy families, because they had to pay for their appointments and promotion. Non-commissioned officers came up through the ranks. Conscription was introduced only in World War I. Before that, recruiting officers toured the country to encourage young men to join the Army. Criminals might also be offered the option of joining up, especially in wartime.

Until the establishment of the various Army colleges, beginning in 1802 with officer training, any instruction needed was given by the unit to which a soldier was posted. As equipment became more specialized, especially in the 20th century, apprenticeships were offered to those wishing to acquire a particular skill.

LOCATING ARMY RECORDS

Finding and putting together records relating to Army ancestors is not easy: this is a highly specialized area of research. Although there are many records (mainly pre-20th century) in TNA, individual regiments may have their own archives and many also have museums where papers may be lodged. There is also the National Army Museum in London. Many records relating to soldiers in the World Wars

Significant dates in the history of the Army

Note that the establishment and name changes of all the different regiments, as well as many support departments, have been omitted.

1660/1 Standing army established.
1716 First separate artillery regiment created.
1717 Corps of Engineers formed.
1741 Royal Military Academy created at Woolwich, East London, initially to train artillery officers and later engineers and signals personnel.
1796 Chaplains' Department formed.

1802 Royal Military College created at Great Marlow and later moved to Sandhurst, Berkshire, to train officers of the cavalry and infantry divisions.
1857 Military Music School (currently Royal Military School of Music) created at Kneller Hall, Middlesex.
1858 Staff College created at Camberley, Surrey.
1858 Veterinary Medical Department (currently the Royal Army Veterinary Corps) formed.
1877 Military police introduced.
1897 Army Nursing Service (currently Queen Alexandra's Royal

Army Nursing Corps) formed.
1916 Tanks introduced into warfare.
1920 Separate Corps of Signals created.
1939 Conscription introduced.
1940 First Parachute Corps formed.
1947 National Service introduced (abolished in 1961).
1947 Royal Military Academy amalgamated with the Royal Military College at Sandhurst.
1949 Women's Royal Army Corps (WRACS) formed.
1952 Special Air Service Regiment formed.

Flags, furled while marching, provide a rallying point for soldiers who have become lost or cut off from their comrades on the battlefield. The crests on the flags originated in the days when most people could not read.

were destroyed by bombing. The majority of recent records are still with the Ministry of Defence; they are not on open access, and a fee is charged for research. The family historian researching a soldier ancestor must therefore find out where he served and, for both World Wars, his service number, if possible.

FURTHER HELP

Cantwell, J. *The Second World War: A Guide to Records in the Public Record Office* (HMSO)

Fowler, Simon *Army Records for Family Historians* (TNA Readers' Guide No. 2)

Pimlott, J. *The Guinness History of the British Army* (Guinness 1993). This has an appendix summarizing the histories of divisions and regiments (detailing name changes), which is useful for the family historian trying to work out in which modern-day regiment an ancestor was serving at a particular time.

TNA Military Records Information 3 *Civil War Soldiers 1642–1660*

TNA Military Records Information 4 *Army: Officers' Records, 1660–1913*

TNA Military Records Information 5 *Army: Soldiers' Discharge Papers, 1660–1913*

TNA Military Records Information 6 *Army: Soldiers' Pension Records, 1702–1913*

TNA Military Records Information 7 *Army: Muster Rolls and Pay Lists c.1730–1898*

TNA Military Records Information 9 *First World War, 1914–1918: Soldiers' Papers 1914–1920*

TNA Military Records Information 10 *First World War: Army Officers' Service Records*

TNA Military Records Information 11 *First World War: Army War Diaries*

TNA Military Records Information 14 *Army: Other Ranks: Useful Sources if You are Getting Nowhere*

TNA Military Records Information 15 *First World War: Disability and Dependants' Pensions*

TNA Military Records Information 17 *The Army Lists*

TNA Military Records Information 22 *Army: Courts Martial 17th–20th Centuries*

TNA Military Records Information 23 *Army: Campaign Records, 1660–1714*

TNA Military Records Information 24 *Army: Campaign Records, 1714–1814*

TNA Military Records Information 25 *Operational Records of the British Army, 1816-1913*

TNA Military Records Information 68 *Second World War: Army Operations*

TNA Military Records Information 73 *Army: Officers' Commissions*

TNA Military Records Information 75 *Army: Courts Martial: First World War 1914–1918*

TNA Military Records Information 76 *Armed Service: Campaign Medals and Other Service Medals*

TNA Military Records Information 77 *Armed Services: Gallantry Medals*

TNA Military Records Information 78 *Armed Services: Gallantry Medals, Further Information*

The Ministry of Defence's website has a section with links to various Army and regimental museums www.army.mod.uk/ceremonialandher itage/museums_main.html ssi

Royal Air Force records

Royal Airforce pilots in an overseas airfield in 1964. A photograph such as this in a family member's archives might be where your research in military records begins.

The Royal Air Force (RAF) was created comparatively recently, and so researching family members who served in it can be simpler than working on other branches of the armed forces. By the beginning of the 20th century, bureaucrats were better at record-keeping, and there are fewer records to search.

THE BEGINNING OF AERIAL WARFARE

As early as 1804, experiments using balloons were being conducted at the Royal Military Academy in Woolwich, London, and they were used in wars in Africa and China at the end of the 19th century. There was even a School of Ballooning at Aldershot, Hampshire. These balloons came under the responsibility of the Royal Engineers, which were part of the British Army, so any records relating to ancestors who worked with them will be in Army records.

It was not long after the first flight in a heavier-than-air machine in 1903 that the potential for aeroplanes and,

later, airships in warfare was recognized. On 1 April 1918, the Royal Air Force was formed by the amalgamation of the Royal Flying Corps and the Royal Naval Air Service.

The RAF is divided into commands – different sections responsible for particular types of activity. There are currently only two (Strike Command, and Personnel and Training Command),

but in the past there were more, such as Bomber Command, Fighter Command, Training Command, etc. Each of these Commands contained a number of groups, divided into squadrons. A squadron consisted of a number of airplanes, the crews (pilots, navigators, gunners and signallers) who flew in them and the ground crew who maintained and repaired them. The airfields

---

RAF ranks

Commissioned officers
Marshal of the Royal Air Force
Air Chief Marshal
Air Marshal
Air Vice-Marshal
Air Commodore
Group Captain
Wing Commander
Squadron Leader
Flight Lieutenant
Flying Officer, Pilot Officer

Non-commissioned officers and other ranks
Warrant Officer/Master Aircrew
Flight Sergeant
Sergeant
Corporal
Senior Aircraftman/woman
Leading Aircraftman/woman
Senior Technician
Junior Technician

The shark's mouth was a motif used by 211 squadron in World War II.

Significant dates in the history of the RAF

1912 Royal Naval Air Service (RNAS) and Royal Flying Corps (RFC) established.
1918 RNAS and RFC merged to form Royal Air Force (RAF).
1918 RAF Nursing Service created, becoming Princess Mary's RAF Nursing Service in 1923.
1918 Women's Royal Air Force (WRAF) created (abolished in 1920).
1920 RAF College opened at Cranwell.
1939 Women's Auxiliary Air Force (WAAF) created.
1994 WAAF integrated into the RAF.

from which they flew also needed medical and administrative staff, stores, transport – all the usual back-up involved in any large organization.

WRAF AND WAAF

The Women's Royal Air Force (WRAF) was formed at the same time as the Royal Air Force in 1918. It was disbanded in 1920, but re-established as the Women's Auxiliary Air Force (WAAF) in 1939. In World War I, the role of women was confined to administration, but in World War II they did work in some technical and mechanical grades as well. They were not allowed to join operational aircrews, although there were women pilots in Ferry Command and the Air Transport Auxiliary (ATA), which flew aircraft from one place to another.

Very few records relating to women officers from World War I have survived, although ordinary airwomen's records are in TNA, where there is an index to all Air Force personnel, which includes women, and gives service numbers.

RESEARCH AND DEVELOPMENT

The government played a great part in the research, development and manufacture of aircraft, airships and radar systems. Many of the records are in TNA, and the RAF Museum also has a substantial collection, as well as many old aircraft.

NURSING SERVICES

At the outbreak of World War I, advertisements were placed in nursing journals to recruit personnel for the Royal Air Force Nursing Service (RAFNS). At first this service was intended to last only as long as the hostilities, but after the war the government decided to make it a permanent part of the RAF. In 1923, it became Princess Mary's Royal Air Force Nursing Service.

If your ancestors were among the very first volunteers, information about them might be in TNA, which mainly holds documents relating to the establishment of the RAFNS and the decision to continue it. Otherwise their records will be with the RAF.

Nursing staff on an exercise to learn to help air crash victims.

LOCATING RAF RECORDS

Records relating to servicemen whose service number was between 1 and 329000 (largely those who served in the RAF during World War I) are mainly in TNA, where there is an index of service numbers. The records of anyone who was still serving in the RAF at the outbreak of World War II, however, will still be with the RAF's records.

The RAF Museum at Hendon, North London, holds many records, including log books and officers' diaries, as well as a card index of every aircraft belonging to the RAF.

FURTHER HELP

Fowler, S., Elliott, R., Nesbit, R.C. and Goulter, C. *RAF Records in the PRO* (TNA Readers' Guide No. 8)
TNA Military Records Information 28 *Royal Air Force: Research and Development*
TNA Military Records Information 49 *Royal Air Force: Airmen's Service Records*
TNA Military Records Information 50 *British Air Forces: Tracing an Individual*

TNA Military Records Information 74 *Records of Women's Services, First World War*
Royal Air Force Museum, Aerodrome Road, Hendon, London NW9 5LI
www.rafmuseum.org.uk
Williamson, H.J. *The Roll of Honour, Royal Flying Corps and Royal Air Force for the Great War 1914–18* (Naval and Military Press) lists officers and men of the RFC and RAF who died in World War I.

The militia, posse comitatis and volunteers

In addition to regular or professional soldiers, a reserve of men who could be called upon in times of war was needed. In England, these reserves, or militia, date from Saxon times. In the Middle Ages, all healthy men between the ages of 15 and 60 were required to do archery practice on Sundays and, according to their income, to provide themselves and their sons over the age of 7 with armour and weapons. Lists of men who could be called upon to serve and those who could give money were made by each county. These were called muster rolls.

With the introduction of a standing army in 1660, these volunteers were stood down, but they were revived in 1757 as a force to protect the country in case of invasion.

THE MILITIA

Each year parishes drew up a list of men capable of serving, and a ballot was held to provide militiamen. They were then trained by the parish, often under the leadership of a member of the local gentry, and the term "trained bands" is often used in records to describe them. Many categories of people, such as clergymen, magistrates, apprentices and parish constables, were exempt. Service was also unpopular among people who had businesses to run, so the better-off members of the community often paid substitutes to serve in their place.

Men served for three years between 1757 and 1786, and for five years after that. They were based at home, except in times of war. While they were away on service, their wives and children were paid an allowance.

A Loyal London Volunteer chose to serve rather than be conscripted.

THE POSSE COMITATIS

During the panic caused by the prospect of invasion at the time of the Napoleonic Wars, a list of the posse comitatis for each county (the strength, or able-bodied men, of the county, effectively the medieval muster) was drawn up in 1798. In addition to listing all the men in the county capable of bearing arms, the list included bakers and owners of barges, horses and wagons. Buckinghamshire is the only county for which a complete record survives, and this has been published, but a number of individual parishes' lists survive from elsewhere. In 1803–4 the Levée en Masse, literally "mass enlistment", collected similar information. With the end of the Napoleonic Wars, fear of invasion declined, and no more general surveys of this kind were made.

VOLUNTEERS

In addition to the militia, in which most men were forced to serve (although there were some volunteers), a number of purely voluntary forces were created. These included the Volunteers, who would not be obliged to serve abroad, and the Yeomanry, who were a cavalry force. Along the coastline, forces of Sea Fencibles (seafaring men under the command of a naval officer) were raised to defend the country against invasion. The various voluntary forces came under the aegis of the Lords Lieutenant of the counties.

19TH-CENTURY DEVELOPMENTS

The end of the Napoleonic Wars in 1815 brought a period of comparative peace to Britain. As a result, it was no longer considered necessary to conscript men to serve in the militia, and the last ballot took place in 1829; thereafter, it was a completely voluntary force. In 1881, militias became linked to local regiments and were renamed as battalions or reserve units. The Rifle Volunteers, a separate organization, was founded in 1859.

20TH-CENTURY DEVELOPMENTS

The two World Wars meant that there was a continuing need for voluntary forces to serve at home.

Territorial Army

In 1908 the militia became the Territorial Army (TA), which continues to the present day, and at the same time the Yeomanry became part of the TA.

Home Guard

During World War II, the militia was revived under the name Local Defence Volunteers – later renamed the Home Guard – in which men between the ages of 17 and 62 were called upon to serve their country.

LOCATING RECORDS OF THE MILITIA, POSSE COMITATIS AND VOLUNTEEERS

Finding references to individual militiamen is not easy, as the records are scattered between a number of repositories. Lists of militia officers were published from 1794, and records relating to them are held in TNA, along with muster and pay books for everyone. Militiamen were eligible to become Chelsea Pensioners after a certain length of service or if they were invalided out, and these records are also in TNA, as well as information on deserters and those who were court-martialled. CROs hold miscellaneous papers, including the ballots.

Other material may be in the regimental museums to which the various volunteer and militia forces were linked after 1881, when a large-scale reform of the Army and auxiliary forces was made.

Local newspapers often covered the activities of the militia in detail. Family History Societies and individuals have produced booklets and microfiche listing individuals who served in their area, which should be in CROs.

USING MILITIA AND POSSE COMITATIS RECORDS

During the period of the ballots to provide militiamen, most parishes listed every man between the ages of 18 and 45, and noted those who were unfit through blindness or other disability. A few lists also included children. Consequently, they form a kind of local census and should be consulted both to locate ancestors and to see whether they had any physical or mental problems.

Unusually long gaps between the births of children can, of course, be due to a number of reasons, but a three- or five-year gap during times of war may suggest that your ancestor was serving in the militia away from home. Women often had to apply to parish officials for support while their husbands were serving, and their appeals will be found in parish records in the accounts of either the overseer of the poor or the churchwarden.

Posse comitatis lists are useful because they can help you to gauge your agricultural ancestors' level of wealth from the number of horses and carts they owned. People's occupations are also often given.

FURTHER HELP

Gibson, Jeremy and Dell, Alan *Tudor and Stuart Muster Rolls* (FFHS)
Gibson, Jeremy and Medlycott, Mervyn *Militia Lists and Musters* (FFHS)
TNA Military Records Information 18 *The Militia 1757–1914*
TNA Military Records Information 72 *Auxiliary Forces: Volunteers, Yeomanry, Territorials and Home Guard, 1769–1945*
Spencer, William *Records of the Militia & Volunteer Forces 1757–1945* (TNA Readers' Guide No. 3)

RIGHT Each county was responsible for raising a militia force. These soldiers are from Buckinghamshire.

137

Royal Navy records

K nown as the Senior Service, the Navy is the longest-established branch of the armed services, having its roots in the 9th century. There are some medieval and Tudor records relating to it, but most date from the post-Commonwealth period. Samuel Pepys, the famous diarist, was from 1660 a civil servant who rose to the top of the Navy Board. He reformed many aspects of naval practice and introduced many of the systems that survive today. He also laid down methods of record keeping for which the genealogist should be grateful.

The *Henry Addington*, festooned with flags of many nations, fires her guns on a ceremonial occasion in 1802 at West India Docks, London.

SECTIONS OF THE ROYAL NAVY

The Royal Navy (RN) is divided into four sections: Ships, Royal Marines, Fleet Air Arm and Submarines. In addition, there is the Women's Royal Naval Service, which has formed a permanent part of the Royal Navy since 1939.

Ships

The history of the vessels themselves is largely one of developments in technology, as ships changed from being made of wood to metal. They were first powered by sails, then steam, then diesel, and, in the case of submarines, nuclear power. With the changes in technology came the need for more specialized and trained personnel, which led to a variety of job titles.

Royal Marines

The Marines were originally soldiers who served at sea. They were founded in 1664 as the Admiral's Regiment. In 1755 they came under the control of the Admiralty and were, like sailors, entitled to enter the Greenwich Hospital after discharge.

The Marines, first formed in 1755, had four divisions, depending on where they were based, and they usually remained with the same division throughout their career. The first three bases were Chatham, Portsmouth and Plymouth, and during 1805–69 the fourth was at Woolwich. Records for 1793–1925 are in TNA, but those relating to officers after 1925 are held at the Royal Marines' Historical Office. There are also some 20th-century records in the Fleet Air Arm Museum. The Royal Marines

---

Navy ranks

There are a bewildering number of titles and ranks in the Royal Navy, which have changed over the years. The following is an abbreviated list.

Commissioned officers
Admiral
Commodore
Captain
Commander
Lieutenant
Mate/Sub-lieutenant
Master (after 1808)
Midshipman

Other ranks
Warrant Officer
Boatswain/Bosun
Gunner
Carpenter
Chaplain
Purser
Schoolmaster (18th century)/
Naval instructor
Cook
Rating (the ordinary seaman)

Museum at Southsea also has many documents, diaries and other records relating to individuals' experiences.

Fleet Air Arm

This section of the Navy is responsible for aircraft of all kinds launched from on board ship. In World War I, it also operated armoured cars transported by ship to the battlefields.

Submarines

The first British submarine was launched in 1901, and by the outbreak of World War II there were 74 submarines in service.

Women in the Royal Navy

From early times, women were frequently, but unofficially, found on board ship. Between the mid-17th century and the mid-19th century, warrant officers were allowed to take their wives to sea, but they rarely appear in the muster books. During battles, women carried ammunition and tended to the wounded. Petitions requesting financial help if their husbands were killed in action and as recompense for their own work as nurses may be found at TNA.

Reports of women disguising themselves as men to serve on board ship are occasionally found. They were immediately discharged when their gender was discovered. It was not until World War I that the Women's Royal Naval Service (WRNS – pronounced "Wrens") was formed. It lasted only a year (1918–19) but was reformed in 1939 for World War II.

MUSTER BOOKS

Ships' muster books, to be found in TNA, list all members of a crew on a particular ship when it began a new voyage, and this is the main way of tracing a rating's career. Ships had to take their support services with them, and so, in addition to the officers and sailors, crews would include surgeons, chaplains, cooks and carpenters, who might all be found in muster books.

Until 1853, commissioned officers and sailors were paid off at the end of each voyage, although warrant officers were generally regarded as belonging to a particular ship. Officers were put on half-pay until they received a new commission, but the ratings had to fend for themselves. Many ratings would try to remain in the service of a particular captain because they had become accustomed and loyal to him.

APPRENTICESHIPS

Before 1794, naval officers could begin an apprenticeship when they were only 7 years old. They were generally known as midshipmen, and after a period of on-the-job training and study in navigational skills, they passed an examination to qualify as a lieutenant. Ships usually had someone on board to educate children and

---

Significant dates in the history of the Navy

As an island, England has always needed ships for defence, so the Navy's origins pre-date the Norman Conquest.

1642 Permanent Navy structure established.

1652 Creation of the post of "able" seaman, senior to and more experienced than the "ordinary" kind.

1660 Samuel Pepys became Clerk of the Acts at the Navy Board. Between this date and his resignation in 1689, by which time he had been promoted to Secretary of the Admiralty, he created an administrative system that lasted into the 19th century.

1694 Foundation of Greenwich Hospital.

1733 Royal Naval Academy founded (became Royal Naval College in 1806).

1755 Royal Marines transfer from Army to Navy control.

1795 Issue of lemon juice to prevent scurvy introduced.

1820 RN began surveying and mapping the seas.

1824 First attempts to standardize uniforms.

1825 Rum ration halved.

1831 Beer ration abolished.

1830 Gunnery School created.

1835 Register of Seamen introduced.

1840s Steam-powered ships introduced, requiring stokers to feed coal into the engines.

1859 Royal Naval Reserve established.

1871 Flogging in peacetime suspended (1879 suspended totally, but not actually abolished).

1873 Royal Naval College transferred to Greenwich.

1880 Royal Naval Engineering College opened.

1901 Submarines introduced.

1903 Osborne section of the Royal Naval College opened on the Isle of Wight.

1918 Women's Royal Navy Service (WRNS) created.

1937 Fleet Air Arm transferred from RAF to RN control.

1963 First nuclear-powered submarine introduced.

1994 WRNS integrated into the RN.

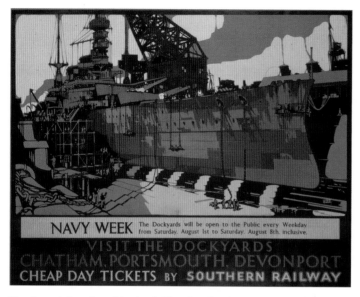

NAVY WEEK The Dockyards will be open to the Public every Weekday from Saturday, August 1st to Saturday, August 8th, inclusive.

VISIT THE DOCKYARDS CHATHAM, PORTSMOUTH, DEVONPORT
CHEAP DAY TICKETS BY SOUTHERN RAILWAY

Devoting a whole week to celebrating the Navy shows how important it was in the nation's consciousness in the 1930s.

ancestor working in a marine occupation suddenly disappears, this may be because his ship sank, but it might also be because he was press-ganged into the Navy, so it is worth checking out both possibilities.

Local papers in maritime areas might report riots or fights caused by people trying to prevent their menfolk being taken. This might also have led to criminal proceedings.

After 1859, this unusual recruiting practice was regularized through the formation of the Royal Naval Reserve, whereby merchant seamen could be called up into the Royal Navy as the need arose.

young sailors. From the early 19th century, some chaplains were also acting as schoolmasters. Warrant officers could also become lieutenants. Promotion thereafter was largely through ability, though the patronage of senior officers was also essential. Midshipmen received certificates, called Passing Certificates, on becoming qualified, and these are held at TNA.

ROYAL NAVAL COLLEGE
A training school for young naval officers was founded at Dartmouth in 1863. It was initially based in two hulks moored on the River Dart, but in 1905 a college was built. The junior section of the Royal Naval College was set up at Osborne on the Isle of Wight to educate boys who would progress to the College at Dartmouth.

As well as attracting the sons of the middle and upper classes, who were sent there to learn to be officers, the Navy provided a convenient way of

providing for orphans, and various organizations and charities sent boys into the service.

PRESS GANGS AND THE ROYAL NAVAL RESERVE
Although attracting naval officers was relatively easy, it was not quite as simple to get ordinary sailors, or ratings, to serve. In times of war, young men condemned to death for a crime might be offered the alternative of enrolling in the Navy, and men might be legally pressed into service, which was effectively kidnapping.

Not all men were in danger of this, however, because the last thing the Navy needed was those who were unaccustomed to the sea and who might imperil their fellow sailors or the ship through seasickness or ignorance. Press-ganged landlubbers were therefore usually released if taken on board, while the press gangs went in search of merchant seamen and fishermen. If an

NAVAL DOCKYARDS
Naval dockyards, where ships were built and equipped, employed a range of skilled workmen: shipwrights, ropemakers, carpenters, and so forth, as well as general labourers. The ships also had to take their food with them. Both sections came under the ultimate authority of the Admiralty. Supplying guns, however, came under the Board of Ordnance. Surviving records for Britain date from the late 18th century. In addition to establishments in Britain, the Navy maintained dockyards all over the world, and some of these records go back to the beginning of the 18th century.

RESEARCH AND DEVELOPMENT
Most naval R&D was carried out by private firms under the patronage of the Admiralty. It is possible that some information may exist in company archives, but, since the development of ships and weapons would have been confidential, most records will be in TNA. Patents on inventions before 1853 are also held in TNA. After that they are with the Patent Office.

GREENWICH HOSPITAL

The Greenwich Hospital was opened in 1694 and closed in 1869. Until then, seamen who had served in the Royal Navy (but not the Merchant Navy) were entitled to live there. The rules were stringent – basically no wine, women or song – so many sailors who had reached retirement age or had been invalided out of the Navy chose to live outside but still collect their naval pensions. The records are in TNA.

LOCATING RECORDS OF THE ROYAL NAVY

Printed lists of officers were published as the Navy List during 1782–1914. Records relating to officers entering the service after 1890 and ratings after 1892 remain with the Ministry of Defence Royal Navy records. Before that date, most are in TNA. The National Maritime Museum holds a

large collection of naval portraits and photographs of ships and sailors. The Royal Naval Museum holds many private documents, pictures and photographs, donated by former and serving men and their families, which date back to the late 18th century. These show what life at sea was like over the years.

RIGHT Lists were kept of those protected from being press-ganged.

FURTHER HELP

Commissioned Sea Officers of the Royal Navy 1600–1815 (National Maritime Museum 1954)
Fleet Air Arm Archive 1939–1945 www.fleetairarmarchive.net
Fleet Air Arm Museum, Royal Navy Air Station, Yeovilton, Ilchester, Somerset BA22 8HT www.fleetairarm.com
National Maritime Museum, Greenwich, London SE10 9NF www.nmm.ac.uk also contains the Caird Library
TNA Military Records Information 30 *Royal Navy: Officers' Service Records*
TNA Military Records Information 31 *Royal Navy: Ratings' service records 1667–1923*
TNA Military Records Information 32 *Royal Navy: Log Books and Reports of Proceedings*
TNA Military Records Information 33 *First World War: Naval Operations*
TNA Military Records Information 35 *Operational Records of the Royal Navy*

1660–1914
TNA Military Records Information 38 *Naval Research and Development*
TNA Military Records Information 41 *Naval Dockyards*
TNA Military Records Information 43 *Ships Wrecked or Sunk*
TNA Military Records Information 45 *Royal Marines: Other Ranks' Service Records*
TNA Military Records Information 46 *Royal Marines: How to Find a Division*
TNA Military Records Information 47 *Royal Marines: Officers' Service Records*
TNA Military Records Information 48 *Royal Marines: Further Areas of Research*
TNA Military Records Information 56 *Royal Navy: Nurses and Nursing Services*
TNA Military Records Information 60 *Royal Navy: Pay and Pensions Records: Commissioned officers*
TNA Military Records Information 61 *Royal Navy: Pay and Pension: Warrant*

officers
TNA Military Records Information 62 *Royal Navy: Pension Records: Ratings*
TNA Military Records Information 69 *Royal Navy: Operational Records 1939–45*
TNA Military Records Information 71: *The Royal Naval Volunteer Reserve 1903–1919*
TNA Military Records Information 79 *Royal Navy: Officers' Service Records, First World War and Confidential Reports 1893–1943*
Rodger, N.A.M. *Naval Records for Genealogists* (TNA Handbook No. 22)
Royal Marines Museum, Southsea, Hampshire PO4 9PX www.royalmarinesmuseum.co.uk
Royal Naval Museum, HM Naval Base (P66), Portsmouth, Hants PO1 3NH www.royalnavalmuseum.org
Royal Navy Submarine Museum, Haslar Jetty Road, Gosport, Hampshire PO12 2AS www.rnsubmus.co.uk

Merchant Navy records

Although merchant seamen were not officially part of the Royal Navy, in practice men worked for both, particularly in wartime. As a maritime nation, exporting and importing goods over the globe, merchant seamen played an important role in the development of British history.

LOCATING RECORDS OF MERCHANT SEAMEN

Surviving records of ships' musters from 1747 and crew agreements for 1835–60 are held by TNA. Thereafter records are divided among a number of repositories. Ten per cent of crew agreements and those for famous vessels are held by TNA. The National Maritime Museum holds the remaining 90 per cent for 1861, 1862 and every year thereafter that ended in "5", until 1939. Some local record offices took documents from the other years, but the majority went to the Maritime

History Research Collection at the Memorial University of Newfoundland in Canada. The Manx National Heritage Library took those records relating to ports on the Isle of Man. Crew agreements for 1939–50 are held by the General Register and Record Office of Shipping and Seamen in Cardiff.

SHIPS' NUMBERS

In order to access the records, you need to know the official number of the ship on which your ancestor served, and the dates. From 1786, each ship above a certain size had to be registered by its owner with the customs office of its home port. It was given a number, which remained the same as long as it was in service, and a certificate. A copy of the certificate was sent to Customs House in London. In 1814, a fire destroyed these centrally held copies. CROs or local record

During World War II, the Merchant Navy kept Britain and her allies in supplies.

offices may hold original port documents including details of the certificates. The TNA holds post-1814 records. These are useful in researching ship-owning ancestors, as well as mariners, because many merchant ships were owned by a number of people from a variety of professional backgrounds with shares in its profits (or, of course, losses).

In 1825, all ships had to be re-registered, but at any time an individual vessel might need a new certificate if there was a change in ownership or it moved to a new port. There is an index of ships giving their numbers on microfiche, which is held by a number of repositories. Two annual publications, Lloyd's Register of Shipping and the Mercantile Navy List, also contain lists of ships with their official numbers.

Seafarers might work on local fishing boats before joining the Merchant Navy and then serving in the Royal Navy.

LLOYD'S OF LONDON

As an insurer of ships and cargoes, Lloyd's of London compiled registers of captains and mates of merchant vessels who held masters' certificates and who were working during 1869–1947. These Captains' Registers contain details of each man's career, and some information recorded in them goes back to 1851. Details of men who held masters' certificates but did not serve as captains or mates in 1869–1911 and 1932–47 are also included. These registers generally do not contain information about men working on fishing vessels, coasters, colliers and ferries, but they do include those who were involved in foreign trade, who needed different certificates.

Lloyd's List, published since 1697, is a newspaper produced by Lloyd's of London containing news about commercial shipping. Issues from 1741 survive in a number of archives. Over

Food from overseas being unloaded near Tower Bridge in London.

the centuries it has changed in format and name and has had supplements added, which are of great use to family historians, enabling them to track the journey of merchant seamen ancestors and, perhaps, discover records of their deaths in wrecks and losses.

RANKS

The hierarchy on board merchant ships is not quite as complicated as that on Royal Navy vessels. Master mariners, mates and engineers were the officers on board merchant ships, and seamen were the equivalent of the ratings in the Royal Navy. No qualifications were needed to work on merchant ships until 1845, and they were initially voluntary.

Masters and mates who wished to pilot their own vessels in and out of British ports without a pilot were examined by the Corporation of Trinity House in order to receive an exemption certificate. Registers of certificates for 1850–1957 and examination results for 1864–1986 are all held in the Guildhall Library.

FURTHER HELP

Guildhall Library Leaflet No. 1 *Lloyd's "Captains Registers" at Guildhall Library and Related Sources Elsewhere*
Guildhall Library Leaflet *The Corporation of Trinity House – Family History Sources at Guildhall Library*
Hogg, Peter L. *Using Merchant Ship Records for Family Historians* (FFHS)
Manx National Heritage, Manx Museum and National Trust, Douglas, Isle of Man IM1 3LY www.isle-of-man.com/interests/genealogy/sources.htm
Memorial University of Newfoundland, St Johns, NF A1C 5S7, Canada www.mun.ca/
NMM Research Guide No. C1 *The Merchant Navy: Tracing People: Crew lists, agreements and official logs*
NMM Research Guide No. C2 *The Merchant Navy: Tracing People: Master mariners, mates and engineers*
NMM Research Guide No. C3 *The Merchant Navy: Bibliography*

NMM Research Guide No. C4 *The Merchant Navy: Sources for Enquiries*
NMM Research Guide No. C5 *The Merchant Navy: Sources for Ships' Histories*
NMM Research Guide No. C6 *The Merchant Navy: The Mercantile Navy List*
NMM Research Guide No. C7 *The Merchant Navy: Shipping Listed in Parliamentary Papers*
NMM Research Guide No. C8 *The Merchant Navy: Wrecks, Losses and Casualties*
NMM Research Guide No. C9 *The Merchant Navy: World War One*
NMM Research Guide No. C10 *The Merchant Navy: World War Two*
NMM Research Guide No. C11 *The Merchant Navy: The Handy Shipping Guide*
NMM Research Guide No. C12 *The Merchant Navy: Ship Registration and Custom House Duties*
NMM Research Guide No. H1 *Lloyd's:*

Lloyd's List: Brief history
NMM Research Guide No. H2 *Lloyd's: Resources at the National Maritime Museum*
NMM Research Guide No. H3 *Lloyd's: Captains' Registers*
NMM Research Guide No. H5 *Lloyd's: Registers Held at the National Maritime Museum*
TNA Source Sheet 38 *Merchant Seamen Records in TNA*
TNA Military Records Information 37 *Merchant Seamen: Royal Naval Reserve*
Registrar General of Shipping and Seamen, PO Box 165, Cardiff CF4 5FU
Smith, H., Watts, Christopher T. and Watts, Michael J. *Records of Merchant Shipping and Seamen* (TNA Readers' Guide No. 20)
Watts, Christopher T. and Watts, Michael J *My Ancestor Was a Merchant Seaman: How Can I Find Out More About Him?* (SoG)

Other maritime occupations

As a collection of islands, the United Kingdom was dependent on the sea for imported and exported goods, and so a fair proportion of its inhabitants have at some time been involved in maritime occupations.

THE ROLE OF TRINITY HOUSE
The Corporation of Trinity House, which received a royal charter in 1514, has been responsible for overseeing a range of activities linked to the sea. Officers of the Royal and Merchant Navies were eligible to become members, called Younger Brethren. From their numbers, a ruling council, called Elder Brethren, was elected. In addition to the responsibilities listed below, the Elder Brethren were

A boatman ferries a couple across the Thames in 1804.

involved in the examination of Royal Navy pilots and pupils of the mathematical school at Christ's Hospital, who trained to be sea captains. They also oversaw the ballasting of ships on the River Thames and heard cases in the Court of Admiralty involving collisions.

CHARITIES
Trinity House maintained almshouses for ex-seamen and their widows. It also gave financial assistance, in the form of pensions or other payments, to mariners and their families anywhere in the United Kingdom. Those who wanted to take advantage of these services had to submit a petition, and the records of these petitions for 1787–1854 have been indexed.

A major port such as Liverpool needed hundreds of workers to support its shipping trade.

144

WATERMEN AND LIGHTERMEN IN LONDON

Until the 19th century, there was only one bridge, London Bridge, across the Thames, and so people used boats to cross the river instead. They also used them to travel along the Thames, since roads then were as crowded as they are today and in a far worse state of repair. The operators of these boats, called watermen, were regulated either by Trinity House, which licensed mainly ex-mariners, or by the Company of Watermen, one of the London livery companies, which was also responsible from 1700 for lightermen, who unloaded and loaded goods on ships. The company's area of authority extended from Gravesend to Windsor.

Like the other companies, the Company of Watermen had an apprenticeship system. Since 1721, an annual race for the prize of Doggett's Coat and Badge has been rowed on the Thames by six watermen within a year of completing their apprenticeships. (The prize was named after Thomas Doggett, an actor who initiated the race, and the winner receives a coat bearing an embroidered badge.)

LIGHTHOUSES

As the general Lighthouse Authority for England, Wales, the Channel Islands and Gibraltar, Trinity House was, and still is, responsible for supplying and maintaining lighthouses, light vessels, buoys and beacons. Before 1841, some lighthouses were privately owned. Ships had to pay a sum of money when entering or leaving port, which went to maintain the lights.

PILOTS

Ships coming into port needed pilots – men who knew the currents and the physical hazards, such as sandbanks – to guide them. Trinity House was

The only access to Beachy Head lighthouse, off the south coast of England, was by aerial railway.

responsible for examining and licensing about two-thirds of the pilots working in England, Wales and the Channel Islands. Its main area of responsibility was London and the River Thames from the estuary to London Bridge (for which it had responsibility from 1604), but there were forty other ports for which it issued pilots' licences after 1808. Masters and mates in the Merchant Navy could be granted exemption certificates by Trinity House if they wanted to pilot their own vessels and were qualified to do so.

Trinity House was not responsible for pilots working at Liverpool, Bristol and some of the ports in the north-east of England. In addition, it had no responsibility over the river pilots needed along the major inland waterways, such as the Thames.

LOCATING THE RECORDS OF TRINITY HOUSE

Since its founding in 1514, Trinity House has occupied a number of different buildings within London. Some were burned down, and in World War II the surviving records relating to

lighthouses and light vessels were destroyed by a bomb. Most of those that remain are in the Guildhall Library in London, but access to the 20th-century records is restricted.

Scotland, with the exception of the port of Leith, and Ireland did not come under Trinity House's aegis, and so records relating to these two countries will be found in their own national or local archives. Leith's Trinity House records are in Edinburgh.

LIFEBOATS

Lifeboat stations were originally run by local authorities, and any surviving records before 1824 will be with CROs. In 1824, the Royal National Lifeboat Institution (RNLI) was set up to co-ordinate the provision of stations around the coast of Britain. The crews were, and still are, volunteers, so information about individual crewmen, especially in the early days, is sparse. They were simply fishermen who could be called out in the event of an emergency. The RNLI does, however, have records of coxswains (helmsmen) and the honorary secretary of each station, as well as lists of those killed and medals awarded for bravery. Newspapers reported cases of shipwrecks and rescues.

FURTHER HELP

Guildhall Library leaflet *Records of the Corporation of Trinity House*
Guildhall Library leaflet *The Corporation of Trinity House: Family History Sources at Guildhall Library*
Guildhall Library leaflet *Records of Watermen and Lightermen*
Guildhall Library leaflet *Doggett's Coat and Badge Race*
Royal National Lifeboat Institution Headquarters, West Quay Road, Poole, Dorset BH15 1HZ www.lifeboats.org.uk

Lifecycle checklist

On the opposite page is a list of the events that occur in most people's lives. It is included as a reminder of the kinds of records the family historian needs to look for, with an indication of where they are most likely to be found. Of course there is no such thing as an "average" life – everyone's is different in some way from the norm – but the following points may help in your research.

ADOLESCENCE

Men were at their most mobile between the ages of 15 and 21, at the time of taking up apprenticeships or beginning work. They also moved the greatest distance during this period in their lives. In Victorian times, servants aged 12–15 were the most mobile of all male workers.

MARRIAGE

Contrary to popular belief, our ancestors rarely married before the age of 20. There were child marriages (or, more precisely, betrothals), but these were arranged between landowners for financial and dynastic purposes, and the couples concerned rarely lived together until they were in their mid- to late teens.

In the early 17th century, the average age at first marriage was 28 for men and 25 for women. These figures dropped over the 18th century, and by the beginning of the 19th century they were 26 and 24 respectively. By the early 20th century they had fallen again, but since the last quarter of the 20th century they have been rising again. These figures seem to have been linked to economic factors, such as industrialization, which meant that young people could earn a comparatively good wage at a younger age. Couples waited until they had accumulated enough money to set up a separate home – multi-generational households, or those consisting of extended families, were rare. A widowed parent might live with a child and in-law, especially in industrial areas where women needed to work, and would provide childcare.

Marriage was the time at which women were at their most mobile. Although they tended to marry in their home parish, they usually went to live in their husband's place of residence. Most couples lived within 32km (20 miles) of each other, presumably because they met at fairs and markets, and 16km (10 miles) was about the limit of how far people were prepared to walk.

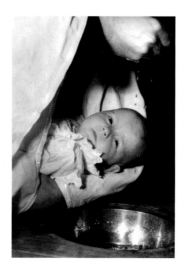

A baby's birth is celebrated by its family, and recorded by the state.

FAMILY SIZE

The high death rate among babies and young children in the late 18th century meant that the average number of children a couple could expect to survive was six. This number had dropped to five in the mid-19th century. By the 1920s the average number of children in a family was just two, but this figure represents a deliberate decision to limit family size rather than a massive growth in child mortality.

LIFE EXPECTANCY

Until the 20th century, the average life expectancy at birth was roughly 30–40 years at different times during the preceding centuries. This apparently low figure is because so many babies died in the first two years of life. A person who survived to the age of 20 could, however, expect to live to 50; at 30, people could expect to reach 60; and those who survived to 60 had a good chance of reaching 70 or even 80. A few then achieved 90 or even 100. These figures were for the country as a whole, disguising the difference between a relatively wholesome life in the country and life in cities, which, until the Victorian era brought improved sanitation, was dangerous.

Clean water, efficient sewage disposal systems and better personal hygiene had a greater effect on increasing life expectancy than advances in medical treatment until the last half of the 20th century. The introduction of antibiotics after World War II brought the next leap in public health improvement. Further advances mean that today more and more people live to 100 years and beyond.

From the cradle to the grave

AGE	EVENT	RECORDS	LOCATION OF RECORDS
0	BIRTH	After 1837 – birth certificate	FRC
		Before 1837 – parish registers	CRO
0+	BAPTISM	Church of England parish registers	CRO
		Nonconformist churches	FRC or CRO
		Roman Catholic churches	Church or DRO
4-18	SCHOOL	Public schools	Published or with school
		Church schools	CRO/denominational archives
		Local Education Authority	CRO
14+	UNIVERSITY	Alumni lists	Published
14-21	APPRENTICESHIP	Indentures	Private papers
		1710–1811 Apprenticeship tax records	TNA
		Poor Law records (for parish apprentices)	CRO
7+	WORK	Directories	Published
		Censuses	FRC
	PROFESSIONS	Published lists/membership of professional bodies	Libraries
	BUSINESS	Company archives	Libraries/CRO
	ARTISANS	Guild membership	CRO
7+	MILITARY SERVICE	Service records	TNA/museums
15+	MILITIA SERVICE	Militia ballot	CRO
		Pay and musters	TNA
	VOLUNTEERS	Pay and musters	TNA/CRO
21+	PROPERTY	Deeds	TNA/CRO
	ACQUISITION	Ratebooks	CRO
		Directories	Published
	FRANCHISE	Poll books	Published
		Electoral registers	CRO/British Library
12/14+	MARRIAGE	After 1837 – marriage certificate	FRC
		1753–1837 – Anglican parish church	CRO
		Before 1753 – denominational church	CRO/FRC
		Marriage licence	CRO/DRO
	CHILDREN	After 1837 – birth certificate	FRC
		Before 1837 – church records	CRO
		Illegitimate children – bastardy examinations	CRO
	LEGAL	Crime	CRO/TNA
	PROCEEDINGS	Property disputes	TNA
	INTERNAL	Settlement certificates/examinations	CRO
	MIGRATION	Removal orders	CRO
	EMIGRATION		
	Voluntary	Government schemes	TNA
	Transportation	Crime and prison records	TNA/CRO
	ILLNESS	Hospital records	CRO/other repositories
		Workhouse records	CRO
	DEATH	After 1837 – death certificate	FRC
		Before 1837 – burial registers	CRO/FRC
		Obituaries in newspapers/periodicals	CRO/British Library
	INQUEST	Coroners' records	CRO/TNA
		Newspaper reports	CRO/British Library
	WILL	After 1858	Probate Registry
		Before 1858	CRO/DRO/TNA

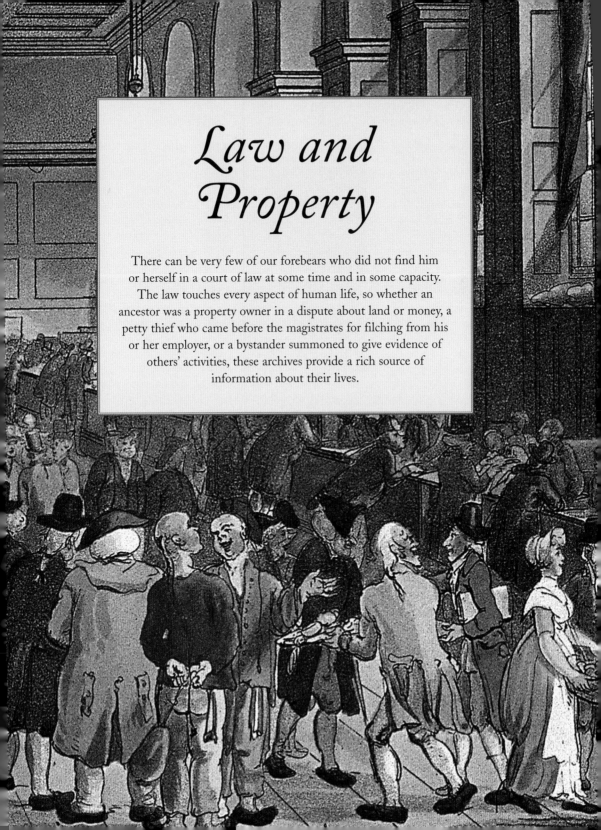

Law and Property

There can be very few of our forebears who did not find him
or herself in a court of law at some time and in some capacity.
The law touches every aspect of human life, so whether an
ancestor was a property owner in a dispute about land or money, a
petty thief who came before the magistrates for filching from his
or her employer, or a bystander summoned to give evidence of
others' activities, these archives provide a rich source of
information about their lives.

Researching legal records

Britain's complex legal system grew and developed over centuries. This is why the family historian will find records relating to ancestors, who might appear as official, counsel, plaintiff, defendant or witness, in a wide variety of courts. The complexities of the legal records, some in a jargon based on Latin and Norman French, will make this a challenging form of research.

THE DEVELOPMENT OF THE LEGAL SYSTEM

Before the Norman Conquest in 1066, the law was administered through local communal courts in the shires and hundreds, which were divisions within shires. The law in one county was not necessarily the same as that in another, reflecting the fact that England grew out of a collection of separate kingdoms. King William grafted on to this a system of law brought from Normandy but administered through these local institutions. The law was the same across the whole of England and was therefore called "common law".

The king and his council, called the Curia Regis, ruled England. The Curia Regis was not a court of law in a fixed place; rather, it accompanied the king as he moved around his domain, settling disputes and carrying out the business of state. In the early medieval period, power was mainly in the hands of large landowners, but as the Crown grew stronger, their might decreased.

In addition, individuals, or groups of individuals, were commissioned to carry out certain duties, such as the Domesday Survey, and some of these commissions had legal purposes, such as trying criminals. These commissions accumulated written records, making a permanent office to store them necessary, and Westminster, where the king had his main court, was the logical place for this. Written records of court proceedings and judgements were necessary because the law was, and is, founded on precedents – what had been decided before. Although laws were passed by parliament, which was established in 1264, they were interpreted through the principles of common law.

MAIN TYPES OF COURTS

As the state grew, more courts were established to handle different aspects of the law. In addition to the temporal courts, the Church, both as a landowner and a spiritual authority, had considerable power and had its own courts. The four main types of court were:

- manorial courts, which dealt mainly with land but also with personal disputes
- criminal courts
- civil courts, which handled cases concerning property and money
- Church courts, which proved wills before 1858 and dealt with cases arising from them. They also had jurisdiction over any immoral behaviour. These courts also administered canon law, matters involving the clergy, Church officials and their parishioners.

ABOVE Three clerks record Edward I's judgement in a lawsuit in the late 13th century.

LEFT The Court of Wards and Liveries meets to deliberate how to protect the interests of a rich orphan in 1747.

In addition, the High Court of Admiralty heard cases concerning maritime issues, both civil, such as disputes over wages, and criminal, such as piracy. It also had a "prize" jurisdiction. The seizure of ships and cargoes ("prize") was common practice, especially during wartime, and members of the capturing crew received a certain proportion of the value of what they had seized. The ship was supposed to be taken to a port in the captor's country, where a court (in Britain the High Court of Admiralty) would determine if the action was legal.

APPEAL COURTS

People who were unhappy with the manner in which their case or trial had been conducted (rather than simply not agreeing with the unfavourable verdict) could appeal to a higher court. The Court of King's/Queen's Bench was the court of appeal for common law courts in both criminal and civil cases, and above it, from 1585, was the Court of Exchequer Chamber. The High Court of Delegates acted as the appeal court for the civil side (known as the Instance Court) of the High Court of Admiralty.

In 1875, the Court of Appeal was created, replacing the other courts. The House of Lords was, and still is, the ultimate appeal court, the highest in the land and also in any British territories overseas.

OTHER COURTS

The major courts in which cases were heard are described in the rest of this chapter, but there were four other courts that operated until the Commonwealth period:

- The Court of Augmentations and Revenues of the Crown (1535–55) dealt with matters arising from the Dissolution of the Monasteries.

A pregnant woman swears in front of a judge that her baby was fathered by the nobleman on the left, who holds up his arms in denial as he is berated by his wife, 18th century.

- The Court of Requests (1483–1642) was intended for those too poor to go to other courts and servants of the monarch.
- The Court of Star Chamber (1487–1642) had jurisdiction over a wide range of civil and criminal matters.
- The Court of Wards (1540–1646) administered the property of orphans who were minors and those who were mentally incapable of acting for themselves.

FINDING ANCESTORS IN COURT RECORDS

The piecemeal growth of the legal system led to cases that, on the surface, seem similar being heard in different courts. A case might therefore not be found in what looks like the most obvious place.

Until 1733, records were kept in Latin (except during the Commonwealth period), but even after that date they retained a highly specialized jargon, partly Latin and partly Norman French, which was usually abbreviated. All this, added to the problems of

reading old handwriting, can be very confusing, so the records of the higher courts, which are stored in The National Archives (TNA), are probably best left until you have accumulated some experience of research. Alternatively, you may prefer to hire a specialist to conduct this research for you.

When you write up your findings, it is worth noting a few conventions. In criminal courts, it is the king or queen who *prosecutes*, because crimes are held to damage the whole community and are therefore an offence against the Crown. The person who loses is *found guilty* and is *convicted*. In civil courts, an individual or corporate body *sues*, because it is their private interests that have been damaged. The person who loses is *held liable* and may be *penalized* in some way.

FURTHER HELP

TNA Legal Records Information 3
Court of Star Chamber 1485–1642
TNA Legal Records Information 4
Court of Requests 1485–1642: A Court for the "Poor"

Church courts

Archdeaconry and diocesan courts proved wills before 1858 and dealt with cases arising from them. This is the area with which the family historian will be mainly concerned. These courts also covered a wide range of other matters. In addition to administrative concerns, such as disputes over tithes, they had jurisdiction over a variety of personal and moral issues, such as non-attendance at church, incest, adultery, fornication, blasphemy, slander, scolding and the like. This responsibility for moral behaviour led to them being called the "bawdy courts". The Church's jurisdiction over the laity was abolished in 1860.

Church courts also dealt with transgressions by clergy and parish officials. These involved such activities as unlicensed preaching, conducting irregular or clandestine marriages, unseemly behaviour and failure to maintain the church and churchyard properly.

PUNISHMENTS AND PENALTIES

The Church could not impose such harsh penalties as the criminal courts, so any wronged people who felt particularly vindictive might prefer to take their complaint to the latter. Most punishments consisted of penances, with transgressors being required to confess their sins before the congregation in church or some other public place, often dressed in a white sheet and carrying a candle.

If offenders refused to repent or to comply with the court's judgement (such as in disputes over tithes), they might be excommunicated, which meant that they were forbidden to

attend services and were denied the sacrament and a Christian burial. In more serious cases, they might also be excluded from all Christian company. While this would be of no great concern to Nonconformists, it would be a severe threat to Anglicans, who might find themselves cut off from the whole congregation. Being denied a Christian burial was also a serious matter at a time when many people believed that their entry into heaven depended on it.

APPEAL COURTS

The Court of Arches was the consistory court of the Province of Canterbury and acted as the appeal court for the archdeaconry and consistory courts within its province. It was also the first court to which all "peculiars" (those that did not come under the jurisdiction of a bishop) were subject. It still deals with matters involving clergymen and church officials. The Chancery Court of York was the equivalent for the province of York.

Above both of these was the High Court of Delegates, set up by Henry VIII in 1533 as a court of appeal for matters heard in Church courts. In 1832, it was abolished and its responsibilities in respect of Church courts were taken over by the Privy Council.

DIVORCE AND SEPARATION

Before 1857, divorce was possible only by a private Act of Parliament, which effectively restricted it to the wealthy and influential. Those people who wanted to end their marriage, but who found the cost of an Act of Parliament prohibitive, could turn instead to the Church courts for a legal separation, with alimony paid to the wife, though the parties could not remarry until after the death of one of them.

Matrimonial cases tended to be long-drawn-out, and many were never successfully resolved: either the parties ran out of money to pursue them or one party simply fled. Even if the outcome of the case is unknown, the court records can give a lot of detail about the couple's lives and information about the witnesses, frequently servants, who gave evidence.

Most people lower down the social scale simply left to live with a new partner. Bigamy was a crime, so many of these new relationships were never formalized. Records relating to bigamous marriages will be found in the criminal courts.

Wife-selling was a form of poor man's divorce. The husband would take his wife, often led by a halter, to a suitably public occasion, such as market day, and offer her for sale. This is not quite as demeaning and patriarchal as it seems, since the buyer was usually her lover, and the three parties had colluded in the "sale". Wife sales were rare and sensational, and therefore they tended to be reported in local papers, but, since they had no legal sanction, they do not appear in any court records.

INVALID MARRIAGES

Some people, rather than trying to get a divorce or separation (which usually required proof of gross cruelty), would go to the Church courts to try to show that the marriage had never been valid, which would leave the option of remarriage open. Their grounds were:

- non-consummation
- the two parties being related within the prohibited degrees, e.g. brother and sister
- lunacy at the time of the ceremony (although if one of the parties went mad afterwards, this was not grounds for an annulment)
- lack of consent, which usually involved a degree of force

After 1753, marriage where one of the couple was under the age of 21 and did not have the written consent of the parent or guardian was null and void.

CRIMINAL CONVERSATION

In cases of adultery, the cuckolded husband would sometimes try to extract financial compensation from his wife's lover rather than take him to court. This might be done informally or perhaps with a legal document drawn up by a lawyer. The alternative was an action for criminal conversation, usually abbreviated to "crim. con.", whereby the husband sued the lover. These cases were heard in the Court of King's/Queen's Bench (Plea Side) or the Court of Common Pleas. Action in these courts was expensive, and involved travelling to London for those who did not live there, and so this action was restricted to the well-off.

FINDING CHURCH COURT RECORDS

The records relating to divorce, separation and other matrimonial issues, such as restitution of conjugal rights, before 1857 will be found in the Church courts. Such cases usually started out in the local diocesan court but might later have been transferred to a higher court.

In 1857, the government took over the administration of divorces, which were heard in the Court of Divorce and Matrimonial Causes. These records are in The National Archives with indexes at the Family Record Centre (FRC) Those cases of divorce that did come to court, both before and after 1857, were usually reported in great detail in newspapers.

Records relating to Church consistory courts will be found in Diocesan Record Offices (DROs) or County Record Offices (CROs). The records of the Court of

Arches are in Lambeth Palace Library, while those of the Chancery Court of York are in the Borthwick Institute. TNA holds the records of the High Court of Delegates.

153

Manorial records

Many people assume that, since manors have their roots in Anglo-Saxon England, manorial records relate just to the medieval period and before, and are therefore only of use to the family historian before the advent of parish registers. In fact, the manor, which comprised not only the manor house but also the lands attached to it, continued to have jurisdiction over some aspects of its inhabitants' lives until 1926.

THE ADVENT OF THE MANOR

Originally all the land in the country belonged to the king. He could grant the use of this land to people in return for various services, which is the basis of the feudal system. Later on, the Crown started to sell land, thus giving up its rights to it.

In the past, there were some 60,000 manors in England and Wales. They were originally estates held from the Crown by a lord, hence the title "Lord of the Manor". Many of these lords were great landowners who had manors all over Britain. They usually consisted of agricultural or pastoral land, but today the remains of some of these manors may be within towns or cities. Even the square mile of the City of London once contained open land, so there are a few manorial records relating to areas within it.

COURT PROCEEDINGS

Manorial courts were usually held twice a year, on Lady Day (25th March) and Michaelmas

(25th September), and the proceedings were divided into three: the View of Frankpledge, the Court Leet and the Court Baron.

The View of Frankpledge

The reciting of the customs of the manor was not done at each court session, but it was done every few years to remind people of the customs or when a new lord of the manor took over. Different manors had different customs, and so there was no one way of doing things all over the country.

A list of tenants of a manor in Pembrokeshire gives names, acreages and the amount they paid.

The Court Leet

This was attended by every male over the age of 16, whether he was a tenant or not, who had lived for a year and a day in the manor. After the Middle Ages, it seems that the Court Leet was held annually, rather than every six months. It was also, particularly in the early days, held in the open air in a place deemed to be magical, such as a crossroads or under an oak tree. Later the court might meet here but immediately adjourn to a place indoors.

The first decision to be made concerned the amount of the common fine. The fines people paid were based on this unit. Someone might be amerced (fined) four times the common fine or perhaps twice for a lesser transgression.

Next came the election of officials: bailiff, constable, etc. These occupations tended to be hereditary, and so an election would be necessary only if an official had died. Although tenants chose the officers, the lord of the manor appointed the steward (also called the seneschal), who kept the minutes. From the 17th century, this post was usually held by a lawyer. A new jury was also elected. It would comprise between four and twelve men, depending on the size of the manor.

After these elections, the main business of the Court Leet took place, divided into two sections:

● Essoins, which were apologies for absence. Those absent without good cause were amerced.

- Business, which was largely concerned with anti-social acts against the lord of the manor or other tenants, such as allowing animals to stray, or damaging crops in some other way.

The Court Baron

The third part of the proceedings dealt with land tenure. Until 1926, land could be held in three ways:

- Freehold – land held as freehold was subject to common law, not manorial law.
- Leasehold – the tenant paid a sum of money to use the land for a fixed period.
- Copyhold – the tenant held the land by custom. The steward made a copy of the court roll entry relating to the property and gave it to the holder. This method of holding land started to die out in the 16th century.

Land could be transferred between individuals but only with the permission of the lord, his steward or the court. In the event of a tenant's death, it passed to his or, in some cases, her heir. If this person was a minor, i.e. under 21, a ward might be appointed to look after his or her interests. Each time land was transferred, a fine (which was not a punishment) had to be paid to the court by the heir. This was called the heriot. Originally this was the best beast, but it could be and, from the 18th century, increasingly was commuted to a sum of money.

People could also surrender copyhold property "to the use of will", which meant they were registering their will in advance of their death and thus avoiding transfer fees. A registered will was binding on the court at the tenant's death. This was often used by women to bequeath land to their children before the Married Women's Property Act (1882), but this applied only to property within the manor.

OTHER MANORIAL RECORDS

In addition to the minutes of the various court meetings, the steward of the manor might occasionally prepare a manorial survey, which listed who occupied which piece of land, especially when a new lord took over. These surveys sometimes include a map. There might also be rent books related to payments for the various holdings.

LOCATING MANORIAL RECORDS

Manorial records are private property. Although most have been deposited in CROs, a number remain in private archives and other repositories, such as university libraries. The National Registry of Archives has records of all the parishes within a county, with lists of the manors either wholly or partly within them. The Register of Manorial Documents lists who owns the records and where they are located. Both of these registers are held by The National Archives.

RESEARCHING MANORIAL RECORDS

Until 1733, records were written in Latin (except during the Commonwealth period). They also had a specialized jargon, which reflects their Anglo-Saxon and medieval roots. Most of the books in the "Further Help" section below contain a list of the vocabulary used. To accustom yourself to this, it will probably help to read some of the published records of manorial courts before tackling the documents themselves, because reading unfamiliar words in what might be semi-legible handwriting is frustrating, and you may be tempted to give up without getting the information you need. Note that the manor did not necessarily have the same boundaries as the parish.

In the absence of a will (which was often copied into the manorial records), the transfer of land between one person and another suggests that one had died and the person who took it over was the heir. There was usually a set hierarchy to the inheritance. Naturally, the deceased person's children (sons first, then daughters) were the prime candidates to inherit, but in the case of someone dying without offspring, rights would pass to brothers and sisters. This was (and still is) the usual practice outside manorial land too. If, however, there were no siblings, some manors would go to the mother's side of the family for the next heir, if this was where the land had originally come from. This is different from non-manorial land, where the father's side of the family was always favoured. This may give the family historian some useful clues about parentage.

Tenants often held land in more than one manor. If the records of one manor where your ancestor lived no longer survive, search the records of the surrounding ones as well. Even if you do find your ancestor in one manor, check others in the same area to see whether he or she was a tenant there too.

FURTHER HELP

Ellis, Mary *Using Manorial Records* (TNA)
Palgrave Moore, Patrick *How to Locate and Use Manorial Records*
Park, Peter B. *My Ancestors Were Manorial Tenants* (SoG)
TNA Legal Records Information 1 *Manorial Records in the Public Record Office*
TNA Legal Records Information 9 *Manor and Other Local Courts Rolls 13th century–1922*
Stuart, Dennis *Manorial Records* (Phillimore)

Crime and punishment

There never was a golden age when all citizens were upright and law-abiding. The reasons why people break the law were as hotly discussed in the past as they are today. Ways of punishing crime have also gone through fashions. The family historian will almost certainly find that at least one ancestor has appeared in the criminal courts, either as defendant, plaintiff, witness or even member of the jury. All those appearing before the criminal courts went through several stages, all of which leave records that will reveal whether you are descended from saints or sinners.

The early records of assize courts are in Latin.

THE CRIMINAL COURT SYSTEM

In the early medieval period, judges from Westminster toured Britain every few years, hearing, among other matters, criminal trials. This court was known as the General Eyre. There were also commissions of *oyez and terminer* (from Anglo-Norman *oyer* to hear and *terminer* to judge), which applied to major crimes; gaol delivery, when all the people held in gaol awaiting trial were tried; petty sessions; quarter sessions and assizes (see below).

PROSECUTION

Before the establishment of a police service, from about 1830 onwards, it was largely the responsibility of the injured party to prosecute an offender. If the injured party had died as a result of what had happened, the coroner would issue a warrant to commit the offender for trial. Using the courts cost money, both in fees paid to them and in working time lost attending them, so local authorities would sometimes offer compensation or a reward to individuals in order to encourage them to report a crime. As the police force grew, from the mid-19th century it took over the prosecution of offenders.

Prisoners at the bar in London's notorious Old Bailey court.

PETTY SESSIONS

The first step in a criminal case was to go to petty sessions to make allegations about a crime. Petty sessions were held by Justices of the Peace (JPs), sometimes in their own homes and sometimes in the vestry of the parish church. In the City of London they were held at the Guildhall. These JPs dealt with a variety of matters. They carried out settlement and bastardy examinations, and arbitrated in minor cases, such as non-payment for work done. Their main function, however, was to examine witnesses to decide whether there was a case to answer in court. If they decided that the matter should be taken further, they would refer it to quarter sessions. Offenders, if they had not fled the scene of the crime, were committed to the House of Correction to await trial there. The JPs also issued recognizances – a bond to forfeit a sum of money if prosecutors and witnesses did not appear at the quarter sessions.

Very few early records of these petty sessions survive, but those that do should be in the CRO. From 1848, however, petty sessions records had to be passed to the quarter sessions, so the survival rate is much higher.

QUARTER SESSIONS

The next stage in the process was to hear a case at quarter sessions. As the name suggests, these were generally held four times a year in a county town or city. Individual boroughs also held their own sessions.

In addition to hearing criminal cases, quarter sessions carried out a range of other business. They issued licences to a variety of people; arbitrated in disputed cases of settlement and bastardy; heard oaths of allegiance (including sacrament certificates); dealt with various taxes, bankrupts and debtors, and the militia; and heard presentments about public nuisances, such as the failure of a parish to repair roads. Coroners' expenses and papers were also handed in to these sessions.

Among the quarter sessions records relating to criminal trials should be lists of jurors, indictments and prisoners. There may also be witness statements, called depositions. The Clerk of the Peace also kept a minute book, in which he noted the major points of the proceedings, including sentences. All these records are held in CROs. After 1971, quarter sessions and assize courts were replaced by crown courts.

ASSIZES

For the assizes, two judges were sent from Westminster, the seat of government, to go around ("on circuit") a group of counties once, twice or three times a year. The number of visits depended on the number of people within the jurisdiction of each circuit, which affected how many cases had to be heard there. The judges tried more serious crimes than those dealt with at quarter sessions. Initially they held investigations into civil matters concerning land, but the verdicts were usually sent to Westminster, where further action was heard, so they began to confine themselves to criminal matters.

In 1876, the counties in each circuit were reorganized, but the assize system continued until 1971, when it was replaced by crown courts. Assize records are in TNA. Before 1733, the records were written in Latin (except during the Commonwealth period, 1649–60).

EXCEPTIONS TO THE ASSIZE SYSTEM

The exceptions to this system were the palatinates of Chester, Durham and Lancaster, which each had their own courts. The City of London and Middlesex did not have assizes either.

LEFT Many prisoners died every year in Newgate Gaol, so the keys to the burial ground were in constant use.

Jack Sheppard, a famous thief, managed to escape from Newgate Gaol, despite being heavily shackled. He was executed in 1724.

Name, Nº ___ Henry Miller - 6456 ___ 16 Aug 73
and Aliases ___
Description.
Age (on discharge) ___ 15
Height ___ 4ft 11½
Hair ___ Brown
Eyes ___ Blue
Complexion ___ Fresh
Where born ___ Boro.
Married or single ___ Single
Trade or occupation ___ Labourer
Distinguishing marks Scar
on back

Address at time of apprehension ___ 9 Kaal Street
Boro Road.
Place and date of conviction ___ Southwark 5 Aug 73.
Offence for which convicted ___ Simple Larceny J.U.
Stealing a loaf of Bread.
Sentence ___ 10 Days Hard Labour & whipped.
Date to be liberated ___ 14 August 1873
Intended residence after liberation ___ 9 Kaal Street
Boro Road

Previous Convictions
Summary
By Jury

Remarks, antecedents &c.

Henry Miller, 15, was sentenced to prison for stealing a loaf of bread in 1873.

Instead, sessions were held mainly at the Old Bailey.

Eight sessions of hearings were held each year between October and July. Transcripts and summaries of trials here were published and sold from the late 17th century onwards. Initially, only cases of particular importance were reported in any detail, but from about 1712 all cases were at least listed, and by 1730 the records included transcripts of the evidence from shorthand notes. These reports were published as *The Proceedings on the King's Commission of the Peace, Oyer and Terminer and Gaol Delivery held for the City of London and the County of Middlesex*. This cumbersome title is usually abbreviated to the *Proceedings of the Old Bailey*. The records of the courts themselves, however, are split between the London Metropolitan Archives (LMA) and the Corporation of London Record Office (CLRO). There is relatively little genealogical evidence in them, although some relatives might be mentioned if they were involved with a crime.

The Ordinary (prison chaplain) of Newgate published the confessions of condemned criminals from the mid-17th to mid-18th century. These give considerable biographical detail, but some of the condemned refused to co-operate. A great number of surviving copies are in the British Library, but there are individual issues elsewhere.

From 1791 there are registers of criminals tried in Middlesex in The National Archives. In 1834, the Central Criminal Court, which incorporated parts of the counties of Surrey, Kent and Essex within its jurisdiction, replaced these Old Bailey sessions. The number of times it sat increased to twelve. The records of the Central Criminal Court are in TNA.

Wales and Chester

Wales and the palatinate of Chester were not part of the assizes circuits until 1830. Before then, Wales had the Court of Great Sessions, the records of which have been deposited in the National Library of Wales. After 1830, Wales and Chester were joined into an assize circuit, which in 1876 was divided into two: North Wales and Chester formed one and South Wales the other. These assize records are in TNA.

THE COURT OF KING'S/QUEEN'S BENCH

This was the highest court in England and Wales. Its work was divided into two "sides": criminal cases were held on the Crown Side and civil cases on the Plea Side. As TNA's information sheet explains, the records are very complex.

Actions here on the Plea Side covered a wide range of crimes, some very

Despite his youth, this boy had already committed several crimes and was placed on the habitual criminal register in 1873.

start with these if they are available. If not, newspaper accounts of proceedings at the quarter sessions and assizes may be the best way of starting your search, especially if you only suspect that your ancestor was involved in a trial at some time.

If the quarter sessions and assizes of the county where your ancestors lived have not been indexed or had a calendar of their proceedings made, it can be a long and frustrating task to find out whether they were involved in criminal proceedings. One clue is to look for a gap in the births of children in a family. There may be many reasons for this, but one of the causes might be a period of imprisonment of

Julia Ann Crumpling, 7, stole a pram and was sentenced to seven days' hard labour, one day for each year of her life.

minor. Most began in lower courts, because appeals from lower courts were made here. There are relatively few cases on the Crown Side, apart from those that presented some legal difficulty and those in which the Crown had an interest, such as state trials. Some coroners' papers from London and Middlesex from 1675–1845 are found here. This court became a division of the High Court of Justice in 1875. Until the first part of the 18th century, papers from coroners' inquests where the verdict was not murder or manslaughter, which were dealt with by the assizes, were sent on to the Court of King's/Queen's Bench. Most circuits had stopped referring coroners' papers by 1750, but the Western circuit (Cornwall, Devon, Dorset, Hampshire, Somerset and Wiltshire) continued to do so until about 1820.

RESEARCHING CRIMINAL RECORDS

Many CROs have calendars or indexes to quarter session proceedings, and some have been published. Always

Locating records of convicts and prisoners

Each stage of a criminal's journey from crime to transportation or completion of a prison sentence in England and Wales was documented, although of course not all the records survive. Magistrates at quarter sessions were able to sentence people to transportation, and details of these will be in the relevant CRO. Most other records are in TNA.

Records can be found in:
- petty sessions
- quarter sessions/borough sessions
- sheriff's cravings, which list all the expenses incurred in keeping prisoners in jail while awaiting trial at assize courts, and the costs of the court proceedings
- sheriff's payments and treasury warrants, which record money paid by the government to the sheriffs
- assize records
- calendars, which list all those indicted

- minute books
- indictments
- annual registers, which list all those indicted and the sentence, or verdict in the case of those found not guilty; these were produced from 1791 covering Middlesex and the City of London, and from 1805 for other counties
- assize vouchers, which list all those sentenced at assizes
- prison records
- prison journals kept by the governors, which might mention individual prisoners or contain copies of correspondence with other authorities
- Home Office records, which cover a variety of topics, such as correspondence with prisons; these might mention individuals, although they are mainly concerned with policy

Australian settlers became increasing unhappy about the transportation of criminals from Britain, which finally ended in 1868.

one of the parents. This might be the starting point for a search.

Places mentioned in indictments are where the offence was committed, not the home of the accused. Other information given at criminal trials should be treated with caution – people both in and out of the dock often had good reasons for not telling the truth.

Courts were usually more lenient on first-time offenders, so someone on a repeat appearance might well give an alias instead of their real name. The young and very old were also treated less harshly, which might be a motive for giving a false age.

If you are looking for ancestors who might have been tried at the Old Bailey, start with the printed *Proceedings of the Old Bailey*, which have been put on microfilm and indexed. Unfortunately, the names of prosecutors and witnesses are not in the index. From 2003 the whole *Proceedings* are being

digitized and put on the internet, which will allow a search by names or keywords.

PUNISHMENTS

The punishment of criminals is still a much-debated issue. Is the aim to inflict pain in revenge; deter others from wrongdoing; rehabilitate, or simply remove a source of crime from the community?

Forms of punishment

Before the middle of the 19th century, long prison sentences were not often used as a punishment. In fact, it was rare for anyone to be imprisoned for more than two years, except for debt. Instead, people found guilty of minor offences were fined or sentenced to some physical punishment, such as being put in the pillory, whipped or branded, while those who had committed more serious crimes were

sentenced to transportation or death. The death sentence was often commuted to the lesser punishment of transportation for life.

Those who were transported might return on the expiration of their sentence, which typically lasted for either seven or fourteen years, although they had to pay for or arrange their own passage back. Sometimes transported convicts managed to escape before their sentence was completed. If they were then recaptured, they were hanged.

Prisons

The aim of imprisonment in Britain was to reform the criminal. During the early 19th century, it became evident that short sentences did not give enough time to achieve this, so, from the middle of the century onwards, especially after transportation ended, more and more prisons, able to hold a greater number of people for longer, were built, and sentences lengthened.

It was always recognized that some criminals were not responsible for their actions, so those who were found to be insane were sent to special institutions, such as Broadmoor hospital for criminal lunatics.

Outlaws

People who refused to attend court to defend themselves against accusations were declared outlaws. They could be imprisoned or executed (if they were eventually caught), and their possessions were forfeited. This concept was finally abolished in 1938, although it had long fallen into disuse by this date.

RESEARCHING PRISON RECORDS

Originally the words "gaol/jail" and "prison" had slightly different meanings. A jail was a lock-up or house of correction where people were held awaiting trial, like today's remand centres. After sentence, they might be committed to prison or jailed in a house of correction. This semantic difference might help you to decide where to look for further records of your ancestor.

Do not assume that an execution followed automatically if a person was sentenced to death. Before 1868, about two-thirds of those sentenced were reprieved and transported. Young men might also be given the option of joining the Navy or Army rather than being executed or transported. Unfortunately, the London records of those who were executed have not survived, but newspapers usually contain the details of who was pardoned and who was hanged.

If the assize records for the period you are researching have not survived,

FURTHER HELP

Gibson, Jeremy *Quarter Sessions Records for Family Historians* (FFHS)
Hawkings, David T. *Criminal Ancestors: A Guide to Historical Criminal Records in England and Wales* (Sutton Publishing)
TNA Legal Records Information 12 *English Assizes 1656–1971: Key to Classes for Civil Trials*
TNA Legal Records Information 13 *Criminal Trials at the Assizes*
TNA Legal Records Information 14 *English Assizes: Key to Records of Criminal Trials*
TNA Legal Records Information 15

Welsh Assizes, 1831–1971: Key to Classes for Criminal and Civil Trials
TNA Legal Records Information 24 *Outlawry in Medieval and Early Modern England*
TNA Legal Records Information 34 *King's Bench (Crown Side) Records 1675–1875*
TNA Domestic Records Information 78 *Tracing 19th-Century Criminals in the PRO*
TNA Domestic Records Information 88 *Sources for Convicts and Prisoners, 1100–1986*
www.oldbaileyonline.org

details about prisoners may be found in the sheriff's records and other documents that may give details of the crime. Descriptions of prisoners are sometimes given, and from 1869 photographs can be found.

There had to be an inquest on every person who died in prison, whether it was clearly due to natural causes or not. These may include why the person was there and how long he or she had been in prison.

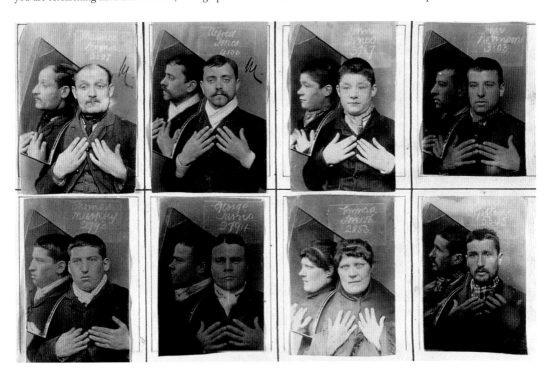

These early photographs of prisoners from Wormwood Scrubs, c.1880, are annotated with the name and number of each person.

Transportation records

Transporting criminals overseas continued for almost three centuries. This served several purposes: it removed the criminal from society, provided the possibility of rehabilitation and also helped to people British colonies.

A HISTORY OF BRITISH TRANSPORTATION

From Elizabethan times onwards, transportation was used to provide the labour force for the growing number of overseas colonies. The first Act to implement this policy was passed in 1597, and for the next 150 years or so criminals were transported to America and the West Indies, particularly Jamaica. The government handed over the responsibility for transportation to contractors, who were paid per convict.

From about 1670, slave labour from Africa replaced criminals in the Caribbean, since the plantation owners preferred slaves. From 1775, America was no longer a possible destination for them because of the War of Independence. In 1782–4, the government considered schemes to send convicts to Africa. Although some people were sentenced to be transported to Africa, only a few went as soldiers. The rest remained either in gaol or on disused ships, called prison hulks, along the Thames as far as the estuary, and at Plymouth and Portsmouth. Given the number of convictions that carried a severe sentence, these quickly filled up.

In 1787, the first fleet of transportees sailed to Australia, which remained the major destination for transported criminals until 1868, although after 1836 some were sent to Gibraltar or Bermuda. When transportation ended in 1868, offenders were once more imprisoned in Britain.

LOCATING RECORDS HELD IN BRITAIN

As well as the court records and newspaper reports on those crimes that led to sentences of transportation, records of convicts sent overseas will be found in TNA among the following records:

- assizes, where the contractor or master of a ship signed a document agreeing to transport named criminals; the name of the ship and destination are usually included
- hulks, where those convicted awaited transportation
- petitions from convicts and their families or friends appealing against their sentences
- pardons granted to prisoners both before and after transportation
- registers of transported convicts
- expenses incurred in transporting criminals
- medical logs of doctors on board ships carrying transported criminals
- lists of convicts, mainly those sent to New South Wales and Tasmania, but also a few of those sent to Bermuda in 1823–28

In addition, *Hue and Cry* (from 1828), later renamed the *Police Gazette*, carried information on crime and criminals, including those who had escaped custody both in Britain and overseas.

Transportees being put on a prison ship in Portsmouth harbour before embarking on a journey to the other side of the world.

The case of the Tolpuddle Martyrs, transported for forming an association, caused public outrage and demonstrations.

Most official records relating to people transported to the American colonies are held in Britain. The agents who arranged their transportation obtained certificates of landing from the ships' captains, which were returned to London. Some have survived and are now in the CLRO.

LOCATING RECORDS HELD OVERSEAS

Advertisements in newspapers will be the main source of information about convicts transported to the American colonies. They were used to notify settlers of the arrival of British convicts, who were then sold to the settlers in the same way that African slaves were. Although they were generally chained and shackled, some convicts managed to escape, and their masters advertised for their return in local newspapers and on handbills. Of course, not many managed to get away, and those that did would have taken good care to disguise their origins, probably changing their names.

Convicts had the right to appeal to the governor of the state where they were placed and individual petitions may survive in official archives in the USA. There may also be mention of them in the private papers of the plantation owners who took them and for whom they worked. After the expiry of their sentences, some returned to Britain but most would not have been able to afford the fare.

LOCATING RECORDS HELD IN AUSTRALIA

The records relating to convicts sent to Australia are held in state archives, primarily in New South Wales, where the majority of convicts were sent, but also in Tasmania and Norfolk Island, both of which were penal settlements. Anyone who committed a further

offence in Australia was usually transported to Tasmania, which was known as Van Diemen's Land, from 1642 to 1855. The kinds of records include:

- tickets of leave – documents that allowed the convict to find employment, as long as it was in a legal occupation, and exempted him/her from government work
- conditional pardons, which were given to those sentenced to transportation for life. They did not allow the person to return to Britain: he or she was free only in Australia
- absolute pardons, which did allow the person concerned to return, as they gave total freedom. These might be granted in response to legal action in Britain by the friends or family of the convict if there had been a miscarriage of justice, so the researcher needs to check the relevant records in both countries.
- certificates of freedom, issued on completion of sentence

Other records that might mention convicts are magistrates courts and

A certificate of freedom confirmed that a convict had served his sentence.

petitions to the authorities. Convicts had to apply to the Governor of Australia for permission to marry. The musters of land, stock, victualling, servants employed by officers, settlers, military people and convicts made between 1788 and 1837 can also help the genealogist to trace criminal ancestors in Australia.

FURTHER HELP

Coldham, Peter Wilson *Emigrants in Bondage, Complete Book of Emigrants in Bondage 1614–1775* and the Supplement (3 volumes), *More Emigrants in Bondage 1614–1755* (Genealogical Publishing Co., Baltimore) and *The King's Passengers to Maryland and Virginia* (Westminster, Maryland) are directories of convicts transported from England to America.
Hawkings, David T. *Bound for Australia* (Phillimore)
Hawkings, David T. *Criminal Ancestors: A Guide to Historical Criminal Records in England and*

Wales (Sutton Publishing)
Individuals and Family History Societies in Australia have published lists of convicts, sometimes including information about what happened to them subsequently.
TNA Domestic Records Information 78 *Tracing 19th Century Criminals in TNA*
TNA Domestic Records Information 88 *Sources for Convicts and Prisoners, 1100–1986*
TNA Legal Records Information 16 *Transportation to America and the West Indies*

Equity law: property and money

In the various courts dealing with property and money are cases that can throw light on the extent of an ancestor's wealth, and on relationships with family, friends and neighbours.

THE DIFFERENT COURTS OF EQUITY

The medieval General Eyre started out to hear cases concerned with civil matters, particularly land.

The Court of Exchequer, set up in the 12th century, heard cases relating to money, especially those that might affect the Crown's revenue. This was defined widely – it could include cases concerning mineral rights, debts and tithes. In 1841, this court was abolished and its functions transferred to the Chancery Court.

The Court of Common Pleas was created in 1215 as a direct result of the Magna Carta, and lasted until 1875, when it became part of the High Court of Justice. In 1880, during

LEFT Signing a lease, if it was badly drawn up or not registered properly, could involve a man in lengthy litigation. It might even continue after his death.

BELOW LEFT A government bond raising money to invest in the South Seas Company, which crashed in 1720, a few months after this bond was issued. Many people were financially ruined.

another reorganization of the legal system, it transferred into the Queen's Bench Division. It heard disputes over land or debts in which the Crown was not involved.

The Court of Chancery was established towards the end of the 14th century. It mainly dealt with disputes over land, both when the Crown was involved and when two private individuals were in dispute. It also had a function of acting on behalf of those who were mentally incapable of looking after their own interests, through either mental incapacity ("idiots") or mental illness ("lunatics") after the Court of Wards was abolished.

The stages of an equity case

The process of cases in the courts of Exchequer and Chancery was in seven stages. *The Bill of Complaint* (1) was drawn up by the plaintiff, setting out the case. If the litigant was the Crown, it was called an "information". It was sent to the defendant, who gave an *answer* (2), which was sent to the plaintiff, who issued a *rejoinder* (3). This went back to the defendant, who issued a *replication* (4). (These last two stages might be repeated as the two parties made claims and counter-claims.) If the parties decided to proceed, the next stage was to draw up *interrogatories* (5) – a series of questions from both parties, which were either sent to witnesses or put to them in court. The deponents (witnesses) produced their *depositions* (6). The judges then considered the evidence and finally produced their *decree/order/sentence* (7).

It was a long and cumbersome process, and at any stage the parties might decide to withdraw the case or settle out of court. If either of the parties was unhappy with the conduct (rather than the verdict) of the hearings, the case might go to appeal to the Court of King's/Queen's Bench (Plea Side).

RESEARCHING THE COURTS OF EQUITY RECORDS

There are calendars to the cases in TNA, where all the records are held, but the records of these courts are complicated to use, and papers to a case might not be filed together. The Bill of Complaint, the interrogatories and the answers may all be found in different files.

Charles Bernau (1878–1961) drew up a card index to Chancery proceedings, covering plaintiffs and defendants, as well as an index to Exchequer cases for 1558–1695. It is not immediately

obvious how the index relates to TNA's classification system, so you need to understand how the Bernau Index works. There is a microfilm copy of the index in the Society of Genealogists (SoG), and the Church of Jesus Christ of Latter-day Saints (LDS) also has a film copy, which can be consulted at their Family History Centers.

The Great Card Index in the SoG contains some references to equity cases. It also has an index of Exchequer proceedings continuing from the Bernau Index up to 1800.

The Court House, Chancery, depicted here c.1808–c.1811, dealt with property cases and was notorious for the slowness of its business.

Large families might create an entail to prevent estates being divided.

Mortgages

There were other, more straightforward, ways of buying property, of which the mortgage is still familiar today. The buyer borrows a sum of money in order to purchase property, agreeing to pay it back in a specified term of years. If the buyer is unable to repay the amount, the lender of the money can foreclose and the property will be sold to recover the loan.

Estates in fee entail

Creating an entail became a popular way of preventing the lands of Cavaliers being confiscated during the Interregnum. Later they were used in order to prevent large estates being broken up and sold off, perhaps by a spendthrift son, or passing away from the family if only a daughter were left to inherit. Until the 1878 Married Women's Property Act, everything a woman owned became her husband's on their marriage.

An entail was set up by stating in a document, usually a will, that the land should be passed down through a specified series of people, who did not become owners but were life tenants. Mortgages could not be raised on the property. This could involve creating a trust administered by named people to ensure that the original owner's wishes were respected. Alternatively, there might be a settlement that, in addition to creating the entail, detailed such other matters as daughters' dowries, widows' pensions, sums of money given to younger sons, etc.

The properties of landed gentry were often not divided up between the chidren as this would devalue the estate.

Entails could be broken by a private Act of Parliament or by a recovery. From the 1870s, there have been Acts to rule that settlements cannot be perpetual: they can last only until the coming of age of an unborn person. A man might therefore leave his property entailed only on his son and on any sons his son might have after the man's death. What often happened in practice was that, as soon as the son's son became 21, pressure was put on him by the trustees to recreate the entail. This pressure usually involved the trustees refusing to hand over any money until he agreed.

Sales and advertisements

Information on property transfer may also come from details of sales, either in estate papers or in newspapers. These might be the result of a number of events, such as the end of a tenancy, the effects of bankruptcy or the foreclosure of a mortgage. Sometimes a family might simply need to realize the capital tied up in the property.

INHERITANCE

Other countries, such as Scotland, had strict inheritance laws, but in England and Wales a person was, generally, free to leave property to anyone he or she chose (unless the estate was entailed). It is therefore not always the most obvious person who inherits property and money, especially in the absence of a direct heir. A surprisingly large proportion of the landed gentry either never married or left no children to inherit. It has been estimated that in the 18th century about a fifth of all property was not passed to an eldest son.

RIGHT Signing the marriage register used to have significant implications for the bride, as she frequently signed away her name, and also all her property, to her husband.

It was also the custom, in England at least, not to divide up the property between children, since, over a few generations, this division would mean that individuals' holdings of land would be uneconomically small and might therefore be sold off.

A combination of both these factors led to considerable property either being left to a daughter or passing to a more distant relative, such as a male cousin or nephew. If either of the latter were descended from a female member of a family, he would have to change his name in order to benefit from the legacy so that the property owner's name would not die out. The family historian therefore needs to be aware that the name he or she bears might not have been the one with which the family started out.

MARITAL PROPERTY

There is another practice that researchers need to bear in mind: most families preferred to marry a rich heiress to an equally or better endowed man. This led to couples owning houses and lands in different parts of England. The wife's property might be used to accommodate relatives or as a source of potential income in times of financial hardship. This needs to be borne in mind by those who are researching how an ancestor came by a house, as well as those investigating their descent from the property owners.

CHANGE OF NAME

From the end of the 19th century, those who wished to make a formal declaration, perhaps because the inheritance of property was dependent on taking a particular name, could do so by deed poll and, after 1914, by making an announcement in the *London Gazette*. Before that, however, it was simply a matter of using the new name. People have always been free to call themselves what they wish, unless a new name is for fraudulent purposes.

There may be a number of other reasons for wishing to change a name, however: a pseudonym for professional purposes; the commemoration of a relative. The family historian should not assume a name change only means marriage or inheritance.

169

INSURANCE

One of the many avenues to explore in researching your ancestor's property is insurance. The first fire insurance companies appeared in London not long after the city's Great Fire in 1666, and provincial companies were established from the early 18th century. Some businesses restricted their interests to their immediate area, while others, especially the London-based ones, grew into national organizations with local agents.

Maps produced for the insurance companies, which were very detailed, can provide a great deal of information about where your ancestors lived, and the insurance records themselves give indications of the size and extent of the property.

TENANTS' RECORDS

Even if your ancestors were not landowners, there may be information about them in the records of those who owned the land on which they lived. Many jobs brought the right to housing – so-called tied properties – especially in the countryside on large agricultural estates. In cities, people may have lived in rented property owned by an organization, such as the Church, a charity or a large company, or even an individual employer such as a shop or innkeeper.

REGISTRATION OF TITLE DEEDS

Proving ownership of land and the exact extent of the property is problematic in the absence of a written document. Documents can be stolen or illegally acquired, so the practice of noting in public records details of changes in land ownership began in medieval times. A statute of 1536 laid down that sales of land were not valid unless a deed was produced and

LEFT William Shakespeare was not only a successful playwright but also a shrewd investor in property around his home town, Stratford-upon-Avon.

OPPOSITE Registering deeds to prove ownership when land was sold became a legal obligation in 1536.

enrolled within six months either in a local court or in Westminster. The regulation did not cover leasehold or copyhold land, which means that lease and release agreements were often used to evade enrolment.

A national land registry was set up in 1862, but entries were made only on a voluntary basis until 1937, when it became compulsory. HM Land Registry gives legal title to property in England and Wales. The Land Registry is not open to the general public.

Yorkshire and Middlesex Deeds Registries

Acts of Parliament at the beginning of the 18th century required the registration of all documents, such as deeds, wills or conveyances, affecting freehold land and land leased for more than 21 years in Yorkshire and Middlesex (excluding the City of London). These are the only British counties to have been obliged to create registers of deeds. They cover 1704–1970 in Yorkshire and 1709–1938 in Middlesex.

LOCATING ESTATE PAPERS AND TITLE DEEDS

Estate papers may be in a number of repositories. Some are still with the organizations or families in question, especially if they still occupy the property. Others have been deposited at CROs or libraries. The National Archives can help to locate them. In addition to estate papers, check whether there are any manorial records in the area.

The National Archives has a large collection of deeds, divided between many classes. The Middlesex Deeds Registry is in the LMA, the North Riding of Yorkshire in the CRO in Northallerton, the East Riding in Beverley and the West Riding in Wakefield. Details of land transfers

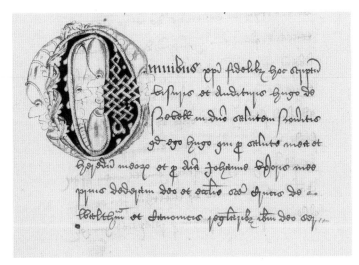

in all counties should be in the relevant CRO. Not all land will appear in the registries. If, for example, the ownership or lease has not been transferred since 1899, there would have been no legal obligation to record it.

THE ACQUISITION OF WEALTH

Methods of acquiring money, which usually brought a rise in social status, varied over time. In the 16th and early 17th century, corruption meant that those with some kind of official job were in the best position to exploit that to enrich themselves. The increase in and cost of legal actions (many over property) meant that lawyers also derived financial benefits.

From the mid-17th century, the pickings from wars gave senior members of the Army and Navy great wealth. The growth of the British Empire from the 18th century and the Industrial Revolution in the 19th enriched not only traders, particularly those who worked in the slave trade or in India, and businessmen, but also bankers, who dealt with all the money. Finally, politics, then as now, has always been a potentially lucrative area

of life. The family historian needs to ask where an ancestor's wealth came from as well as how it was spent, for further avenues of research to explore. Perhaps there may be money or estates "in chancery" awaiting the family historian, but this is very rare.

FURTHER HELP

Cornwall, Julian *An Introduction to Reading Old Title Deeds* (FFHS)
County Hall, Northallerton, North Yorkshire DL7 8AF
www.northyorks.gov.uk
East Riding Archives, County Hall, Beverley, East Yorkshire HU17 9RA
www.eastriding.gov.uk
GL *Fire Insurance Records at Guildhall Library*
LMA Information Leaflet No. 7 *The Middlesex Deeds Registry 1709–1938*
TNA Domestic Records Information 86 *Enclosure Awards*
TNA Legal Records Information 2 *Feet of Fines 1182–1833*
TNA Legal Records Information 21 *Money (Funds) in Court*
West Yorkshire Archives Services
www.archives.wyjs.org.uk (This is the website for a consortium of record offices in the area.)

Taxes

Originally only raised when the government needed money, over the centuries, taxes have become a permanent part of most people's lives.

LAND TAXES

Although people move around, land stays where it is, which makes it easy to tax. The value and size of properties taxed changed over the years, and anyone not paying the tax they owed was taken to court.

A history of land taxation

The first tax on land, levied on both those who owned it and those who benefited from it by living on it or by earning their income from it, was introduced in 1692. It was intended only as a temporary measure in order to fund the current war against France, but it was renewed again and again. Although this tax was generally called "land tax", movable property was included in assessments until 1833.

Survival of records until 1780 is patchy. From this date, copies were generally made for the quarter sessions in order to establish who was entitled to vote, although some courts had been keeping earlier records since an Act of 1745. Tax was levied only on occupied land.

Until 1798, parliament voted on the continuation of land tax annually, but after that it became a permanent tax. People could choose to pay a lump sum equivalent to a number of years' tax to redeem their obligation, rather than paying annually, although they went on being included in lists because their right to vote depended on property. Redemption was made compulsory in 1949, and the tax was abolished in 1963.

Locating land tax records

The majority of land tax assessments are found in CROs, but some, especially before 1780, may be found in parish records and private papers. TNA's holdings relating to land tax mainly date from after *c*.1798.

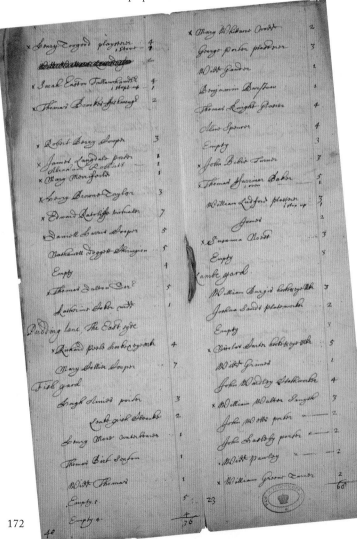

LEFT This Hearth Tax return for 1666 includes Thomas Farrinor, the owner of the hearth in which the Great Fire of London began.

Researching land tax records

The records name both the owner of the land and the occupier or tenant. They also describe the kind of property. Although this may simply say "house", sometimes there is a more precise description, such "shop" or "inn". The sum assessed is also included, and in the early days this gives an accurate assessment of the property's worth. Only the head of the household is generally named. When one person disappears from the records to be replaced by another of the same surname, this is usually an indication that the first person has died and the property has been inherited by a widow or other relative.

OTHER TAXES

Taxes were collected by local officials and passed to central government, which means that there may be copies of records in both CROs and TNA. These taxes were often, like land tax, linked to particular needs, such as to fund a war. Tax records are useful to the family historian for two reasons: they show where an ancestor was living at a particular time, and they give an indication of his, or occasionally her, level of wealth.

A history of taxation in England and Wales

As well as taxing land, the government found that money could be raised by imposing levies on a variety of goods and services. What was liable for tax changes over the years.

The 16th century and before

In medieval and Tudor times, there were two taxes: the lay subsidy and the poll tax. The lay subsidy was a tax levied during 1290–1663 on people not in holy orders, based on their movable goods, land or wages above a certain amount. The poll tax was a sum of money that everyone but the very poor was meant to pay. It was collected by parish officials, so surviving records should be in CROs. Before 1660 there are some records in TNA. The latter records continued from time to time until 1697.

The 17th century

The Restoration in 1660, after the Commonwealth period, saw a number of attempts to raise money for the monarch, of which a tax known as the free and voluntary present to King Charles II was the first. It was raised in autumn 1661. Some people gave money, while others merely promised they would, so there was a follow-up the next year to try to collect these pledges. Most of the king's better-off subjects did eventually contribute.

The hearth tax was the next and most comprehensive tax. It was levied on the occupiers of houses, depending on the number of hearths there were (which is a guide to the size of the property and therefore the wealth of an ancestor.)

Ship money to fund the Navy was collected in ports during 1634–40, and a tax to build thirty warships was collected in 1677.

The marriage tax was collected during 1695–1706. Although called the marriage tax, this was also levied on births and burials. Bachelors over 25 and childless widowers had to pay this tax as well.

The trophy tax, to pay for military drums and colours, was levied during 1690–1715.

The 18th century

From the 18th century, the government generally preferred to tax expenditure. Over the years it chose a variety of luxury goods, so records relating to them will include mainly the names of the well-to-do. Tax that was levied on goods (such as alcohol) at source did not, of course, generate records relating to individuals. Those taxes that did, include:

- window tax (1696–1851). Not many records survive; those that do date from after 1715 and do not always include names.
- apprenticeships 1710–1808
- duty on carriages (1742–82)
- duty on silver plate (1756–77)
- employers of servants: those of male servants were taxed during 1777–1830 and those of female servants during 1785–1792. Occasionally the lists contain the names of the servants themselves.
- horses for riding or husbandry (1784–1830)
- armorial bearings (i.e. a coat-of-arms) (1793–1830)
- ownership of dogs (1796–1830)

The 19th and 20th centuries

Income tax looms large in all our lives today, but it was not levied on most people until the beginning of the 20th century, though it began in 1799 to fund the Napoleonic Wars. It was abolished in 1815 but reintroduced in 1842.

TNA records are closed for 75 years, so few records from the 20th century are open to researchers. The records that are available mainly relate to government and royal employees, but there are samples of payments under Schedule D (self-employed people) for 1887–1918. There are also records of people who were imprisoned during the 19th century for non-payment of taxes.

FURTHER HELP

Gibson, Jeremy *The Hearth Tax and Other Later Stuart Tax Lists and the Association Oath Rolls* (FFHS)
Gibson, Jeremy and Mills, Dennis *Land Tax Assessments c.1690–c.1950* (FFHS)

Customs and Excise and the Coastguard

The increasing number of taxes being levied on the British people had to be collected by someone, and so the Board of Customs and the Board of Excise were set up to collect tax on imported and home-produced goods respectively. The Coastguard aided the Customs by helping to prevent smuggling, as well as protecting Britain's shores against invasion.

A HISTORY OF CUSTOMS AND EXCISE

The Board of Customs had the responsibility for collecting taxes on imported goods from medieval times. Throughout the 17th and 18th centuries, there were high duties on alcohol, tea, tobacco and various luxury

ABOVE The Customs House on the Thames in London was one of hundreds in ports around the British Isles.

BELOW A page from the records of the Board of Customs and Excise, Newcastle Upon Tyne, 1771–1772.

Date of the Original Orders	Date of ye Orders for continuing ye Allowances to the present Officers	Officers' Names	Employments	Place of Residence	Established Salaries ye annum	Incident Salaries ye annum
1708 September 30.	1769 December 19.	Langdale Sunderland	Collector	Newcastle	100	30
1770 March 17.	1770 March 17.	Nicholas Armstrong	Riding Surveyor	Cullercoats	60	40
1723 Novem. 28.		Vacant by the Death of William Galway 20th July 1771.	Boatman North Shield	North Shields		25
Do.	1771 May 10.	William Thoburn	Do.	Do.	Howdenpans	25
1724/5 Jan.y 16	1767 Octo. 27.	John Shotton	Do.	Newcastle	South Shields	25
Do.	1765 May 9.	William Robson	Do.	Shield	Do.	20
Do.	1770 July 5.	Ralph Robson	Do.	N. Shields	North Shields	25
Do.	1771 May 14	William Ward	Do.	So. Shields	South Shields	25
1726 April 2.	1726 April 2.	John Lawson	Do.	Do.	Do.	25
Do.	1768 July 12.	Jeff. Dennison	Do.	Do.	Do.	25
February 16.	1750 April 2.	Rob. Jackson	Coll. McQueens Dittisman Content at Blyth	Blyth oct.		40
Do.	1760 February 19	John Robinson	Dittism at Do.			30
1736 July 8. Do.	1761 February 26.	John Wilson	Tidesurveyor at Do.	Do.	30	10
1726 May 16.	1766 November 18.	William Hague	Tidesman	Do.	10	20
1725/6 Feb. 7. 10.	1764 September 28.	William Atwell	Boatman at Blyth	Do.		25
Do.	1766 Novem. 22.	Peter Craithwaite	Do.	Do.		20
1726 April 21.	1726 April 21.	Joseph Ingo	Do.	Do.		25
1726 Do. 21.	1732 Septem. 20.	Henry Byng	Do.	Do.	Howdenpans	25
1723 Octo. 22.	1762 February 7.	John Wilkinson	Do.	at Cammas	Cammas	20
Do.	1763 June 14.	William Sample	Do.	Do.	Do.	20
1729 July 12.	1765 May 1.	Geo. Clennell	Riding Officer	Cullercoats		40
1733 Septem. 8.	1755 June 21.	William Hall	Nightwatchman	Newcastle		18. 5
Do.	1764 April 21.	Tho. Snowball	Do.	Do.		18. 5
1769 Aug. 22.	1769 Aug. 22.	Jn. Fawcett	Waiter & Searcher R. P.	Cramell. L. S.	25. 5. L. 285	5. 591. 10

items, such as lace. A permanent force, known as preventative officers, was established in 1698 along the coasts of Kent and Sussex, which were nearest to Europe. In addition to collecting levies, these men had, in times of war, a role in checking passengers, who might be spies, and keeping an eye out for potential invasions. From the end of the 18th century, they covered the whole of England and Wales. Scotland had a separate Customs service.

The Board of Customs had offices in ports and their own ships to intercept smugglers off shore. They also had a force of men called riding officers throughout the counties, whose job was to track goods that had evaded the Customs officers.

The Board of Excise was responsible for the collection of taxes on goods produced in the United Kingdom. Records date from 1695. It also had ships of its own and employed its own riding officers, who were stationed all over the country.

Riding officers were not, naturally enough, popular men. They were therefore posted away from their place of origin so that links of family and friendship would not corrupt them. Inevitably, however, some were bribed.

In 1809, the government created another body – the Preventative Water Guard – which was supposed both to intercept smugglers at sea and check the Customs' vessels (to make sure that they weren't colluding with the smugglers, or smuggling themselves). By 1816, a decision to appoint shore-based men as a back-up force was made, resulting in the Coast Blockade.

The degree of confusion resulting from this duplication of bodies all carrying out the same functions needed to be resolved. In 1821, the Coast guard was formed by the amalgamation of the Preventative Water Guard,

ABOVE Tea was regarded as a luxury and was therefore taxed, which made it worth smuggling.

LEFT Customs officers row out to a ship before it can unload its cargo.

the revenue cruisers and the riding officers. It came under the authority of the Board of Customs. Ten years later, the Coast Blockade was also absorbed into the Coastguard.

THE COASTGUARD

The Coastguard had a double role: it was there partly to protect Britain against foreign invaders and partly to prevent smuggled goods being brought ashore. In the last half of the

19th century, other duties were added, including assisting vessels in distress and taking over wrecked ships. As many employees had joined the Coastguard after leaving the Navy, they also formed a reserve of seamen who could be called up in wartime.

Locating Customs, Excise and Coastguard records

Most records are in The National Archives, but some CROs have records from ports in their counties.

Trials of smugglers and dealers in illicit goods will be found in the usual records relating to criminals, including newspaper reports. These may include testimony from government officials.

People within the Customs, Excise and Coastguard were entitled to pensions, and some genealogical information may be found in them.

FURTHER HELP

TNA Domestic Records Information 38 *Customs, Excise, Tax Collectors and Civil Servants*
TNA Military Records Information 44 *The Coastguard*
Rodger, N.A.M. *Naval Records for Genealogists* (TNA Handbook No. 22 1988)

Rich man, poor man checklist

The checklist opposite will help in identifying and locating records that are likely to mention ancestors according to their wealth and social standing. It serves as a reminder of places to look but is not exhaustive, and you need to remember that people of all incomes and classes can be found in the same documents. Criminal records, for example, are more likely to include the rich and middle-classes as victims of crime or on juries and the poor as criminals, because of the link between crime and poverty. But even well-off people turned to crime so do not assume that no one rich will be found in the dock. People from all classes of society could fall on hard times and find themselves in prison for debt, or in receipt of charity.

CLASS AND MONEY

In Britain the determining factors of social status were class and money. The two did not necessarily go together: there were many people who were richer than members of the aristocracy but were not admitted to the upper echelons of society, because their money came from trade. Their well-endowed children, however, would be welcomed in marriage by impoverished aristocrats. The practice of leaving the bulk of the family property and money to the eldest son or a single heir meant that younger sons and daughters whose fathers could not afford to give them a good dowry could easily slip down the class hierarchy. Between the rich and the poor existed the middle classes. The upper middle-class consisted of people at the top of their profession or trade, like university professors. The middle-middle class were professionals who were climbing the ladder. The lower-middle class were those who were starting out, like clerks and small shopkeepers. Members of the middle classes were mainly either on the way up or down. Within the working class there were skilled artisans, such as shoemakers and tailors, and unskilled workers of all kinds. The family historian needs to be alert to this social mobility and decide in which direction his or her forebears were travelling, because this will affect the type of documents where mention of them will be found.

INCOMES

In the late 17th century a Duke's income was some £3,200 per year. A member of the landed gentry had about £280, while a prosperous merchant might obtain £400. Officers in the armed forces got an average of £70, while common seamen earned £20 and soldiers £14. The average clergyman had about the same as a small farmer, shopkeeper or artisan, between £40-£50. At the bottom of the social scale were labourers and paupers who could expect only £6 10s (£6.50).

By the end of the 19th century, these amounts had gone up. This was partly due to inflation but more to the growth of the country's wealth. The gap between rich and poor greatly increased over the two centuries. It is difficult to know exactly how much those at the top of the hierarchy received, as the better-off considered discussion of money to be vulgar. The

The possessions of the upper classes, such as land, horses and carriages, and even servants, were subject to taxation.

The poor received alms, but even well-off people might be reduced to receiving charity.

Duke of Westminster, however, received about £250,000 a year solely from the properties he owned in London, which formed only part of his income. The average clergyman got about £400 a year, skilled workers perhaps £150. Around these averages, however, there were great variations.

More uniform were the incomes of those at the bottom of the scale. Factory workers, as young as seven, started on about £6 p.a. while a skilled man might earn £78. A general labourer's family would have a total income of just over £1 a week, perhaps £55 per year, but this would include money

The destitute and homeless often had no alternative to begging.

earned by the wife and children working at home with him. Even very young children might bring in a couple of pennies a week by running errands, scavenging rubbish and the like if they lived in a town or city. In the countryside, agricultural labourers earned about £40 but would be able to grow some of their own food and gather fuel. Women and children could supplement the family's income by doing work, such as at harvest, for a daily rate of 9d or 1s (4p or 5p). With the growth of trade unionism throughout the 20th century, wages for a wide range of jobs became more standard.

Where to look: for the rich or the poor

THE UPPER CLASSES	Kinds of Records	Location of Records
National Government posts	Government records	TNA, CRO
Land ownership	Deeds	CRO, private papers
Taxes	Government records Parish records	TNA, CRO
Enclosure awards	Government records Quarter sessions	TNA, CRO
Manors	Manorial records	Private papers, TNA, CRO
Elections	Poll books	CRO
Armed Services (as officers)	Service records	TNA
Bank accounts	Banks	Banks' own archives, CRO
Investments	Government bonds, companies	TNA, CRO, companies' own archives
Charities (as patrons)	Charity records	CROs, charities' own archives

THE MIDDLE CLASSES	Kinds of Records	Location of Records
Taxes	Government records Parish records	TNA, CRO
Rates	Ratebooks	CRO
Parish officials and administrators	Parish records	CRO
Professional memberships and licences to practise	Guilds, professional and trade associations, freemasons	Organisations' own archives, CRO, Borough archives
Armed services (as officers & NCOs)	Government records	TNA

	Kinds of Records	Location of Records
Elections	Poll books	CRO
Trials (as jurors)	Quarter Sessions, Assizes	TNA, CRO
Recipients of charity, especially linked to trade	Charity and almshouse records	Charities' own archives, CRO

THE WORKING CLASSES		
Guild membership	Guild records	Guild archives, CRO, borough archives
Licences to practise	Quarter Sessions	CRO
Memberships of friendly societies & trade unions	Society and union records	Organisations' own archives, CROs, university libraries
Armed services (as non-officers)	Government records	TNA
Militia	Quarter Sessions, parish records	CRO
Settlement examinations and removal orders	Parish records, Quarter Sessions	CRO
Bastardy examinations and bonds	Parish records, Quarter Sessions	CRO
Workhouses	Parish records	CRO
Recipients of charity	Charity records	Charities' own archives, CRO
Trials	Quarter Sessions, Assizes	CRO, TNA
Inmates of prisons	Prison records	CRO, TNA

Migrant Ancestors

Before the 20th century, Britain had always had a relatively open-door policy, though it did keep a fairly close eye on immigrants and foreigners once they were here. This is fortunate for the family historian, because references to immigrants can be found for the last 600 years or so.

Researching migrant ancestors

Conditions in their home countries, such as religious persecution, political upheavals or recessions, brought foreigners to Britain, so the family historian needs to be aware of what was happening both in Britain and abroad in order to deduce when ancestors might have arrived, and why. This will give clues about which records to investigate.

DENIZATION AND NATURALISATION

People who arrived from overseas could apply either for a patent of denization, which was granted by the sovereign and gave the right to live in Britain, or

Naturalisation certificates can provide details about the applicant and their family.

for naturalisation, which was conferred by an Act of Parliament and gave foreigners citizenship (i.e. the full rights of the native-born). These applications were not necessary for those coming from the expanding British Empire, who were automatically citizens and therefore did not need any special arrangements to be made. It was not until the middle of the 20th century that there were limits put on immigration from the Commonwealth.

It was not obligatory to get either denization or naturalisation, and many people, especially the poorer ones, did not bother.

Original documents are in The National Archives (TNA), but denizations and naturalisations before 1800 have been published by the Huguenot Society of London and include all foreigners, not just Huguenots. After 1800 there are indexes in TNA.

LEGISLATION

It is usually a war that makes governments aware of aliens (people who come to a foreign country but do not intend to settle there) and immigrants (people who come to a foreign country in order to settle there), who might be spies or potential troublemakers. For this reason, new legislation is usually connected with some form of hostilities and tends to be most enthusiastically applied in times of crisis. In times of economic hardship, restrictions may be brought on foreigners' employment in order to protect the interests of the indigenous population. These restrictions also produce useful records.

The 16th century

There was relatively little legislation affecting the registration of foreigners in Britain during this period. Most of the laws that applied to people from other countries concerned money and their property and employment rights under the law. Regular surveys were made of strangers in London, but elsewhere very little official government documentation of immigrants survives.

Guilds varied in their willingness to admit strangers to the freedom of their towns and cities, and the records of the guilds, particularly those in the City of London, contain a number of cases of enrolled immigrants.

Acts of naturalisation in this period often related to the children of English people born abroad, as there was uncertainty about whether it was the parents' nationality or the child's place of birth that was more important in establishing the child's legal position.

The 17th century

Fears that foreigners would work for less money than native-born British people continued, especially in London. There was an economic crisis in the early years of the century, and this caused old laws that had fallen into disuse to be reapplied. Aliens, and those people employing them, may therefore be found in records from Quarter and Borough Sessions.

A survey of strangers was carried out in 1622, and lists for several provincial towns, as well as London, do still survive in TNA. The London returns have been published by the Huguenot Society.

The 18th century

In 1793, the French Wars brought the first requirement for foreigners arriving in ports to register themselves immediately. They also had to notify the local Justices of the Peace (JPs) of their presence. In 1797, householders had to tell parish officials of any aliens in their homes. This information was recorded at Quarter Sessions, which should be found in CROs.

The 19th century

The Napoleonic Wars ended in 1815, but regulations about registration in ports and notifications to JPs continued. In 1826, the Aliens Act introduced certificates for those arriving in Britain, which had to be completed by the master of the ship on which they arrived. The certificates themselves have not survived before 1836, but there is an index to them in TNA.

The 20th century

In 1914, the outbreak of World War I brought in a requirement for all aliens to register with the local police force. Surviving registration cards will be with police records, most of which have been deposited in the relevant CRO, apart from the Metropolitan Police records, which are in TNA.

RESEARCHING MIGRANT ANCESTORS

The regulations applying to immigrants changed over the years, so the most important fact to establish, therefore, is the approximate date of an ancestor's arrival in Britain.

If the birthplace of a child is somewhere in Britain, but his or her parents are recorded as having been born overseas, then census returns in the 19th century may help in estimating the date of their arrival. If you find "British subject" as an entry in the

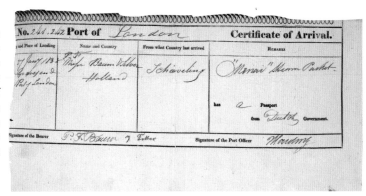

A certificate of arrival shows from which port an immigrant sailed, but this may not be the country of origin.

"birthplace" column in the census returns, it should also state the country of birth. If it doesn't, check the indexes to denization and naturalisation in TNA. If your ancestor is not there, he or she could well have been born in British territories overseas.

Before the Act of Union in 1707 (which united England, Wales and Scotland to create the United Kingdom of Great Britain), and a further Act in 1801 (which created the United Kingdom of Great Britain and Ireland), Scots and Irish people were also regarded as aliens and so can be found in lists of strangers.

The certificates of arrival completed between 1826 and 1905 state the last overseas port from which the people sailed. This may not, however, have been where they originally came from, since emigrations were often undertaken in stages.

The larger foreign communities had charities to assist their compatriots, so these records should also be consulted. The French Huguenots, for example, established charities to care for the old and infirm, to educate children and to provide money to help Huguenots from particular areas of France. It

was usually on first arrival or at the end of their lives that people needed most assistance.

Information supplied to the government relates only to people arriving by sea until 1951. There are no records of airline passengers in TNA.

Those intending to research their immigrant ancestors in the country from which they originated should try to find a book written for genealogists in that country, since this is likely to contain the best advice and information.

FURTHER HELP

Currer-Briggs, Noel *Worldwide Family History* (Routledge & Kegan Paul) contains a broad outline of records of interest to the family historian intending to do research in overseas archives. It has a large section on immigrants in America.
Huguenot Society of London Quarto Series Vols VIII, X, XVIII, XXV. XXVII, LVII
Kershaw, Roger and Pearsall, Mark *Immigrants and Aliens* (TNA 2000)
TNA Domestic Records Information 49 *Grants of British Nationality*
TNA Domestic Records Information 50 *Immigrants*

Jewish ancestors

Jewish ancestry is inherited through the female line, which is very logical, since, as genealogists agree, maternity is a matter of fact, paternity a matter of opinion. Judaism, unlike Christianity, does not seek converts. Until the 20th century, Jews married mainly within their own communities. Those who "married out" were those who had decided to leave their faith. This was sometimes because certain professions were barred to them, and sometimes because of genuine conversion.

The interior of the Spanish and Portuguese synagogue in London in the 18th century.

THE ARRIVAL OF JEWISH MIGRANTS

Until World War II, Jews faced at best discrimination and at worst active persecution in Europe. Britain was relatively tolerant, so many Jews found refuge here, either permanently or as a staging post on the way to America.

The Middle Ages to the 17th century

There was a Jewish community in Britain in medieval times, but in 1290 they were expelled from the country. Some 350 years later, they were allowed to re-enter. In the intervening years, a few came illegally from Spain and Portugal and pretended to be Roman Catholics: they attended Mass for show, while practising their own religion secretly. They were known as New Christians. The declaration of war against Spain in 1654 was the triggering factor in revealing their true faith, as the Government now believed them to be enemy aliens as well as Catholics, who were always regarded with fear and suspicion. In 1656, Jews were allowed to settle in Britain legally.

The 18th century

In 1701, the first arrivals built a synagogue in Bevis Marks, just outside the city wall in London. They were followed by others, who settled in other parts of Britain, though the main community was in London.

There were two main branches of Jewish immigrants. The first branch was the Sephardim, who were largely of Portuguese and Spanish origins. After being expelled from the Iberian peninsula, they went to Holland and then to England, where they settled in London. The second branch was the Ashkenazim, who came from Eastern Europe, particularly Poland. All the communities outside London were Ashkenazim.

Jewish people brought with them a range of skills, but there were many obstacles to their existence in London. They were forbidden by city ordinances to be apprenticed to a craft (and therefore excluded from the freedom of the City of London), and the

number who could trade as city merchants was limited. This meant that most of their work had to be done outside the square mile. Their inability to comply with the requirement for public officials to take the sacrament in an Anglican church and to swear an oath of allegiance also restricted their employment possibilities.

There was a sizeable Jewish presence in Devon and Cornwall, and the next synagogue to be built was in Plymouth, Devon, in 1762. In the north of England, the first settlement, by 1753, was in Liverpool, and there were communities in the north-east, of which Sunderland (around 1770) was the first. The need for a minimum number of ten men to establish a religious prayer group (called a *minyan*) meant that the Jews tended either to settle together in small communities, where they could establish a *minyan*, or, having settled separately, to choose a particular area in which to meet for their *minyan*.

The 19th century

Following political upheavals in the mid-19th century, more Jews fled to Britain as a first step to emigrating to America. Some remained in Britain rather than going on across the Atlantic. Jews from the Baltic States took advantage of the Baltic trade routes to come to Britain, landing at ports in the north-east, such as Newcastle (1830) and the Tyneside area, and Hull, where they set up communities.

The Industrial Revolution in Britain, which began around 1810, brought new employment opportunities in cotton and wool mills, so Jews began to move away from ports to places further inland, such as Leeds, Birmingham and Manchester (which remains the largest Jewish community in Britain outside London).

Political tensions and persecutions in Russia after 1881 brought the next influx of Jewish refugees. Although most of these settled in London, especially Whitechapel, some joined communities elsewhere. Before the middle of the 19th century, all Jews in Britain followed the Orthodox tradition. The first synagogue of the Reform movement was built in 1870 in London.

The 20th century

The third major wave of immigration began in the 1930s, as anti-semitism revived in Germany. The end of World War II brought some survivors of the concentration camps to Britain, while many others went to America. Postwar, there has been a trend towards assimilation of Jews into the mainstream of secular British society.

RESEARCHING JEWISH ANCESTORS

Britain was almost permanently at war with Spain before the 19th century, and, although relations were better

Many Jewish refugees fled from Germany before World War II.

with Portugal, relatively few non-Jewish people outside the royal court or diplomatic corps came from either country. A Spanish or Portuguese name from this time therefore suggests Sephardic origins.

The various synagogues served different communities, so finding out when Jewish ancestors came to Britain, and where they came from, will help to identify the synagogue most likely to have records of them.

Jewish records use a different calendar. To find the Jewish calendar number for the current year, add 3760 to it. When trying to work out in which year of the Gregorian calendar a Jewish document was written, subtract 3760.

The main types of records relating to Jewish rites of passage are the circumcision record (for boys), kept by the person (the *mohel*) who carried it out, the marriage contract, or *ketubah*, which was generally kept by the wife's family, and the burial certificate.

Like other immigrant groups, the Jews set up their own charities and schools. The first school, the Jews' Free School, was opened in London in

1732. Numerous Jewish charities were established to help their communities, such as Food for the Jewish Poor, which was started in Spitalfields in London in 1854.

Jewish people can be found in the same civil and criminal records as everyone else, such as returns of aliens, denization and naturalisation papers, wills, coroners' inquests, trials at the Old Bailey and in other courts. They are also mentioned in newspapers, of course, including the *Jewish Chronicle*, which began in 1844. Other records relating to the London communities, such as those of the synagogues, are stored in the London Metropolitan Archives (LMA), but they can be seen only with the permission of the Office of the Chief Rabbi or the person who deposited them. The LMA produces a leaflet with details.

Some Jews asked for their children to be recorded in parish registers in order to establish their right to settlement under the Poor Laws. These children were not, of course, baptized, but details of their births were entered. A few were converted to Christianity and baptized as adults.

FURTHER HELP

Gandy, Michael *My Ancestor Was Jewish: How can I find out more about him?* (SoG)
London Metropolitan Archives *Archives of the Anglo-Jewish Community at London Metropolitan Archives*
TNA Domestic Records Information 76 *Anglo-Jewish History: Sources in the PRO, 18th–20th centuries*
Steel, Don and Samuel, Edgar R. *Sources for Roman Catholic and Jewish Genealogy and Family History* (Phillimore for SoG)
Jewish Museum, Woburn House, Upper Woburn Place, London WC1E 6BT

French ancestors

The English Channel, which separates England and France, is, at its narrowest, only about 80 km (50 miles) wide, so it's hardly surprising that many people in Britain have French ancestry.

THE ARRIVAL OF FRENCH MIGRANTS

Many people have family legends that they came from France "with the Conqueror", the "evidence" being that they have a surname, such as Gascoigne, that suggests that their ancestors came from places in France. It is possible that they were among William's followers, but people came from England to France over the centuries for a variety of reasons. They came for trade purposes or as servants, and there are those who were driven out by religious or political persecution.

The first arrivals

When William the Conqueror arrived in England in 1066, he brought not only his Norman followers but also his language, which quickly became the legal jargon of his adopted country.

The 16th to mid-18th century

The biggest group of French people that came to Britain were the Huguenots (Protestants driven out of their country because of their refusal to convert to Roman Catholicism). Some Huguenots were from France; others (the Walloons) were from the Low Countries (the part of Europe today occupied by the Netherlands, Belgium and Luxembourg).

The first influx came in the last half of the 16th century, but a greater number arrived between the 1680s and the

Huguenots who fled religious persecution in Europe faced a dangerous sea journey before they arrived in England.

middle of the 18th century. They settled mainly in the south of England, with communities in London, Kent, Southampton, the West Country and East Anglia. Records from these places have been published. Individuals and small groups who went to other parts of Britain joined local parish churches. Records relating to them are found in the usual genealogical sources.

Some went to Scotland, where they formed a community in Edinburgh, whose records are lost. Their Protestantism, which was much stricter than that of the Church of England, was close to the Scottish Calvinists and Presbyterians. As a result, most Huguenots seem to have joined the local church communities rather than set up separate places of worship, as they did in England.

Those who settled in Ireland went initially to Dublin. Later, as a reward for

their help in fighting for William III, they were given land at Portarlington. Some Huguenots went to the Channel Islands, which were French-speaking. They also settled in America, Canada and South Africa.

By the middle of the 18th century, Huguenot immigration had virtually ceased because persecution in their own countries had stopped.

The late 18th century

The next influx of French refugees came for political rather than religious reasons, fleeing from France to escape the Reign of Terror that formed part of the French Revolution. While the Huguenots had come mainly from the middle-classes or were skilled tradesmen, these new émigrés were typically from the aristocracy and were Roman Catholics. Unlike the Huguenots, they did not set up separate communities. Many had links with the British aristocracy, who helped them and took them into their own houses. In London, they gravitated to the parish of St Marylebone, where there was a Catholic church. As aristocrats, they did not have the practical skills that a lot of Huguenots had, and, as a result, many of them became teachers.

RESEARCHING FRENCH ANCESTORS

It is important to note that the boundaries of European countries have changed over the centuries, so places in present-day France might not have been in the country at different times in the past.

There is no such thing as a "Huguenot name". Their surnames were the same as their compatriots in France or the Low Countries. This makes it difficult to distinguish the people who left their homes for religious reasons from those who left for other purposes. The British struggled

with foreign surnames, which may be misspelled or appear in different documents in their French or English forms.

The Huguenots set up charities to help the poor of their community and schools to educate their children, and they kept minutes of their church activities. Most of the surviving records and registers of their churches have been published in over fifty volumes by the Huguenot Society. It also has an extensive library of material, documents and private papers.

There is less material on later French immigrants. Some papers relating to those who fled the French Revolution, and also records detailing pensions and charitable payments, are in TNA. Information on French prisoners of war is also held at TNA. Most records relate to the Revolutionary and Napoleonic Wars, but there are some on people taken in previous hostilities.

Very few of the Huguenot churches had their own burial sites, so members of their congregations were interred in the Anglican parish churchyards.

FURTHER HELP

Currier-Briggs, Noel and Gambier, Royston *Huguenot Ancestry* (Phillmore & Co.)
Huguenot Society of Great Britain www.huguenotsociety.org.uk/ publishes a series of books, including transcipts of surviving registers, and the *Proceedings of the Huguenot Society*, a regular journal of articles on aspects of Huguenot history and genealogy.
TNA Military Records Information 29

Prisoners of War in British Hands, 1698–1919
TNA Domestic Records Information 50 *Immigrants*
Huguenot Library, University College London, Gower Street, London WC1E 6BT www.ucl.ac.uk/library/huguenot.htm
Anglo-French Family History Society www.anglo-french-fhs.org/home.htm (for those with non-Huguenot French ancestry).

Significant dates in the history of French immigration into Britain

1066 William the Conqueror arrived from Normandy to take the English throne.
1550 Edward VI granted a charter permitting immigrants and strangers of the reformed religion (the Church of England) the right to hold their own services in England. Most immigrants at this time were from the Low Countries, though some came from France. French churches were established as a result of this charter.
1550 French Church in Threadneedle Street in the City of London founded.
1565 Walloon Church in Norwich established.

1572 Massacre of St Bartholomew's Eve in France brought many Protestant refugees to England.
1598 Edict of Nantes granted French Protestants a measure of toleration, so some refugees returned. Immigration to Britain slowed down.
1661 Erosion of the rights granted to French Protestants under the Edict of Nantes began. Refugees again started to leave France.
1685 Revocation of the Edict of Nantes. Main wave of French Huguenot immigration began.
1750s Local persecutions in the south of France, especially in the Dauphiné, brought the last French

Huguenot refugees.
1789 French Revolution began.
1793–4 Reign of Terror, when anyone thought to oppose the regime's government was executed. This was when most refugees left.
1793 French Revolutionary War declared against Britain, the Netherlands and Spain. This merged into the Napoleonic Wars, which lasted from 1799 to 1815. During this time, some prisoners of war were held in England. Most returned to France, but a few decided to remain.
1945+ Following World War II, many French people settled in Britain, mainly in the London area.

German and Dutch ancestors

The map of Europe changed many times over the centuries in response to wars. The frequent boundary changes mean that some places in present-day Germany and the Netherlands might have been in other countries at some time in the past.

GERMANY AND THE LOW COUNTRIES

During the 16th and 17th centuries until 1648, most of the Low Countries (today's Netherlands, Belgium and Luxembourg) were under Spanish rule, and much of present-day Germany was part of the Hapsburg Empire, ruled from Austria. Other parts of Germany were ruled by Poland. In 1871 Germany was united – previously it had been a collection of independent states.

Belgium, an area ruled first by the Spanish and then by the Austrians, did not exist in its present form until 1839. Today the two communities in Belgium – the Flemings and the Walloons – have different languages and cultures reflecting their separate histories. There was a Flemish community in the City of London in medieval times. In 1550, the Flemings were given their own church at Austin Friars, in the City.

THE ARRIVAL OF GERMAN MIGRANTS

Miners from Germany were invited to come to Wales in the 14th century and to Cumbria in the 16th century, but the largest German community was in London. Most Germans were Lutherans, so the majority of their churches were for this denomination.

In 1707, the Elector of Hanover, one of the German states, became George I. Two years later, wars on the Continent brought a wave of immigration from Germany. Most immigrants remained in Britain for a relatively short time, preferring after a few decades to go to America.

George I, and the kings who followed him, remained rulers of Hanover as well as Britain, so there was a lot of immigration, both from Hanover and the other German states that continued to experience social and economic problems. Although the link with Hanover was severed when Victoria became Queen (women were barred from the Hanoverian throne), her husband, Prince Albert of Saxe-Coburg and Gotha, was another German, and so the close ties between the two countries continued until World War I.

The first Lutheran church was founded in the City in 1669 and served mainly merchants and other business people. Part of Whitechapel, where most immigrants started their lives in Britain, was known as Little Germany. Other German Protestant denominations set up churches in London, but none has survived. There was one German Catholic church (still in existence today). Before it was built German Catholics attended services in the Austrian and Bavarian legation chapels. There was even a German hospital in Dalston, north London, which existed between 1845 and 1948, and a German school in Islington.

Outside the capital, there were German churches in Hull, Bradford, South Shields, Sunderland, Liverpool and Manchester, indicating the locations of other major German communities.

The Dutch king, William of Orange, became King of England in 1688 and was co-ruler with his wife Mary.

Significant dates in the history of German and Dutch immigration into Britain

12th century Flemish community of merchants formed in the City of London.

1281 Hanseatic League formed by a group of German merchants in London.

1550 Church of the Austin Friars in the City of London given to the Dutch Protestant community.

1688 William of Orange invited to take the throne as William III. Ruled Britain with Mary.

1714 The Elector of Hanover became George I, who founded the house of Hanover.

1838 Queen Victoria, whose mother was German, became Queen.

1914 Outbreak of World War I led to internment of Germans resident in Britain.

1930s Political tensions in Germany led to Jewish immigration.

1939 Outbreak of World War II again led to internment of Germans and also the setting up of camps for prisoners of war, some of whom remained in Britain after 1945.

THE ARRIVAL OF DUTCH MIGRANTS

From the early 16th century, Dutch people were brought to East Anglia, where their experience was invaluable in a scheme to drain the Fens, and low-lying land in Essex. When James II was deposed in 1688, his daughter Mary and her husband, William of Orange, who came from the Netherlands, reigned as William III and Mary. Many of his compatriots followed him to Britain, settling especially in East Anglia, where they found other Dutch people and also Dutch-speaking Huguenot communities.

RESEARCHING GERMAN ANCESTORS

In the Returns of Aliens, compiled in the 16th and early 17th centuries, people born in German towns are often called "Dutch".

Ports on the east coast of Britain had long-established links with north-west Europe. Apart from London, Hull was the major trading port with Germany, and most immigrants came through these two ports. So from 1836, aliens' certificates and passenger lists of people arriving through these ports may include your ancestors. As well as people emigrating from Europe, individual sailors from ports in Germany, Scandinavia and the Baltic States might have settled in ports in north-east England and Scotland.

Many German immigrants were actually intending to go on to America. Some never managed to raise the fare, or decided to remain in Britain, but others stayed just long enough to earn the money to travel across the Atlantic. This might have taken some years, so there may be information about them in official sources.

In addition to Christians (Protestant and Roman Catholics), there were many Jewish immigrants from Germany and Eastern Europe, so Jewish records are worth checking too.

Between 1753 and 1837, marriages of Germans living in Britain would have taken place in Church of England parish churches rather than the denominational churches.

Registers of various German chapels and churches were surrendered to the government after 1837, and the originals are in TNA. Transcripts and indexes of some are in the Family Record Centre (FRC); others have been published. Indexes to the four main German churches in London are also available.

When World War I broke out with Germany, there was immense hostility to Germans in Britain, many of whom anglicized their names. Personal announcements of these changes were made in newspapers as a way of proving loyalty to Britain.

RESEARCHING DUTCH ANCESTORS

There was a fairly continuous flow of merchants, sailors and others moving between Britain and the Netherlands. Inevitably, many Dutch people settled in Britain.

As they did not arrive as refugees from problems in their own country (apart from the Huguenots), there are none of the kinds of records generated by mass immigration. Instead, they arrived separately, probably worshipping with their compatriots, marrying and assimilating into British society. Note that the Dutch would have said that they came from the Low Countries or the Netherlands.

From 1753 to 1837, marriages of Dutch living in Britain took place in Church of England parish churches instead of the denominational churches.

FURTHER HELP

LMA Information Leaflet No. 17
The German Community in London
The Anglo-German Family History Society www.feefhs.org.uk/frgagfha.html

Black ancestors

Genealogists are usually aware that they might have ancestors from mainland Europe because of the trade and social links with Britain. Black ancestry is also a distinct possibility.

THE ARRIVAL OF BLACK MIGRANTS

Black people in Britain have a long history: there is evidence that some African soldiers arrived with the Roman army. Britain did not become involved in the slave trade until the middle of the 17th century (although John Hawkins, an Elizabethan naval commander, made three not very successful attempts in the late 1500s to trade in African slaves). There are, however, occasional references to black people from the reign of Henry VIII

LEFT An elaborately dressed black pageboy was fashionable among the wealthy in the 17th and 18th centuries.

BELOW LEFT Ships involved in the slave trade did not bring black people directly to Britain.

onwards. Most were probably captured from the Spanish and Portuguese, who began dealing in African slaves in the 15th century.

The 16th and 17th centuries

When Britain started to colonize America and the West Indies, from the late 16th century, labour was needed to develop the land. At first, indentured servants and criminals were used, but they found the climate difficult and there were not enough of them. The solution was to import slaves from Africa, and in 1662 the Royal African Company was formed from groups of merchants who had begun to trade in slaves and was given a charter to operate. In 1697 its monopoly was withdrawn.

The 18th century

The removal of the Royal African Company's monopoly meant that the 18th century saw a great increase in the number of

black people shipped from Africa to British possessions in the New World. There the majority worked in the fields on plantations, but others became domestic servants and sailors. It was people from these latter groups who came to Britain. The domestic servants were brought by plantation owners returning home, either on business or to settle here.

In 1772, Lord Mansfield ruled that black servants could not be sent back to the colonies without their consent, and a few years later the American War of Independence (1775–83) took place. These two events combined to produce a great increase in the number of black people, particularly men, who arrived in Britain. Some of these were Loyalists who had fought on the British side during the war, others were the servants of white Americans who decided to remain British, but most seem to have come because it was widely believed that the Mansfield Judgement had freed black people in Britain.

The 19th century

With the end of the British slave trade the number of black people coming to Britain fell. Slavery in the colonies was finally abolished in 1834. During the 19th century, therefore, the majority of people of African origin in Britain were sailors or students, and so they tended to be transient visitors.

The 20th century

Soldiers from the colonies served in the British Army during the two World Wars, and there were long-standing communities in ports such as London, Liverpool, Bristol and Cardiff. Some of the mariners here were Afro-Caribbeans, while others were from Africa.

It was after World War II that the major immigration of black people from the Caribbean began. In 1948, the *Empire Windrush* arrived, the first of a number of ships bringing workers to Britain. Most of the first arrivals settled in areas of London, mainly related to the island from which they came, such as the Jamaicans in Brixton.

In 1948 the *Empire Windrush* was the first ship to bring Caribbean workers to Britain.

RESEARCHING BLACK ANCESTORS

Most black people settled in ports. London, Bristol and Liverpool were the main ones involved in the slave trade, but, because many black immigrants were sailors, they can be found in almost every coastal parish. However, because it was fashionable in the 17th and 18th centuries for wealthy people to have black servants, isolated individuals can be found throughout Britain. These were mainly men who married white women, but there were also black women who married white men. The latter are far more difficult to research, as women took their husband's settlement status on marriage.

If the trail comes to a dead end in the 18th century, consider whether your ancestor might have been black. There are a number of clues that, put together, can indicate black ancestry. The clues are:

- adult baptism
- a surname that is the same as the employer or the place where he or she lived
- birthplace in the Caribbean or (before 1783) America

Check employers' wills: sometimes they mention the colour of a servant. If the will mentions property in America (before 1783) or the Caribbean, this is evidence of a link.

In the 19th century, birthplaces given in census returns and physical descriptions in official documents and newspapers are the main ways of identifying black ancestors.

In the 20th century, family memories and photographs will be the best indication. In addition, local libraries in areas with a large black community may have history projects that will give background information about your ancestors' lives. It is difficult to identify black people in official records,

FURTHER HELP

Fryer, Peter *Staying Power* (Pluto Press) This is the standard work on the history of black people in Britain.

because there was never any legal discrimination or segregation in Britain, as existed in its overseas colonies. Colour and/or ethnic origin were mainly given in baptism and burial registers, because birthplace was relevant under the Poor Laws. Generally such information does not appear in marriage register entries, wills or criminal indictments.

Documents that give a physical description, such as prison, Army and Navy records, may say that someone had a "black" or "brown" complexion, but these words were also used for dark-skinned British people. Newspapers consistently identify black people. Census returns up to 1991 asked for birthplace, not ethnic origin. There are therefore no records specifically related to black people.

Before 1948, small black communities lived in British ports, such as Tiger Bay, Wales.

Indian ancestors

Today curry is one of Britain's favourite foods and India has contributed many other things to British culture. Chutney, bungalows, verandahs, chits (an official piece of paper) are only some of the hundreds of words of Indian origin in everyday use.

THE ARRIVAL OF INDIAN MIGRANTS

Britain's long involvement with the Indian sub-continent means that Indian servants and sailors regularly travelled to Britain. They seem, however, not to have intermarried with British women in the way that men of African origin did. There appear to have been fewer baptisms of Indian servants, too. The reasons why are not clear, though it was probably partly to do with religion and partly to do with caste. The Indian caste system was as rigid as the British

class system, and marrying a white woman was frowned upon.

What is certain, however, is that many British men in India married or had children by local women. In the

ABOVE A colonial household during the period of the British Raj in India c.1910.

1780s, a third of the wills left by men in India mention local wives or mistresses and children by them. This does not mean that a third of all men there had interracial unions, because those who left wills were from the wealthier section of the community, but it is an indication of how common such relationships were. Children were generally sent to Britain to be educated.

The 19th century

Racial prejudice grew in the Victorian period, so the practice of interracial unions had greatly reduced by the mid-19th century. Eurasians were looked down on by both British and Indians, so it was people further down the social hierarchy, mainly soldiers, who married these mixed-race women in the 19th century. Even so, there were a number of interracial unions at all levels of British Indian society.

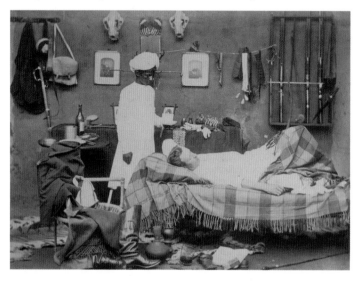

Under the blanket is a British officer whose servant might travel with him to Britain, either on visits or on retirement.

During World War I a great many troops were brought from India to fight for the allies, including these Sikh soldiers.

In addition to these mixed-race children, a number of Indians came here as servants or sailors. The latter were known as lascars, and there were boarding houses for them in all the major ports. The Strangers Home for Asiatics, Africans and South Sea Islanders was opened in Limehouse, London, in 1857, but there were many others. Christian missions were also set up in ports to care for lascars. A few, of course, settled down with local wives.

Christian missionaries in India set up schools and orphanages. Their brighter students often came to Britain to study. Indian princes visited England, especially for state occasions, and many sent their sons to Britain for their education. A few princes, having lost their thrones in India, settled in England. Others chose to stay on in Britain after receiving their degrees. Their children and grandchildren married British people.

Other Indians came as entrepreneurs, and what might be called the first Indian restaurant (actually a coffee-house serving Indian food) opened in London in the early 19th century. It must have catered mainly for British people who had acquired a taste for these dishes in India and any expatriates homesick for their native land. Itinerant Indian pedlars and street sellers were also a fairly common sight.

The 20th century

World War I saw a great number of troops brought from India to fight in Europe. At the end of the war, many, particularly sailors, remained in Britain. Students continued to arrive,

and many of them became drawn into political activities from suffragism to the development of the unions. After graduation, those who stayed in Britain usually retained their interest in politics and became involved in local councils. Many married British women.

Indians also fought in World War II, but fewer troops came to Britain than in World War I. There were, however, a substantial number of sailors in the Royal Navy. Even after India achieved independence in 1947, people from the sub-continent continued to arrive, mainly because of the post-war need for labour.

RESEARCHING INDIAN ANCESTORS

The problem with trying to trace Indian ancestors in Britain is that, unlike many other nationalities, they did not need to take out denization or naturalisation: they were already British. Reference to them may be found in ships' passenger lists, but tracking these down does depend on knowing when and where they entered the country.

Another problem is that it is difficult to distinguish between Africans and Indians in parish records: "black" seems to have covered both, and there are references to "negroes" whom the clerks noted were born in India.

Students will be found noted in universities' published lists of alumni; soldiers, sailors and airmen in the British armed forces will be located in the records of TNA. Indians in other professions will be found in the usual records relating to them.

Other overseas ancestors

People from all over the world have come to Britain. They have formed large and small communities, but, over the centuries, they have assimilated themselves into the British way of life. Family historians must therefore be prepared to find an amazing range of ethnic diversity among their ancestors, particularly if they lived in London, which has always been a magnet for immigrants, or other ports.

AMERICANS

The fact that Britain and the USA share a language has always made it easy for Americans to settle in Britain, and strong business links have led to a constant flow of people across the Atlantic, in both directions.

Before the American War of Independence, many British people moved between the two countries because they owned property in both places, but after the war those who had been loyal to the Crown, both white and black, came to the mother country. For some, it was only a temporary sojourn before they went to Canada or (in the case of whites) the West Indies, but for others it became a permanent settlement. The separation of the two countries involved the setting up of a diplomatic legation, and many Americans came to Britain as part of it.

During the 19th century, the anti-slavery movement led to a number of black Americans coming to Britain to speak at public meetings, and some decided to remain. There was also a fashion for black musicians, such as the Fisk Jubilee singers (a choir that introduced Negro spirituals to Britain) and minstrel bands.

Joseph Grimaldi (1778–1837) was born in London, the son of an Italian dance master.

Both World Wars, particularly World War II, brought American servicemen to Britain, where they were dispersed in bases all over the country. The majority went home when the war ended (often taking British brides with them), but a few settled in Britain.

ARABS

Records have used the term "Arab" to describe people from a number of Middle Eastern countries, rather than giving the actual country of origin, which is what the family historian wants to know. In addition, up to the end of the 17th century, the word "tawney" seems to have been particularly used to describe Arabs, though they were also called "Moors". Since the latter term also referred to people of African origin, it is not of much help to the family historian. Many immigrants were Turks who arrived as captives from the Mediterranean,

where piracy was rife. (Though it should be noted that the Turks were also taking British sailors prisoner.) In parish registers, the occasional conversion from Islam may be represented by an adult baptism.

British involvement in the Middle East in the 19th century meant an increase in the number of people coming from these parts of the world. The Merchant Navy also recruited sailors, particularly Yemenis, who settled in ports such as London, Cardiff, Liverpool and South Shields.

CHINESE

China largely remained closed to outsiders until the 19th century, but a few Chinese men came to Britain in the 18th century, when Chinese servants were fashionable. Some of these servants may have married British women, but there were too few of them to form a community.

Before World War II, Chinese people in Britain were overwhelmingly sailors, working on board East India Company ships initially and then, as trade with China opened up in the last half of the 19th century, on ships of all kinds. The docks in London's East End probably had the largest community (by the early 20th century, the Chinese had their own shops, clubs and friendly societies), but there were other groups in ports such as Liverpool, Cardiff, Bristol and Glasgow. The population was almost exclusively male, so they chose to marry local women.

In addition to working as sailors, the Chinese established laundries and restaurants at about this time. The restaurants they opened catered largely for their compatriots until the 1950s, when British people's eating habits became much more adventurous. These later establishments were usually opened by Hong Kong Chinese. Some of the present-day Chinese community, however, are the descendants of labourers recruited to work in the West Indies after the ending of slavery there. There are therefore several possible routes by which you may have Chinese forebears.

ITALIANS

There has always been a steady flow of immigrants and visitors from Italy. In medieval times, they came to the City of London as bankers, and Lombard Street commemorates where most of them could be found. Later on, fashions for Italian music, painting and architecture brought singers, musicians, artists and architects to Britain.

Political upheavals in Italy caused the arrival in Britain of a number of refugees in the early 19th century, among them well-educated political activists who contributed to intellectual life. Later came a number of poorer people, who, like so many immigrants, started out by selling food to their compatriots and the British, who are usually willing to try a new culinary experience. Ice cream was a particularly successful speciality.

In the 1930s, economic problems in Italy encouraged many Italians to migrate to Britain. They, too, initially sold the food of their country. London, Glasgow and Cardiff had large numbers of Italians, but smaller communities also existed in many other cities. The outbreak of World War II caused men to be interned. Some were offered the choice of returning to Italy but decided to stay, as did many who were captured as prisoners of war.

After 1945, labour shortages led the British government to recruit Italian workers, mainly from southern Italy.

RESEARCHING ANCESTORS FROM OTHER COUNTRIES

These are only a few of the immigrant communities in Britain. Most immigrants form cultural associations, which allow them to meet fellow countryfolk, give help and advice to each other, lobby on behalf of their community members and establish places of worship. The records relating to them may have been deposited in repositories such as CROs, universities or libraries, or they may remain with the association in question.

ABOVE Among the first Chinese people to come to Britain were servants, who replaced black servants as a fashion accessory in the 18th century.

LEFT Italian street vendors brought the pleasures of ice cream to poor people in the 19th century.

Gypsies and other travellers

There were many groups of people whose itinerant lifestyle makes it difficult to trace them. Before the 19th century, there was a deep distrust of people who did not have a regular job – "masterless men", as they were called – and many did their best to avoid the authorities. Note that, although performers are not immigrants, they are included in this chapter because the problems of tracing them are the same as those encountered when looking for Gypsy ancestors.

GYPSIES

The word "Gypsy" is an abbreviation of "Egyptian", as these people were thought to come from Egypt, although it seems that their origins lie in 9th-century India. Today the word "Romany" is also used. They have their own culture and traditions, such as marriage ceremonies, which run in parallel to the practices of British people, so entries relating to Gypsies are rarely found in parish records.

They were often not distinguished from Scottish and Irish tinkers, who also had a nomadic lifestyle, selling crockery and mending pots and kettles, which some true Romanies also

Romanies' and other travellers' distinctive caravans were a common sight until the 20th century, but their owners faced prejudice and official harrassment.

did. The Gypsy families had a number of distinctive surnames, which might give family historians a clue to their origins (see box below).

Horse-dealing was an important part of Gypsy life, so they travelled around the horse fairs, but they also made and sold clothes pegs, and dealt in rabbit skins and rugs. Marriage outside their community was frowned on, but, inevitably, many did marry non-Romanies, settling down in villages rather than continuing an itinerant life.

By World War I, their numbers were reducing, and mechanization, brought

about by the development of cars and farming machinery, reduced the need for horses, so further contributing to their decline. There was a great interest in their way of life in the last part of the 19th century, and books published then are a good source of information.

ACTORS AND SINGERS

From the 16th to the middle of the 18th century, the aristocracy had their own companies of musicians or performers who would entertain their guests. Any surviving records of them should be among the papers of the

Gypsy surnames

Some characteristic gypsy surnames were: Ayres, Cray, Herne, Heron, Lee, Lock, Lovell, Loveridge and Stanley, as well as many others, such as Cooper and Smith, which were shared with a large proportion of the rest of the population.

Romanies sold goods, such as wooden clothes pegs, from door to door.

An itinerant labourer rests between villages where he would look for casual work.

around which a company would tour during the year, usually spending the winters in the most important town. CMB records of actors will be found in the registers of the towns on their particular circuit.

The coming of the railways in the mid-19th century weakened and then ended the circuit system. Many provincial theatres closed due to competition from the cinema in the 20th century. Records of theatres may have been deposited with a local record office or be in the Theatre Museum.

CIRCUSES, FAIRS AND SHOWMEN

In addition to these performers, there were all kinds of other travelling entertainers: individual people with performing animals, such as bears; those who sang and played musical instruments; jugglers and acrobats; and freak shows, where people with unusual physical attributes exhibited themselves.

Many toured with circuses or fairs. Since they were frequently in trouble with the authorities, due to drunkenness and fighting, references to them may be found in Quarter Sessions records and newspapers.

RESEARCHING ITINERANT ANCESTORS

Most travellers of one kind or another did follow regular routes, depending on events, such as fairs, and also on the seasons. Looking at parish and other records, such as newspapers, along these routes could help you to reconstruct your ancestors' lives.

Some parishes were reluctant to baptize the children of non-residents in case they tried to claim settlement or support under the Poor Laws. The parishes that did baptize them marked

employer. Actors, too, needed the patronage of an influential man, or they ran the risk of being whipped as rogues and vagabonds as they toured towns and villages acting at inns or in the open air.

Following the Restoration in 1660, only two theatres in the whole of England and Wales (Covent Garden and Drury Lane), which were both located in London, were licensed for the performance of plays. Unlicensed places got around the prohibition on drama by offering musical programmes interspersed with scenes from a play or burletta – a musical rhyming drama that was a forerunner of the musical. All these performances had to be licensed by local magistrates. From the beginning of the 18th century, many of the magistrates turned a blind eye to the fact that plays, rather than just music, were being offered.

From 1768, provincial theatres began to receive patents that enabled them to put on plays, and companies of actors were openly established. Counties had a number of theatres

the entries with the word "traveller". The word "sojourner" in a register means someone who was there for a short time, and may encompass both itinerants and visitors who were staying with friends or breaking a journey at a local inn.

The trade magazines *Era* (1838–1939) and *World's Fair* (1904–present) may report the activities of fairground and showmen ancestors or suggest further avenues of research.

FURTHER HELP

Floate, Sharon Sillers *My Ancestors Were Gypsies* (SoG)
LMA Information Leaflet No. 28 *Sources for the History of London Theatres and Music Halls at London Metropolitan Archives*
Romany & Traveller Family History Society http://website.lineone. net/~rtfhs/
Sydney Jones Library, University of Liverpool, Liverpool L69 3DA has a collection of material on Gypsies.
The Circus, Theatre and Music Hall Families Page www. entertainer-genealogy.org.uk
Theatre Museum, 1e Tavistock Street, London WC2E 2PR theatremuseum.vam.ac.uk

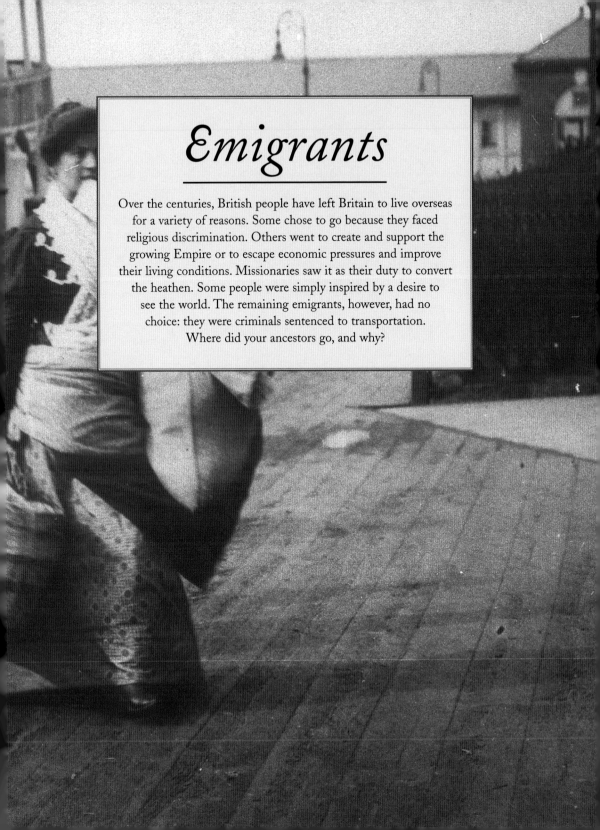

Emigrants

Over the centuries, British people have left Britain to live overseas
for a variety of reasons. Some chose to go because they faced
religious discrimination. Others went to create and support the
growing Empire or to escape economic pressures and improve
their living conditions. Missionaries saw it as their duty to convert
the heathen. Some people were simply inspired by a desire to
see the world. The remaining emigrants, however, had no
choice: they were criminals sentenced to transportation.
Where did your ancestors go, and why?

Researching emigrant ancestors

Over the centuries, Britain has probably been a net exporter of people. Some went voluntarily to seek their fortunes, while others were forcibly transported. Researching ancestors who moved overseas, either temporarily or permanently, is difficult because records will probably be in both their home country and their ultimate destination.

A HISTORY OF BRITISH EMIGRATION

The system of primogeniture, whereby the eldest child (usually a son) inherits all the father's property, meant that in the past younger children had to make their own way in the world. Some, of course, turned to trade and industry, but for the rest there was the growing British Empire, which needed people to administer and develop it. Although many returned home after working abroad, others decided to stay.

The 16th and 17th centuries

The first major wave of emigration from Britain began towards the end of the 16th century in the hope of commercial profit. Soon after, Puritans began to leave for the Americas in order to escape religious discrimination at home. The story of the Pilgrim Fathers is well known, and a great deal of research has been done on them.

As British possessions overseas grew, more settlers were needed to develop the land in the American colonies and the West Indies. Some paid their own passage, while others went as indentured servants, usually through an agent. In return for working for a certain period (usually four years), these servants had their passage, or part of it, paid, and might receive a bonus at the end of their time. This practice lasted until 1785.

There were still, however, not enough volunteers, and so agents resorted to having people kidnapped. Information relating to these unfortunates may be found in court records, but whether any legal action resulted depended on family members finding out what had happened. From 1682, there was a requirement for prospective bonded servants to go before a magistrate to be examined, before their indentures (which may include their father's name and parish of origin) were sworn. The aim was to ensure that those who went were willing to do so. Some of these records survive in County Record Offices (CROs).

The 18th century

A great growth in the territory under British rule occurred during this period. Although the aim of this empire-building was mainly to develop trade, all the European powers were in competition for goods and political influence, so controlling territory by settling government officials and traders there increased. Soldiers and sailors were then needed to protect the settlers' interests.

The greatest British expansion in this period was in India and the Far East, although this had begun in earlier centuries. Australia was also colonized and initially settled by transported criminals. Missionary societies were formed to convert the "heathens" to the Christian faith.

The Pilgrim Fathers called the place where they landed Plymouth, and they named other settlements after the towns and cities of their homeland.

Convicts were transported to Australia from 1788. On completion of their sentences, many remained to build prosperous lives.

CHILDREN

Transportation to the colonies began at the end of the 16th century and continued until the 19th century. It was mainly convicted criminals, some quite young, who were sent, but some poor children went to America as servants from the early 17th century.

During the 19th and 20th centuries, many orphans and other children who were admitted to institutions, either because their families could not support them or because they were illegitimate, were sent to British territories overseas, mainly to Canada in the 19th century and Australia in the 20th. The last of these child migrants left Britain in 1967. Local authorities and religious agencies mainly sent children of primary-school age, but some were teenagers.

The 19th century

This period saw a further growth and expansion of British possessions, and by the end of the century Britain had created an empire on which the sun never set.

Problems in Britain, such as the famine in Ireland and poverty in rural areas, also caused people to emigrate. For example, the Enclosure Acts, which began in the 18th century, drove many people off the land, as the strips they had farmed to support themselves were bought up by large landowners. This led to a huge increase in emigrants all over the globe, not just to British possessions such as Australia and New Zealand, where agricultural experience was valuable, but also to places outside British rule, such as South America. The USA was also a major destination.

There was also an increase in trade and Christian missionary activity in China. Missionary activity peaked between 1880 and 1920, when some 60 societies were involved. In addition to clergymen, both men and women were sent abroad as medical personnel and teachers.

The 20th century

The first half of the 20th century saw attempts to make the British Empire a more important market for British goods, and this, combined with the economic depression of the early 1930s, impelled many people to move overseas. When countries gained their independence after World War II, some people chose to remain abroad, while others returned to Britain.

PASSPORTS

Until the 20th century, passports were not much used. Diplomats and other important people might obtain a licence to pass across the seas, but for everyone else there was little or no bureaucracy needed to emigrate. This is unfortunate for the family historian.

RIGHT Orphaned and abandoned children were sent abroad by local authorities and charitable institutions.

As most of the early settlers in Australia were men, efforts were made to encourage women to emigrate to balance the sexes.

Organizations involved included the following:

- Religious denominations that ran homes for children, such as the Church of England; the Roman Catholic Father Hudson Homes and the Christian Brothers; the Methodists' National Children's Homes; the Salvation Army.
- Dr Barnardo's Homes, which were founded by Thomas Barnardo, who was horrified by the plight of homeless children in London.
- The Young Men's Christian Association (YMCA), which was founded in London in 1844. The organization quickly spread to other countries. It aimed to use Bible study to help young men stay out of the way of temptation, and was unusual for its period in being ecumenical rather than being tied to one faith.
- The Big Brother Movement, which was a juvenile migration scheme founded in 1924 for boys aged 15–17. They were paired with someone in their new country who was supposed to act as a godparent.
- The Dreadnought Scheme, which

arranged for unemployed British youths to make a fresh start in Australia. They were taught agricultural skills to develop the land.

Most records are in the countries to which the children went, but surviving records in Britain should be in a County Record Office (CRO) or still with the organization itself. This is a sensitive subject, because many of the children suffered abuse while in the care of these organizations. Legal action has been taken by some children, so organizations can be reluctant to allow access to their records; they may also be within the hundred years that is generally the period of time for which personal records are closed.

RESEARCHING EMIGRANT ANCESTORS

Governments are naturally less interested in those leaving the country than in those people arriving, and so most information will be found in the country to which individuals went. Deciding why your ancestor left Britain will help you to locate the appropriate records.

- Those who went on government service will mainly be recorded in The National Archives (TNA).
- Missionaries will be recorded in the archives of their particular denomination's missionary service.
- Engineers and technical personnel can be traced through their companies' archives.
- Poor people may be found in records of government schemes to encourage emigrants.
- Details of criminals may be found in court records and TNA.

Middle-class people living overseas often sent announcements of births, marriages and deaths (BMD) to *The Times* personal columns. These were not, unfortunately, included in Palmer's Index after 1837, but there are indexes in the Society of Genealogists' (SoG) library. Some overseas BMD appear in miscellaneous indexes in the Family Record Centre (FRC).

Commercial directories were produced for British communities overseas. These may be helpful in locating a difficult group of people to research: professional people who chose to go and who paid their own passage.

FURTHER HELP

Corporation of London Records Office Research Guide 3 *Transportation and Emigration*
TNA Domestic Records Information 107 *Emigrants*
The British Overseas: A guide to records of their births, baptism, marriages, deaths and burials available in the United Kingdom (Guildhall Library)
Copies of CLRO records have been supplied to many overseas archives.
Missionary collections in the UK: www.mundus.ac.uk is an on-line listing of missionary papers and where they are located in the UK

Ancestors from India and the Far East

The history of the British Empire and its incursions and occupation of India and the Far East is well documented and there are a number of ways in which family tree researchers can trace family members who were involved in setting up and maintaining communities and administrations in these countries.

THE BRITISH SETTLEMENT OF INDIA AND THE FAR EAST

The British East India Company was formed in 1600 to trade with the islands of the East Indies, but other nations were already established there, so the company turned its attention to India and began three and a half centuries of involvement with the subcontinent. This lasted until independence in 1947, when Pakistan became a separate state and was divided into East and West Pakistan. East Pakistan seceded from Pakistan and became Bangladesh in 1971.

Initially, the company simply set up bases, called "factories", in various ports, but war with the French and internal problems in the various Indian territories led, in the middle of the 18th century, to the British gaining control over much of India. From this period onwards, an increasing amount of trade was also conducted with other countries in the Far East, such as China, and the islands in the Pacific Ocean off the mainland of Asia, but India remained the jewel in the crown. The Andaman Islands in the Indian Ocean were occupied in 1789–96. From 1858 to 1845 they were used as a penal colony. When India became independent, they were

transferred to its rule. From the late 18th century to the middle of the 20th century, there was a strong British presence in India and the Far East, which included:

ABOVE The sale room of the East India Company, where fortunes could be made.

BELOW The East India Company operated under government charters.

Haileybury School in Hertfordshire educated children to prepare them for life in Britain's Asian colonies.

- civil servants, who administered the various colonies
- engineers, who built the road and rail systems
- missionaries, who set up schools and hospitals
- settlers, who developed tea plantations and other agricultural or commercial ventures
- armed forces, who protected the British settlers

During the long involvement between England, India, and the Far East, soldiers, sailors and families travelled back and forth between the Far East and Britain, sometimes taking servants with them. British men also married local women in the Far East.

THE EAST INDIA COMPANY

Until 1813, the East India Company (EIC), also known as the Honourable East India Company, or John Company, had a monopoly of trade with India. Initially, it had its own merchant fleet, but from the middle of the 18th century the company chartered vessels and crews, which were commanded by its own officers.

Professional training

The EIC established training colleges for its employees from the beginning of the 19th century. Civil servants were taught at Haileybury College near Ware, Hertfordshire, and there was also a school on the site for those expected to go to the college. The school and college lasted from 1806 to 1858, when the EIC was disbanded.

In addition to its own civil service, the EIC had an army. The recruits were taught at the Royal Military Academy in Woolwich until 1809, when Addiscombe Place, near Croydon, Surrey, was acquired for use as a military academy. It closed in 1861. Books about Haileybury and Addiscombe have been published.

Lunatic asylums

From 1818, the EIC had an arrangement to place employees and members of their families who suffered from mental problems in Pembroke House Private Asylum in Hackney, north London. After that closed in 1870, the company opened its own establishment in Ealing, west London, which closed in 1892. The remaining male patients were transferred to the Royal Naval Hospital in Yarmouth and the females went to Coton Hill Institution in Stafford. Documents relating to these patients for 1830-92 have survived.

THE INDIAN CIVIL SERVICE

Before 1855, senior civil servants were largely appointed on a patronage basis. After that date, posts were filled by examination. Junior positions were usually filled by local recruitment, generally from people of European families resident in India or, before 1791, from Eurasians (the children of mixed marriages). In 1791, the EIC barred Eurasians from employment in its service.

PENSIONS

From 1770, various pension funds covering different occupations existed. They included the Lord Clive Military Fund and the Indian Military Service Family Pension Fund, both of which were for soldiers, particularly officers. The Poplar Pension Fund was for seamen involved in the EIC's merchant navy. There is often some correspondence attached to the payment of pensions, which provides considerable genealogical information.

OTHER BRITISH INTERESTS

In 1784, the British government set up a department – the Board of Control – to deal with those interests it had in the East that were not administered by the EIC. Its sphere of influence covered parts of the Middle East, South and East Africa, China and Japan.

In 1857, the government wound up the EIC, and in the following year it set up the India Office. Burma (now Myanmar) was annexed in 1886 and was administered by the India Office until 1937, when the Burma Office was created.

RESEARCHING ANCESTORS IN INDIA AND THE FAR EAST

The records of the EIC and its successors are now housed in the Oriental and India Office Collection (OIOC) in the British Library. It holds a vast collection of archives relating to the British in the Indian subcontinent and south Asia. There is also a smaller collection at the South Asian Studies Centre Library in Cambridge, which contains newspapers from the area and many private papers.

The OIOC includes returns of BMD sent to Britain from the churches in India for c.1700–1947. They are mainly of Europeans and Eurasians, although a few local converts are included. There is also an index of some births and deaths for 1923–47 in the FRC. Wills, administrations and inventories from 1618 have also been deposited in the OIOC; copies may also be found in the Prerogative Court of Canterbury probate records at the FRC and TNA.

There is also correspondence on a wide variety of matters in the OIOC, including petitions for financial assistance from men working there or the widows of dead employees.

Births and deaths in India and other places in the Far East, including the Dutch East Indies, that were notified to the British authorities from various dates after 1831 are held in TNA, with indexes also in the FRC.

Records of retired soldiers and sailors and pensions paid to them may be found in the registers of the Chelsea and Greenwich Hospitals in TNA. Official correspondence to and from the Treasury to the EIC, the Board of Control and the India Office, which may mention individuals, is held in TNA.

The EIC ruled other parts of the Far East claimed for the Crown, so records relating to these various places before 1857 (when the EIC was wound up) will be found in its archives. Thereafter, records will be found in various government departments in TNA until the countries gained their independence after World War I or World War II.

Many lists of Memorial Inscriptions in churches and graveyards in India and the Far East have been made by individuals. These can be difficult to track down, but the Families in British India Society (FIBIS) should have details.

India was divided into three presidencies: Madras, Bombay and Bengal. Records are divided between these areas, so you need to find out where your ancestors lived in order to locate them. The EIC's army had to be supplemented by the British Army, so you may find military ancestors in either.

If you don't find CMB records in the OIOC, this may be because they were not returned to Britain but are entered in church registers in India, Pakistan, Bangladesh or Burma. They may also be in local registrars' offices in these countries.

FURTHER HELP

Oriental and India Office Collection, British Library, 96 Euston Road, London NW1 2DB www.bl.uk/collections/oriental

South Asian Studies Centre Library, Cambridge University, Laundress Lane, Cambridge CB2 1SD www.s-asian.cam.ac.uk/

Families in British India Society (FIBIS) www.links.org/FIBIS/ This FHS is not just for those with ancestors in British India: it covers all those areas under the control of the EIC and the India Office.

Trade with the East brought tea from plantations in India and Ceylon to Britain, and it is still the UK's favourite beverage.

North America

The American landmass was initially settled by peoples who crossed the Bering Strait while it was still linked by ice to Asia. When the ice melted, they were cut off and developed separately.

THE EUROPEAN SETTLEMENT OF AMERICA

The northernmost part of America was discovered by Norsemen and sailors fishing the icy waters around the Arctic in medieval times, but towards the end of the 15th century Europeans began to look for a new way to the East. Sailing across the Atlantic, they encountered the continent of America. They soon realized that this was a previously unknown landmass and set about claiming it for their sovereigns.

Spain and Portugal colonized South America, while the British, Dutch and French concentrated on

ABOVE The New World promised a better future for its settlers.

BELOW The descendants of the Pilgrim Fathers have their own family history society.

the north of the continent. Spain also retained control of a broad swathe of land from Florida up the East Coast until the middle of the 18th century. Wars in Europe led to the transfer of land in America between the various countries, but the settlers there did not leave the lives they had built up. Thus there are the remnants of different European cultures all across America. Individual towns were also created by people from particular countries.

British settlers

The first British settlement was at Roanoke in Virginia. The settlers disappeared without trace, but there were soon other people eager to replace them. Initially they were inspired by the prospect of trade and growing tobacco, the pleasures of which were introduced to them by the Native Americans. Although they tried to use the Native Americans for labour, this was not successful, so indentured servants, paupers and convicted criminals were brought in. The number proved to be insufficient, leading to the transportation of slaves from Africa, beginning in 1619.

The next group of settlers from England came as a result of religious upheavals, and the first party, known as the Pilgrim Fathers, arrived on the *Mayflower* at Cape Cod in Massachusetts, in 1620. The Pilgrim Fathers were followed by many others who wanted freedom to worship in their own way. Unlike the people who went further south, their industries in New England required relatively little slave labour.

The vast open lands of North America drew not only religious immigrants: others came for political or economic reasons. People tended to move in groups and establish settlements that reflected their religious, national and geographic origins. The New England states, as the name suggests, were where British people originally went, but within that area there were local concentrations of particular social and ethnic groups in specific towns and regions.

Most of the early settlers were Puritans from London and the south-east of England, and their origin is preserved in the regional accent. Pennsylvania attracted Quakers. Boston's large Irish community was primarily the result of economic hardship, particularly the famine in the middle of the 19th century. The southern states had many immigrants from the West Country of England, looking not for religious freedom but for economic reasons to escape poverty at home.

Land grants

Although three countries, the United Kingdom, France and Spain, claimed

ABOVE Most emigrants from Europe could afford only the cheapest class of travel, called steerage.

BELOW Initially relations with the Native Americans were good but later conflict developed.

vast tracts of land in North America, only the British established numerous settlements. Until 1775, Britain considered the land it claimed in America as the property of the Crown and made grants of land to both companies and individuals. Those people who paid for their own passage were granted about 50 acres (123 hectares). Confusingly, these people were sometimes referred to as transportees, even though they were not criminals.

Surrendered interests

The involvement of the French in early 19th-century wars in Europe meant that France had too many problems at home to give attention to developing its claims in the New World. Spain also had its attention diverted elsewhere (concentrating on its colonies in South America), so both countries surrendered their interests to the American government in the early 19th century. The names of towns and villages often preserve the cultural legacy.

and in federal archives. Naturalization records are state-based. Many papers may still be in the local courthouse.

Civil registration of BMD began at different dates in different states during 1880–1900. There was no national registration. Because there is no established Church of America, there were no regulations about how records should be kept, or a designated repository for church registers. Wills are also proved at state level.

Cyndi's List on the internet has an excellent guide to tracing ancestry in the major American sources. It covers BMD records, censuses, adoption, land records, localities and ethnic groups, military records and ships' passenger lists, as well as less obvious sources, such as FBI files and American passport applications.

Censuses were held in the USA from 1790. Until 1850 they listed only the name of the head of the household, with his or her occupation and state of birth. There is only statistical information about the other members of the household. The censuses of

LEFT Poor emigrants left their homelands with only the possessions they could carry.

BELOW The West was settled by families travelling in groups, called wagon trains.

1900 and 1910 should include the year in which an immigrant took up residency in the country. Information about land grants and sales in the USA will be in the national archives if the deal was between state and individual,

or in state archives if it was between individual and individual. Before 1775, there is also information about them in The National Archives in Britain.

Many lists have been published, such as the first settlers, transported

Russians, especially Jews, came to the USA to escape political and social problems in their own country during the late 19th and early 20th centuries.

Emigrants, like this Italian family, came to America from all over the world.

criminals and passengers entering through the many ports in the USA before 1900. There is an on-line database of people passing through Ellis Island during 1892–1924. Later immigrant records are held in the National Archives and Records Administration in Washington.

RECORDS RELATING TO AMERICANS IN BRITISH ARCHIVES

The USA was a British colony until the War of Independence, and therefore much information will be in TNA and other archives. Details of transported criminals, for example, are in Britain. People who owned land in the thirteen states of New England on the East Coast before the War of Independence may have had their wills proved in the PCC in England.

After the War of Independence, many of those who fought on the British side, called Loyalists, submitted claims for their losses to the British government, which are now

held in TNA. Some of these have been microfilmed and so may be available in other record offices. Private papers of families who came back may have been deposited in record offices or libraries, and some remain in private hands. Some British Loyalists went north to Canada.

For 1890–1960 there are passenger lists in TNA of people leaving Britain for all destinations, but they're unindexed, so it is necessary to know the approximate date of departure or the name of the ship. These include details of Europeans for whom Britain was a stage on their journey to the USA.

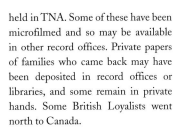

FURTHER HELP

Coldham, Peter Wilson *Child Apprentices in America from Christ's Hospital* 1617–1788 (Genealogical Publishing Co. Inc., Baltimore, USA)

Coldham, Peter Wilson *The Bristol Register of Servants Sent to Foreign Plantations 1654–1686* (Genealogical Publishing Co. Inc., Baltimore, USA)

Filby & Meyer *Passenger and Immigration Lists Index* shows through which port immigrants entered North America, both the USA and Canada, and the West Indies before 1900.

Manross, William Wilson *The Fulham Papers in the Lambeth Palace Library: American colonial section calendar and*

indexes (OUP) is a catalogue of documents held in Lambeth Palace Library mainly related to Church matters.

TNA Overseas Records Information 35 *Land Grants in America and American Loyalists' Claims*

TNA Overseas Records Information 53 *Emigrants to North America after 1776*

www.ellisisland.org/ has a database of immigrants who passed through the immigration controls on Ellis Island during 1892–1924.

National Archives and Records Administration, 700 Pennsylvania Avenue, NW, Washington DC 20408. www.nara.gov/

Canada

Canada has long-standing links with both Britain and France, the two countries which contributed most to its creation and culture. Public records in Canada are held by each province.

THE EUROPEAN SETTLEMENT OF CANADA

The first English-speaking colony in North America, created in 1588, was on the island of Newfoundland. Initially, it was used by seasonal workers, who came there to fish for cod. They came mainly from Ireland and the West Country of England. They were soon followed by fur trappers, many of whom were Scottish. A French expedition had already explored part of the St Lawrence River, and in 1608 a settlement was founded at Quebec.

In 1627, the Company of New France was given authority to establish settlements from Florida to the Arctic Circle. They were not, however, without competition. Further south, the British, Spanish and Dutch were also engaged in struggles to control the whole North American landmass.

In Canada, however, only the British and French were competing. The British Hudson Bay Company, which was granted a royal charter in 1670, came to control the area around the bay. Despite their grand ambitions, the French managed to settle only a strip of land north and south of the St Lawrence River before the Seven Year War between Britain and France in Europe spilled over into their American territories. The French ceded all their territories in North America to the British in 1763, but a small proportion of the land's total population in Canada remained French, retaining their Roman Catholic religion, a feudal system of land tenure and their own laws and language though under British rule.

After the American War of Independence, Canada decided to remain British. Many American Loyalists headed north at this point. Others, although they went to Britain at this time, later decided to relocate to Canada. They were given grants of land, some in Nova Scotia, but the majority settled around the northern edges of Lakes Ontario and Erie.

UNIFICATION

Until 1867, Canada was a collection of separate provinces. In 1867, Quebec, Ontario, Nova Scotia and New Brunswick formed the Dominion of Canada, which took over the Hudson Bay Company in 1869. British Columbia joined in 1871 and Prince Edward Island in 1873. This unification of the country meant that it could be developed. Central government was responsible for defence and foreign affairs, railways, trade and custom duties and company law, but the individual provinces retained the right to pass their own laws and raise their own taxes. They also had control over prisons, hospitals, local railways and education.

The provinces of Saskatchewan and Alberta were formed in 1905. The remaining land, not covered by one or other of the various provinces, became the Northwest Territories, which came under the direct control of the Dominion's government in 1898. The last province, Newfoundland and Labrador, did not join the Dominion until 1949.

LEFT The Hudson Bay Company was established by royal charter in 1670.

THE MOUNTIES

Until the last quarter of the 19th century, very little effort was made to exploit to the full the resources of the middle-west's prairies. Until then, the area had largely been inhabited by native Canadians and fur trappers, who had for all practical purposes been left to their own devices. In 1874, using men largely recruited from Britain, the Northwest Mounted Police, called the Mounties and famous for always getting their man, was formed in order to enforce law and order over this territory. In 1904, the force was renamed the Royal Northwest Mounted Police, and in 1920 it became the Royal Canadian Mounted Police.

DEVELOPMENT OF THE RAILWAYS

In 1871, the Dominion government decided to build a railway across the landmass from east to west, to be completed by 1881. Like most government estimates, it proved over-optimistic. In 1873, the Canadian Pacific Railway Company was founded, but it experienced political difficulties and collapsed, and it was not until 1880, when the company was refounded, that work

The Mounties prided themselves on catching their man and bringing him in by whatever means possible.

really got under way. Funds were partly raised by selling land along the route to settlers, and the railway was completed in 1885.

The construction required engineers and labourers, many of whom came from Britain. Its construction enabled the development of agricultural land, which was mainly turned over to wheat growing, and made settlement possible, because goods could be transported to the interior. More railways followed.

THE GOLD RUSH

The discovery of gold in the Yukon in 1896 led to the Canadian gold rush, with prospectors coming from all over the world. Other natural resources, such as timber, gold, oil and uranium, have led to immigration from people hoping to make their fortunes.

LINKS WITH BRITAIN

The majority of Canadians are of British descent, and Canada retained strong links with the mother country. From 1869, some 100,000 British children were sent to Canada under various schemes. In both World Wars, servicemen came from Canada to Britain to fight. The Canadian Army and Airforce fought in Europe, and

the Royal Canadian Navy played an important part. Individuals also joined the British forces. Although the country became independent in 1931, it retained the sovereignty of the Queen and is still part of the Commonwealth.

RESEARCHING ANCESTORS IN CANADA

Each of the twelve provinces and territories had its own civil registration system and conducted its own censuses. These remain in the archives of each state. The way in which the provinces developed, and the fact that they have their own laws, means that the records they hold will vary. The Hudson Bay Company records are held in the University of Manitoba. Records relating to those Canadians who joined British services during the wars may be found in TNA.

The Canadian Pacific Railway made settlement in the prairies possible.

FURTHER HELP

National Archives of Canada
www.archives.ca
Provincial Archives of Manitoba,
200 Vaughan Street, Winnepeg,
Manitoba, Canada R3C 1T5
www.gov.mb.ca/chc/archives/hbc
a/ has the Hudson Bay Company
archives.

The Caribbean

The West Indies, which stretch across the Caribbean Sea from North to South America, were discovered by Europeans at the end of the 15th century. They were so named because the explorers thought they had reached India by a different route.

THE BRITISH SETTLEMENT OF THE CARIBBEAN

The first island to be settled by the British was Bermuda in 1609. Initially, indentured servants and criminals from Britain were used to clear and develop the islands, but from the 1650s increasing numbers of slaves were transported from Africa to supply labour. The ships that brought them went back to Britain, with sugar, rum and other commodities, before returning to Africa for more slaves. This was the notorious "triangular trade".

Plantation owners were greatly outnumbered by their slaves. They lived in fear of uprisings and passed increas-

Plantation owners tried to recreate the lives of wealthy people in their homelands – and an impressive, well-appointed mansion was an essential.

ingly draconian laws against the black members of the population. But many of the plantation owners had children by their slaves. Mixed white-black ancestry created a class system: the more white blood people had, the higher they ranked in the social scale. On the whole, mixed-race children seem to have been well provided for. Some of them were sent to Britain for their education by the wealthier estate owners, presumably because of the legal discrimination they would face on the islands.

From the 1800s, missionaries of various Nonconformist denominations, mainly the Methodists and Moravians, established churches on the islands.

After the end of slavery in 1834, there was supposed to be a four-year transition period of apprenticeship for the labourers, but this proved unworkable. So many slaves left their masters' service that there was a labour shortage. To compensate for this, Chinese, African and East Indian workers were brought in.

The various islands gained their independence after World War II.

The Caribbean Sea has hundreds of islands whose turbulent past as they were fought over by European powers is reflected in the different languages and cultures there.

RECORDS RELATING TO THE CARIBBEAN

The British Government records, mainly relating to landowners, are in TNA. Between 1812 and 1834 they contain lists of slaves. There are also some returns of baptisms, marriages and burials on the various islands from the 18th century. Occasional censuses, mainly recording only the head of the household, were compiled from the end of the 17th century.

Most of the church baptism, marriage and burial registers have been microfiched by the Mormons. Information from some of these records is on the IGI, but the others can be ordered and consulted at your local LDS Family History Centre.

In the early 20th century, Vere Langford Oliver edited a series of publications called *Caribbeana*, which reproduced some parish registers and other records.

Church records, other than registers, may be either in the library of Lambeth Palace, because the Archbishop of Canterbury was head of the worldwide Anglican Church, or in the Guildhall Library, because the Bishop of London was erroneously assumed to have governance over the islands.

Private papers relating to individual families and estates are scattered across a variety of repositories. Some are still in the Caribbean, while others were brought back to Britain and, over the years, have been deposited in CROs and other libraries.

Local newspapers carry BMD notices of the more important inhabitants as well as news stories.

The West Indies were important to the different European countries that colonized them. Some changed hands as the result of wars, so records relating to them before they were acquired by the British may be in European archives.

Bananas, brought to the Caribbean from Africa, were – and remain so today – an important crop.

Local record offices in the Caribbean have suffered over the years due to natural disasters, such as hurricanes and fires. Where records have survived, they are similar to those in England – wills, workhouses, criminal courts, charities, etc.

RESEARCHING ANCESTORS IN THE CARIBBEAN

As elsewhere, if your ancestors were part of the wealthier, land-owning classes, you will find a great deal of material about them. Land and tax records may be in local record offices or in TNA. If they also had property in America (which was not uncommon before the War of Independence) or in Britain, their wills should be in the Prerogative Court of Canterbury (PCC) records, which are on microfilm in the FRC.

When slavery ended, owners were compensated, and there are documents giving the sums received and other information in TNA. Civil servants and members of the islands' governments will appear in official records. Officers in the armed forces were white but there were several regiments

of black West Indians, as well as the Colonial Marines. These records are in TNA.

There are, unfortunately, few official records relating to slaves before the end of the 18th century. They may be listed in documents relating to their masters, such as wills or estate papers. Slaves also appear in church registers, but the lack of surnames makes reconstructing family trees difficult, if not impossible. The private papers of estate owners may contain more details. On emancipation, some slaves took the names of their masters, either the current one or an earlier one, which may give clues as to where on the islands they came from, but this was by no means standard practice and cannot be relied on.

Manumissions (documents setting slaves free) may be found in wills and in legal documents from the islands, and there are also some among the court records in the Corporation of London Record Office.

FURTHER HELP

Grannum, Guy *Tracing Your West Indian Ancestors* (TNA Readers Guide No. 11)

Manross, William Wilson *The Fulham Papers in the Lambeth Palace Library: American colonial section calendar and indexes* (OUP 1965) is a catalogue of documents mainly related to Church matters held in Lambeth Palace Library.

TNA Legal Records Information 16 *Transportation to America and the West Indies*

Walne, Peter ed. *A Guide to Manuscript Sources for the History of Latin America and the Caribbean in the British Isles* (OUP 1973) shows the location, listed by county, of a range of documents, mainly private and business papers, in the United Kingdom.

Australia

Originally called New Holland, Australia was known to sailors from the early 17th century – such a huge island was difficult to miss. As only a comparatively narrow strip of land around the coastline was fertile, no-one thought it worth colonizing.

THE BRITISH SETTLEMENT OF AUSTRALIA

Although Australia was known to explorers from early on in the 1600s, the distance from Britain and the fact that the land was so inhospitable meant that there were no settlements there until after the American War of Independence in 1783. Until then, criminals had been transported to America, but, with this no longer possible, the government needed to find somewhere else to send convicts. Australia (which had been claimed for Britain by Captain Cook in 1770) was finally chosen, and the First Fleet sailed there in 1787. Penal colonies

Potential settlers were carefully vetted before they were allowed to enter the country.

were established in New South Wales, on Norfolk Island and, later, on Tasmania, then called Van Diemen's Land.

Some free settlers came to Tasmania in 1803, but initially Australia was considered somewhere to dispose of

criminals. At the end of their sentences, most prisoners remained, and Royal Marines, who had gone with the convict ships to guard the prisoners, were granted land if they too chose to stay.

From 1793, free people choosing to come to New South Wales in search of a better life began to arrive. The numbers increased after the end of the Napoleonic Wars in 1815, which brought unemployment among discharged soldiers and sailors. Many of the people in rural areas of England decided to leave and take their chances in Australia, now that its potential for agriculture and sheep-farming was being realized.

The process of enclosure in Britain continued until the middle of the 19th century, displacing many people from their land. It coincided with the settlement of the rest of Australia. Assisted immigration, whereby people wishing to emigrate had their fares paid or subsidized, began in 1832, with an emphasis on people with particular skills and single women.

The Commonwealth of Australia

Western Australia was the first area to be settled, but there were so many problems there that it was not given its own government until 1890. Victoria became a colony in 1855; South Australia in 1856; Queensland in 1859. These colonies, with New South Wales and Tasmania, joined together in 1901 to form the Commonwealth of Australia. It was not until 1911 that the last two colonies (the Northern Territory and the Australian Capital Territory) joined the Commonwealth.

In the earliest days, the only labour in the colony was provided by convicts.

Many British families emigrated to the other side of the world in the 20th century under various schemes which gave financial aid.

Families on sheep stations in the interior were and still are isolated. The Flying Doctor service provides vital help.

RESEARCHING ANCESTORS IN AUSTRALIA

All eight ex-colonies are separate states with their own archives. The Commonwealth of Australia, formed in 1901, has a federal archive in the capital, Canberra. Records of grants of land are held in the individual states.

Civil registration began at different times:

New South Wales	1856
Victoria	1853
Queensland	1856
South Australia	1842
Western Australia	1841
Tasmania	1838
Northern Territory	1870
Australian Capital Territory	1930

Civil records are similar to those in Britain, but there is another source of information that may help you to discover how and why your ancestors went to Australia. Musters of land, stock, victualling, servants employed by officers, settlers, military people and convicts were made for 1788–1837.

Censuses began in New South Wales in 1828, but most were destroyed once the statistical information had been extracted. Only a few of the early ones survive.

Lists of people transported in the early convict fleets, including biographies and descendants (where they can be traced), have been published.

From 1832, the British government gave assistance to those who wished to emigrate. Some of these lists have also been published.

Records relating to child migrants for 1947–53 are held in the Australian national archives, but, in order to find a particular child in them, you need to know the ship on which he or she arrived and the date.

SOUTH PACIFIC ISLANDS ADMINISTERED BY THE BRITISH

A number of other islands in the south Pacific came under British rule and were administered from Australia. These include:

- Christmas Island (1888–1958)
- Nauru (from 1857)
- Norfolk Island, which was claimed by the British in 1788 and became a convict settlement until 1814. Between 1825 and 1855 it was reoccupied as a prison
- Papua New Guinea (until 1975)
- Pitcairn Island, which was where

the Bounty mutineers settled in 1790. It came under formal British rule in 1814. The islanders were moved to Norfolk Island in 1858, but some returned.

- The Cocos, or Keeling, Islands, which were annexed to the Crown in 1857, and from 1886 were ruled by the descendants of John Clunies-Ross, a Scottish seaman who arrived there and built a settlement. In 1955, it came under the auspices of the Australian government, who bought out the family in 1978.

After World War I, a number of previously German possessions, such as German New Guinea, the Bismarck Archipelago and some of the Solomon Islands (until 1978), were transferred to the trusteeship of Australia.

FURTHER HELP

Hall, Nick Vine *Tracing Your Family History in Australia* (Rigby, Australia)
Hawkings, David T. *Bound for Australia* (Phillimore)
Child Migrants Trust, 228 Canning Street, North Carlton, Vic 3034, Australia.
National Archives www.naa.gov.au

New Zealand

New Zealand initially seemed too far away and to have no resources worth exploiting, so it was not until the 19th century that the British decided to settle there.

THE BRITISH SETTLEMENT OF NEW ZEALAND

New Zealand was claimed for Britain by Captain Cook on the same voyage as the one in which he landed in Australia. The history of the two countries is, however, very different. New Zealand was never used as a penal colony, although prisoners who escaped from Australia came here, either brought on ships by sympathetic sailors or by surviving the perilous 2,400-kilometre (1,500-mile) journey in stolen boats. Most convicts were sheltered by, and intermarried with, the Maoris – the indigenous people of New Zealand.

From 1814, missionaries began to arrive, but the British government did not allow other settlers. A private individual, Edward Gibbon Wakefield, organized an expedition, which landed in 1840 on the North Island, where the government had purchased land from the Maoris. This forced the government to send someone to administer the new territory, initially under the authority of Australia, but soon afterwards it was made an independent colony.

For the next 30 years, there were a number of assisted immigration schemes, some privately organized, others government initiatives, with most people coming from Britain. Some came from Europe and others from Australia. The latter, however, had to pay their own passage, and so do not appear in official records. After 1870, the government increased its efforts to encourage immigration.

The government and private individuals continued to buy land from the Maoris without fully understanding that they had a different concept of land ownership. This led to the first

ABOVE The indigenous people, the Maoris, originally came from the islands of Polynesia in the Pacific.

LEFT The Maoris resisted colonization and fought two wars in an attempt to keep settlers from their lands.

RIGHT Both the government and private organizations offered free passage to encourage emigrants from Britain.

Maori War (1845–47). There were fewer Maoris in the South Island, so settlement of British people was encouraged here.

In 1852, New Zealand was given its own government. There was a second Maori War, which lasted from 1860 to 1871.

New Zealand also administers several of the Pacific Island groups, including the Cook Islands, Tokelau Islands, the Ross Dependency and the Keremadec Group. Until 1961 it also administered Western Samoa.

RESEARCHING ANCESTORS IN NEW ZEALAND

The main record office in New Zealand is located in Wellington, with regional offices in Christchurch, Auckland and Dunedin. Civil registration for Europeans began in 1848, but in the initial years there was under-registration of marriages, which were not consistently recorded until 1855. It was not until 1911 that Maori marriages were registered, with births and deaths among Maoris entered from 1913. Separate registers for Europeans and Maoris were kept until 1955 (marriages) and 1962 (births and deaths).

Censuses before 1962 have been destroyed, but there are a few surviving documents in the regional archives.

Passenger lists are held in regional offices, depending on which port the immigrants arrived at, but from 1883 there is a central source of passenger lists of all arrivals in New Zealand, not just settlers, which is held in Wellington. There are card indexes covering different sections of immigrants, mainly sorted according to their nationality.

Child migrant schemes to bring orphans, those whose families could not care for them, and other unaccompanied youngsters continued until 1954.

FURTHER HELP

Archives New Zealand
www.archives.govt.nz/ has links to the regional archive centres.
Department of Internal Affairs is responsible for registration of BMD and has offices all over the country. www.bdm.govt.nz/
National Library of New Zealand, PO Box 1467, Wellington, New Zealand www.natlib.govt.nz/

Africa

As far as the family historian is concerned, the continent of Africa can be divided into the Sahel, Sub-Saharan Africa, East Africa and South Africa, each of which has a very different history.

THE SAHEL

The part of Africa to the north of the Sahara, along the Mediterranean, together with Egypt and Ethiopia (also called Abyssinia) along the Red Sea, was known from medieval times as being important for trade. The Arabs were heavily involved in slavery, both of black Africans and of white people, mainly sailors captured in the Mediterranean whom they used as labour until they could be ransomed. The Turks were also involved in this piracy. In parish records, you will find regular collections to raise money to purchase the freedom of such slaves, to which your ancestors may have contributed. Some of your mariner ancestors were perhaps among those enslaved.

For political reasons, both local and European, there was a strong British presence in Egypt from 1841. After 1882, Britain began to play a major role in government, including the administration of finance and law and order. British diplomats advised the ruler, and officers were sent to train the Egyptian army. Schemes to improve agriculture and the country's infrastructure were also put in place. Unrest in the Sudan led to a joint Anglo-Egyptian administration being established there in 1898. After World War I, the British remained in Egypt and the Sudan until the Suez Crisis of 1956.

Although Egypt never came under official British rule, there was a strong presence of diplomats, businessmen and archaeologists in the 19th and early 20th centuries.

SUB-SAHARAN AFRICA

Although the European powers were heavily involved in the slave trade from West Africa, they had trading posts only along the coastline. It was not until the middle of the 19th century, after the slave trade had been abolished, that the African chiefs allowed white people to enter the interior of the continent south of the Sahara – the part in the centre and also west between the Sahara and South Africa. From 1860, explorers mapped the rivers and the land.

In the 1880s, what is known as the "scramble for Africa" took place, when the various powers carved up the continent between themselves. Of course, it needed intensive military involvement, but civilians were also required to provide a permanent presence. Missionaries were heavily involved in medicine and education. There were always relatively few Europeans in the colonies: an 1881 directory, for example, lists only fifty resident Europeans in the Gambia, though the editor notes that the returns are not very reliable.

EAST AFRICA

The part of Africa next to the Red Sea was not important to Britain until the completion of the Suez Canal in 1869. Thereafter the country of Somaliland (now Somalia) came under British rule, while Kenya, Uganda and Tanganyika (now Tanzania) came under the administration of the Imperial East Africa Company. The island of Zanzibar was ruled by a Sultan with the assistance of a British Resident (a representative of the British government).

By 1901, railways had improved transport into the interior, and settlers, both British and Dutch, began to arrive. They were given land, which was developed for agriculture. Most British people would have come to this area during the period between the two World Wars.

SOUTH AFRICA

On their way to and from the East Indies, European ships called in at what became Cape Town during the 15th and 16th centuries. The Dutch created a permanent settlement there in 1652, and the growth of what was originally just a place to stop off for water and food and to repair vessels was given a boost by a number of Huguenot refugees who arrived in the 1680s. Dutch people, known as Boers, also moved farther into the interior and founded communities. At the end of the Napoleonic Wars in 1814, the Cape Colony became a British possession.

Initially the British had no plans to settle the area, but missionaries arrived to convert the African people living there. A few British people had settled in South Africa from 1660 when it was a Dutch colony. From 1820, there was an assisted passage scheme to foster emigration from the United Kingdom, and later in the century Indians were also encouraged to settle there. The Dutch farmers remained, but following disputes with

This poster dated c.1927–1933 advertises tobacco, one of the crops introduced into Rhodesia by British settlers.

the British government after slavery was abolished in 1834, they moved north to found the Orange Free State, Natal and the Transvaal. All eventually became separate colonies with their own governments.

When diamonds were discovered in 1870 on the border of the Cape Colony, another major influx of emigrants began. Some fifteen years later, gold was discovered in the Transvaal. This too brought more people: engineers to build mines, prospectors and tradesmen. After the Boer War, at the very end of the 19th century, there was a shortage of labour in the Transvaal, and thousands of Chinese "coolies" were brought in.

RHODESIA

Rhodesia was named after Cecil Rhodes, once Prime Minister of South Africa, who in 1889 was granted a charter to develop land north of the South African colonies. In 1923 it became a separate territory, divided into Northern Rhodesia (Zambia), Southern Rhodesia (Zimbabwe) and Nyasaland (Malawi).

By 1965, Britain had withdrawn from all its possessions, except in South Africa. With the coming of independence for the African countries, many white settlers remained, but, post-decolonization, most of the previously British territories have gone through periods of political upheaval and war. Some settlers have remained, others have moved to another country in the continent.

The Boer War between the British and settlers of Dutch origin ended in 1901.

> ### FURTHER HELP
>
> Bull, Esmé *Aided Immigration from Britain to South Africa 1857–1867* (Pretoria)
> Philip, Peter *British Residents at the Cape 1795–1819* (Cape Town)
> Spencer, Shelagh O'Byrne *British Settlers in Natal 1824–1857*
> The Genealogical Society of South Africa has published lists of people, such as those who were sponsored to emigrate and settlers in the various colonies.

Other British territories

In addition to its major colonies in the larger countries around the world, Britain acquired a number of smaller territories, many of them from France in 1814, following the end of the Napoleonic Wars. Since the end of World War II, most of these former colonies have become independent, although many have remained within the Commonwealth. Britain was also involved in the government of places, although they were never officially part of the British Empire. Most had a strategic importance or were occupied to prevent another power establishing itself. Places not included in previous sections are listed below. The dates given are the start and end of official involvement in government, but British people both arrived before and remained after these dates. Records may be in Britain or in the country's archives.

THE MEDITERRANEAN

Gibraltar was ceded to Britain following the War of the Spanish Succession in 1713. Its main importance was as a naval base.

Malta became a British possession in 1815 and was also used mainly as a naval base. The naval Commander in Chief was always the island's governor, supported by a council. The Royal Navy withdrew from the dockyard there in 1950, and it became independent in 1964.

Cyprus was effectively under the control of the British during 1878–1960, although it was nominally a Turkish possession.

THE MIDDLE EAST

Aden came under British rule in 1839, when it was administered as part of India until 1937. Then it became a Crown colony and gained independence in 1967.

Palestine was administered by the British under a United Nations Mandate from 1917, the year in which Arthur Balfour, the Foreign Secretary, declared that the government favoured the establishment of a Jewish state there. Jewish immigrants started to arrive in great numbers, and, after World War II, the United Nations made it into the state of Israel, and the British withdrew.

Although Britain never formally ruled any of the other countries in the Middle East, it did have a strong influence in Syria, Jordan, Iraq,

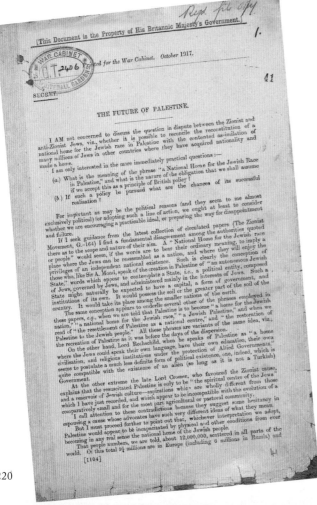

LEFT A copy of The Balfour Declaration, which led to the creation of the state of Israel in 1917.

Even in tropical Tonga the British managed to retain the dress and customs of their homeland.

St Helena was primarily important as a naval base so needed to grow food for all its visitors.

Bahrain, Kuwait, Muscat and Oman, and communities of British people lived in these countries.

THE FAR EAST AND INDIAN OCEAN

British possessions and protectorates in the Far East included Hong Kong (1898–1997), Malaya (1786–1957), North Borneo, also known as Sabah (1881–1963), Sarawak (1839–1963) and Brunei (1888–1984). In the Indian Ocean, Mauritius (1814–1968), the Maldives (1887–1965) and the Seychelles (1814–1976) came under British rule.

THE PACIFIC

In the Pacific, the main areas of British rule were the Fiji Islands (1874–1970) and Tonga (1900–70).

A number of smaller islands came under the Western Pacific High Commission, including the Gilbert & Ellice Islands, now known as Kiribati and Tuvalu respectively (1892–1978); the Solomon Islands (1893–1978) and the New Hebrides, now called Vanuatu, administered as a condominium with France from 1906 (1887–1980).

THE SOUTH ATLANTIC

St Helena's main claim to fame is as the place where Napoleon was imprisoned and died, but its history as a British possession dates back to 1659. It was important even before that as a place for European ships to stop off on their voyages from Africa to the New World. It came under the administration of the East India Company until 1836, when it became a Crown colony.

British sailors played an important role in making the Empire visible to its overseas subjects.

Over the years, many Saints, as the inhabitants are known, relocated to South Africa. Records related to St Helena are divided between TNA and the East India Company's archives.

Like St Helena, Ascension Island's main importance was as a naval base. It became a dependency of St Helena in 1922. Naval personnel made up the majority of the inhabitants. TNA has registers and there is a transcript of BMD records for 1839–61 at the SoG.

Tristan da Cunha was first discovered in 1506 by the Portuguese admiral Tristão da Cunha, when the island was used as a temporary base for whaling ships. The British claimed it in 1816, when there were already a few settlers, and the population grew gradually. In 1938, it became a dependency of St Helena. Following a volcanic eruption in 1961, the whole population of the island was evacuated. They remained in England until 1963, when the majority returned but some remained. There is a register of BMD for 1867–1955 in TNA.

All three of the above islands remain under British rule. There are a number of books on their histories that contain genealogical data.

Other British communities overseas

British communities can be found all over the world, not just in the countries of the old British Empire. You can use this section to research British people who lived or worked abroad for awhile and also ancestors who were born in these countries.

EUROPE

Many people went to Europe for reasons of health, to escape the threat of social shame or imprisonment or to make a limited income go farther. For the gentry, especially in the 19th century, living abroad in genteel poverty was preferable to getting a job in Britain. Such people generally stayed in touch with the diplomatic legation, so references to them will be found in TNA, and their BMD will be in the FRC, but records relating to those who did not stay in touch will have to be sought in local archives. In the 19th

The marriage of Charles II to Catherine of Braganza reinforced links with Portugal.

century in particular, Europe was also a place where people sent their children for an education, to learn fashionable French and, later, German.

France

Despite the long history of hostilities between the two countries, France

remained the epitome of civilization to the British, and many chose to spend time there between wars. Since 1792 there has been a system of civil registration, with the records being held, where they remain, in the office of the local mayor of each *commun*, or community. There are some 36,000 *communs* in France, so it is essential to know where your ancestors lived. Each *département*, roughly equivalent to the English county, also has archives, where a copy of the local records should be deposited. Parish registers were kept before the French Revolution, but many were destroyed. Those that survived are mainly in the departmental archives.

Germany

Before unification in 1871, Germany consisted of a number of small states. They all had their own laws, and this is reflected in which records are kept and what information is included in them.

Portugal and Madeira

The harmonious relations between Britain and Portugal meant that, long before 20th-century holiday homes, there were British communities in Portugal and its dependency, the island of Madeira. This began with the marriage of Charles II to Catherine of Braganza in 1662, but its continuance may have had something to do with the British fondness for port and Madeira wine.

Civil registration was set up in 1832, though non-Catholics were not obliged to comply until 1878, and it was the responsibility, at different times, of the Church and the state. It

Madeira in the Atlantic was, and remains, a favourite destination for British people, either on holiday or as a home.

The English artist John Augustus Atkinson produced this picture in 1803/4 on a visit to his uncle, one of many people working at the Russian royal court.

the University of Leeds (www.leeds.ac.uk/library/spcoll/lra/).

CENTRAL AND SOUTH AMERICA

In Central and South America, Britain ruled only three small areas. Guyana and British Honduras (now Belize) became independent in 1966 and 1981 respectively. The Falkland Islands were originally occupied to protect whaling ships in the area. They were not settled until 1833 and remained under the control of the Navy until 1843, when a governor and legislative council were appointed.

There was, however, a strong British presence in Paraguay, Uruguay and especially Argentina from the middle of the 19th century. Many expatriates went there to develop agricultural land. There was also a Welsh community in Patagonia, on the southernmost tip of the continent, which was established in 1865.

Records relating to these people will be in the archives of the various countries, though individuals may appear in British government papers if they needed assistance from the local embassy.

was not until 1911 that a unified system became fully established. Records are today held in local archives, and national archives in Lisbon.

The small British community in Funchal, the capital of Madeira, built a Protestant church there in the early 19th century. The Roman Catholic Church had previously objected strongly to the Protestant presence and did not allow a burial ground until 1761. Many servicemen were buried there, but it was also used by Protestants from a number of other countries. Copies of the church registers have been made and deposited in the Guildhall Library and with the SoG.

RUSSIA

Merchants established trade links with Russia in the 16th century, and the 1698 visit of Peter the Great to England to study ship-building was part of a long association between the two countries, which lasted until the 1930s. The Muscovy Company, which traded with Russia, was set up in 1555. The largest British community was based in St Petersburg, and from the 19th century included engineers and

other technical experts who helped to build factories and railways, but there were also employment opportunities for British men and women as teachers and nannies.

The records of the English church in St Petersburg are now in the Guildhall Library. TNA has Foreign Office papers related to various British communities and passport records dating from the beginning of the 19th century. Many of the records of companies that worked in Russia are held at

Welsh choral traditions went with settlers to Patagonia in South America, where their descendants still live today.

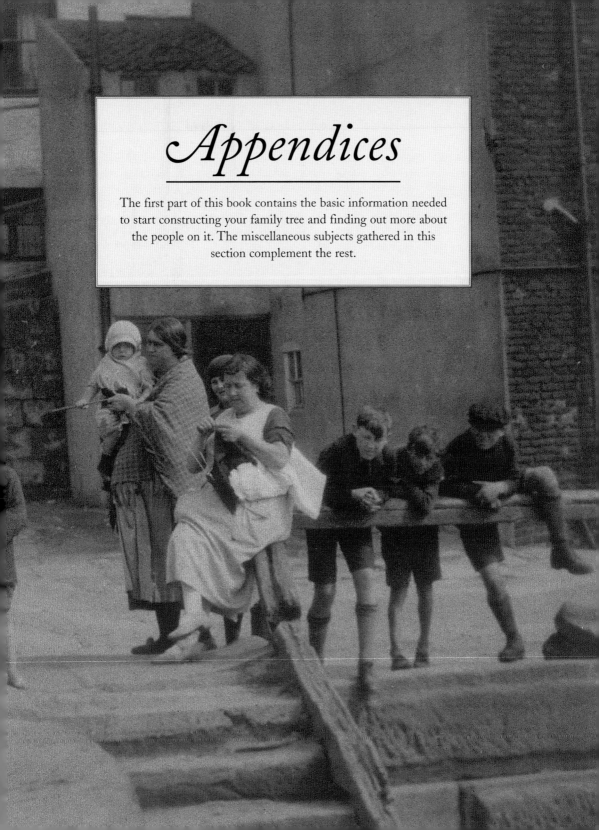

Appendices

The first part of this book contains the basic information needed to start constructing your family tree and finding out more about the people on it. The miscellaneous subjects gathered in this section complement the rest.

Sources for pre-1538 research

If you have successfully traced your forebears back to 1538, and want to extend your research beyond that date, you will find that the work becomes much harder. Constructing a tree for pre-1538 ancestry is feasible only if you can link your family to the nobility or landed gentry. Owning land brought obligations, which means that people who did so were likely to carry out duties that will be mentioned in records. Landownership or occupation was also the basis for taxation, which also produced records.

RECORDS

From parish registers, which recorded, among other things, christenings, marriages and burials, to military and criminal records, you will find a wide variety of written sources by which you

might be able to trace your pre-1538 ancestors. Note that women were considered of relatively little importance, and so rarely appear in documents.

Parish registers

If parish registers for the areas you are interested in have survived, it is possible to trace ancestry of even relatively poor people back to 1538, especially if the family did not move very far. Going beyond that date is much more difficult, however, because fewer records were kept and therefore fewer have survived. History often seems to be a process of increasing bureaucracy, and with bureaucracy come written records, which is why it is easier to trace your more recent forebears and find out more about them than it is to research your more distant ancestors.

In the absence of parish registers it is difficult to reconstruct family trees properly. There may well be a number of people with the same surname in a locality, but rarely anything that indicates whether they are brothers, cousins or more distant relations.

Landownership

When William I (William the Conqueror) came to the throne in 1066 he found that England had a functioning administrative system. In 1086 he ordered a survey of his new possessions, which were recorded in the Domesday Book. Only landowners or occupiers were to be named in the Book, and only a few of these are actually included.

The Church was an extensive landowner throughout the Middle Ages,

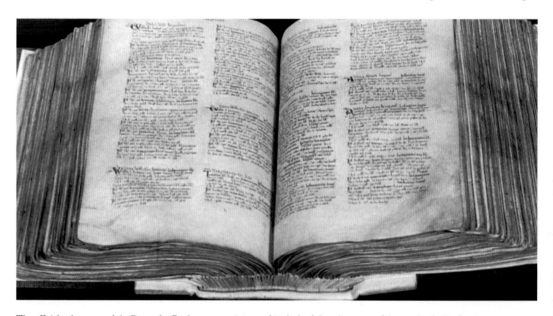

The officials who prepared the Domesday Book were more interested in the land than the names of the people who lived on it.

and cartularies of the possessions of monasteries and abbeys survive. These were administrative registers, containing, among other matters, copies of deeds and leases. Although mainly associated with religious foundations, cartularies were also kept by other landowners. From the late 12th century there are surviving property transfers made through Feet of Fines deeds kept in The National Archives (TNA).

Some manorial records, especially of those manors owned by the Crown, survive and a few predate 1066.

Taxation

The main form of taxation in medieval times was the Lay Subsidies, levied between 1290 and 1332 by statute, which means that they were not collected regularly but only when the Crown had need of revenue and passed legislation to collect it. Another was held in 1524, based on the value of property, income from the land or wages. The records are in TNA, but, unfortunately, the earlier ones do not often include names.

Between 1377 and 1381 a poll tax was imposed on all people over 14, including women. The one levied in 1377 has the best collection of individuals' names.

Borough records

The records of towns granted special status as boroughs free to administer their own affairs are held either locally or in County Record Offices (CROs). In addition to matters relating to property, they may include information about officials, members of guilds and their freemen.

Medieval guilds were rich and powerful. In 1388 the Crown ordered a survey of guilds and chantries (endowments, many of which were set up by guilds, to pay for masses to be said for

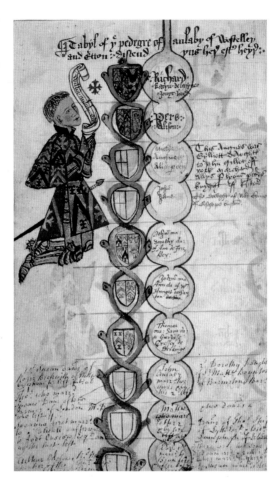

LEFT This pedigree, produced around 1450, shows the descent of the family of a Thomas Anlaby. A rare, pre-1538 document such as this, will be confined to the ancestors of the nobility.

people's souls), and the returns made then, now in TNA, give details of their rules and regulations and landownership, which may mention individuals.

Wills

Some medieval wills do still survive. The earliest one in the Prerogative Court of Canterbury (PCC) dates from 1383, and there are other medieval wills in diocesan courts, now held in CROs or Diocesan Record Offices (DROs). Indexes to, or transcriptions of, these wills may be published or available in the repository holding them.

Inquisitions Post Mortem

When a tenant of the Crown died, an inquiry was held to ensure that the land passed to the rightful heir. This was called an Inquisition Post Mortem, and it should not be confused with an inquest held to determine how a person had died. Some ordinary people were called as witnesses. Escheators, as the officials who carried out this task were called, conducted similar inquiries in the case of minors or people who became incapable of administering their affairs through mental incapacity. These records are held in TNA.

Criminal records

Before the Assize system of courts was instituted at the end of the 13th century, the General Eyre, a court held every few years, toured Britain. It dealt with both serious crimes and property matters. Some records for it survive in The National Archives.

Palatinates, Duchies and Wales

TNA holds records of all kinds for the Palatinate of Durham (abolished in 1536), the Palatinate of Chester and the Duchy of Lancaster. The Duchy of Cornwall, which is still part of the Prince of Wales's possessions, has its own separate office. In addition to Cornwall, this Duchy had holdings in the West Country.

There are few Welsh records before 1284, and they are distributed in a number of places, mainly the National Library of Wales or TNA.

Military records

There was no standing army before the English Civil War. Instead, troops were raised as needed, initially through the obligation of landowners' tenants to do military service. Knights who held land from the Crown had to provide their own men and equipment to fight for their king. Later, this feudal obligation was replaced by a contractual system and the use of commissions, which gave individuals the authority to recruit troops on behalf of the Crown. The use of mercenaries and the payment of men also created records, which are now in TNA.

Published records

Official records from before the 17th century are mainly kept in Latin, or occasionally Norman French, and before secretary hand was introduced court hand was used. This is much harder to read. Begin, therefore, with any printed material.

There are a surprising number of published medieval documents, proportionately more than later records. Early inquests from many counties, for example, have been produced. Calendars to chancery records, relating to grants of land, Exchequer records relating to taxes and the King's/ Queen's Bench Court law, both criminal and civil, are also available.

Armorial bearings

The regulation of armorial bearings did not really begin until the 15th century, but before that people used coats of arms, badges and seals to represent and identify themselves. Tombs in churches often display the armorial bearings of their inhabitants. These are particularly useful to determine the wife's family, since her parentage is rarely mentioned on inscriptions. Heraldic pedigrees are another useful source of information.

OTHER POSSIBILITIES

Even if you can't find your particular ancestors in any pre-1538 records, you may be able to find their origins.

Distribution of names

As mentioned before, surnames were not much used by the majority of the population before the 15th century, although noblemen started using them earlier, in some cases around the time of the Conquest in 1066.

Before names became fixed, the same person might be given different names in different documents. A man might be John the Smith in his home village, to distinguish him from John the Baker and John the Cooper, or John Crisp because he had noticeably curly hair. When he went to the nearest market town, he was

LEFT Transcript of the Assize of Northampton, 1176. The legal reforms of Henry II's reign were of fundamental importance in English constitutional development.

John of Wootton, because that was his home village, and when he wanted to sort out his inheritance on his father's death, he was referred to as John, son of William.

Some surnames are found only or mainly in certain areas, which gives a strong indication that your family ultimately came from that region. A Victorian scholar, H.B. Guppy, wrote *Homes of Family Names in Great Britain* (London, 1890), in which he used early documents to identify in which counties particular names were found in medieval and Tudor times. This book is out of print and not easily obtained, but subsequent compilers of dictionaries have drawn on it and often mention his findings. Other authors have written studies on the names of particular regions, such as Scotland, Ireland, Cornwall, etc., which may be obtainable through your local library or available to read in an academic library.

RESEARCHING ANCESTRY PRE-1538

Apart from the Royal Family, there is only a handful of families that can trace their ancestry back to 1066 and before. If you are descended from a landowning family that did not move around much, and if you are lucky in locating surviving records, the best you may be able to do is to identify a group of people who are plainly related (although, in the absence of parish registers, determining exactly what their relationship to each other was may prove impossible).

By the time you are back to the middle of the 16th century, you have thousands of ancestors. Among them should be a few rare, distinctive names, which will be much easier to find in records. Landowners and tax-payers leave the most records. Trying

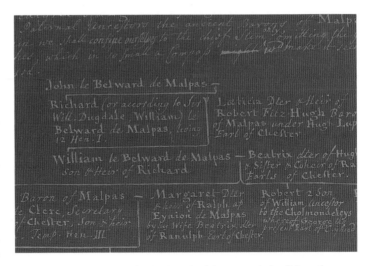

Family trees for many medieval families have already been researched and it's worth checking to see if you connect to one of the branches.

to research the forebears of an agricultural labourer called Smith will be a frustrating and ultimately fruitless endeavour, so pick the branch you decide to research with care.

In the medieval period, the Royal Family were more inclined to intermarry with people lower down the social scale than the Stuarts and later monarchs. Theoretically, every English person is possibly descended from Edward III (1327–77), who had eight surviving legitimate and three illegitimate children. Henry I (1100–35), his great-grandfather, had 20–24 illegitimate children, in addition to his sole legitimate daughter. If you can link yourself to one of these offspring, you will have a ready-made pedigree back to Anglo-Saxon times as well as being related to the Queen.

The *Genealogists' Magazine* and other specialist journals have articles on members of the nobility and their family connections, which go back to the pre-Conquest period.

The majority of records for pre-1538 genealogy will be in TNA.

Borough records and CROs may have some others, and there are large collections of medieval manuscripts in the British Library and the Bodleian.

If you do manage to trace your ancestry back to the 16th century and a rural area, it's a fair guess that your forebears originated in the locality. You can then do a blanket search of all the documents you can find relating to that place, in the hope that the people of that name that are mentioned in them can somehow be fitted together into your family history.

> ### FURTHER HELP
>
> Camp, Anthony J. *My Ancestor Came with the Conqueror* (SoG)
> Hoyle, Richard *Tudor Taxation Records: A guide for users* (TNA)
> Riden, Philip *Record Sources for Local History* (Batsford)
> TNA Military Records Information 1 *Medieval and Early Modern Soldiers*
> TNA Domestic Records Information 5 *Medieval and Early Modern Sources for Family History*

Paleography

Until very recently, all documents had to be written by hand. Over the centuries, a number of handwriting styles have been used for official documents, and the family historian needs to be able to recognize – and read – the different styles in order to understand different source material.

DIFFERENT HANDWRITING STYLES

Before the late 19th century all documents had to be handwritten. A variety of styles were used, depending on the time and whether they were produced by professional scriveners or private individuals.

Copperplate

From about 1700, a style of writing known as copperplate was used. It was called this because it was based on the writing in book illustration, which was produced by engravers on a copper plate. It has thin upstrokes and thick downstrokes. In the mid-19th century, a modified style called cursive was taught to schoolchildren, and the fashion for it lasted until the middle of the 20th century. Both styles present few problems to the researcher.

Italic

This style of writing, which has recently enjoyed a revival, was originally introduced into England in the 16th century. It was considered simpler to write than the court hand then used, and was therefore regarded as particularly suitable for women. Elizabeth I (1533–1601) was taught it as a child, and so it became fashionable first among the aristocracy and upper classes, and then farther down the social hierarchy. Variations on it are found in private papers, which are comparatively easy to read. Fortunately, most parish registers were also kept by people who had learned italic. It was not, however, much used by clerks preparing official documents.

Secretary hand

This style developed out of legal, or chancery, hand, which began in the 15th century. Chancery and secretary hands were used for legal documents until the 18th century, so this is the style of writing that most family historians will encounter in official records.

Most of the lower-case letters look familiar, but there are a few that present particular problems. They often have different forms, depending on whether they come at the end of a word or not:

- c looks like the modern r.
- e in the middle of words can resemble a modern c. At the end of a

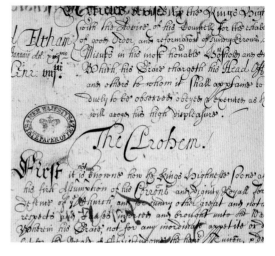

Copperplate writing was used both by officials and ordinary people, and is comparatively easy to read.

Many documents were written in a mixture of italic and secretary hand elements.

word, it often looks like a modern e written backward.

- n and m at the end of words often have an elongated last downward stroke, which may curl back under the rest of the letter.

- s at the end of words often consists of just a circle with an upward flourish.

- th is written in two ways, reflecting two separate sounds. One looks like a y, which is why you find "the" written as "ye" (the familiar "ye olde teashoppe"). In fact, this is an old symbol, called "thorn", which has been dropped from the modern alphabet, and was pronounced "th", not "y". The other way, th, is found in words such as "mother" and "father", which are therefore never written with the y symbol.

- w can look like an i and a v written next to each other.

Capital letters, which gave clerks scope for decorative flourishes, present the greatest problems, which can make reading surnames hard. The capital F was usually written as two lower-case fs side by side. This should not be translated as "ff". People who call themselves a name such as ffinch because they have found it in an old document are making a mistake.

READING OLD DOCUMENTS

If you are finding a word difficult to read, try breaking it down into individual letters by working out how the clerk might have written it. Look for other words in the document that you can read, and use these to compare individual letters.

You may find it easier to get a photocopy of a lengthy document from a record office so that you can puzzle out what it says at home, rather than spend time doing this that you could be using more profitably there.

When you are translating a particularly difficult piece of writing, it's a good idea to number the lines on both the photocopy and your translation. This will make it easier to go back to and find the words you could not read. A highlighter is also useful to indicate words you will need to return to.

FURTHER HELP

Buck, W.S.B. *Examples of Handwriting 1150–1650* (SoG)
Preston, J.F. and Yeandle, L. *English Handwriting 1400–1650* (Binghamton, USA)

If a word or name puzzles you, try saying it out loud and consider what the local accent might have been.

Abbreviations

Clerks frequently abbreviated common words or combinations of letters. They usually put either a horizontal line above the next letter to show that something had been omitted or a full stop to show that the word had been shortened by omitting the last letters.

Spelling

Spelling was very much a matter of individual choice until the 19th century. The same word may even be written in different ways within a single document. How surnames were spelt may also reflect local accents.

Italic handwriting fell out of favour in the late 18th century but was re-introduced in the 20th.

Secretary hand was the everyday style used by official clerks. It was often highly abbreviated and idiosyncratic.

Latin

Before 1733, most legal documents were written in Latin, except during the period of the Commonwealth (1649–60). They were usually also in a highly abbreviated form that is complicated to decipher. If you need to read legal documents before the first part of the 18th century, you have two choices: you can take a course in Latin for family and local historians or you can hire an expert, many of whom advertise in family history magazines.

UNDERSTANDING LATIN

One of the main problems with Latin is that it is an inflected language, that is to say the endings of the words change in accordance with the meaning. Originally Anglo-Saxon was too, but modern English has largely done away with inflections, although some remain. Plurals, for example, usually end in -s today (a parent/two parents), but child/children retains the old form of the plural. The possessive, showing ownership, ends in -'s, e.g. the child's parents. Latin, however, has many more case endings, and verbs also change according to their tense (past, present, future, conditional, etc) and whether they are singular or plural. The word order also changes according to significance, and verbs are generally put at the end of a sentence. It is impossible to work through a document written in Latin with a dictionary, translating word for word.

Useful Latin words

Names
Most names are obvious, but a few might cause confusion in Latin:
Carolus/Caroli = Charles/of Charles
Henricus/Henrici = Henry/of Henry
Jacobus/Jacobi = James/of James
Johanna/Johannae = Joan/of Joan
Johannus/Johanni = John (sometimes abbreviated as Jno)/of John
Ludovica/Ludoviae = Louisa/of Louisa
Ludovicus/Ludovici = Louis or Lewis/of Louis or of Lewis, although Ludovic was a name used by Roman Catholics.
Maria/Marae = Mary/of Mary
Petrus/Petri = Peter/of Peter
Ricardus/Ricardi = Richard/of Richard
Sara(h)/Sarae = Sara(h)/of Sarah
Thomas/Thomae = Thomas/of Thomas
Wilelmus/Guiliemus/Wilelmi/Guiliemi = William/of William

Family relationships
filia/filiae = daughter/daughters
filius/filii = son/sons
frater = brother
gemellae = twins (female)
gemelli = twins (male or where one was a boy and the other a girl)
genetrix = mother
ignotus/ignoti (m.)/ignota /ignotae (f.) = unknown /of an unknown
illegitimus (m.)/illegitima (f.) = illegitimate
mater = mother
pater = father
relicta/relectae = widow/of the widow
soror = sister
uxor/ex uxore = wife/by his wife

vidua = widow
viduus = widower

Other words and phrases
aetas = age
baptizatus/a = baptized
conjugati fuerunt = were married
cum bannis = with banns
cum licentia = with a licence
de = of/from
eodem die = the same day
et = and
defunctus/defuncti = deceased/of the deceased
filius (m.)/filia (f.) populi = son/daughter of the people, i.e. illegitimate
fuit = was
interfectus (m.)/interfecta (f.) = killed
mortuus (m.)/mortua (f.) = dead
parocia = of/from the parish
pestis = plague
sepultus (m.)/sepulta (f.) est = was buried
spurius (m.)/spuria (f.) = illegitimate (literally, false)

Occupations/descriptions
There are far too many occupations and descriptions to list all the Latin translations, but the following are the more common ones found in registers.
ancilla = maidservant
armiger = esquire (literally someone with a coat of arms)
bergensis = burgess/freeman
clericus = priest
faber = smith (faber ferrarius is a blacksmith)
generosus (m.)/generosa (f.) = gentleman/woman
Gwallia/Gwallius (m.)/Gwallia (f.) = Wales/Welshman/woman
Hibernia/Hiburnus (m.)/Hiberna (f.) = Ireland/Irishman/woman
ludimagister = schoolmaster
magister = master, which was what a clergyman who had a master's degree was called
mercator = merchant

READING CHURCH REGISTERS

Some early parish registers and Catholic registers until comparatively late are also in Latin, but the meaning is usually fairly obvious once you have learned a few basic words. Names of men usually end in -us and names of women in -a. The possessive is -i for men and -ae for women. These Latin forms were usually created by simply adding a case ending to the name, e.g. Edward became Edwardus and Elizabeth was Elizabetha or Elisabetha. Edward, son of Edward and Elizabeth Brown, would be written "Edwardus filius Edwardi et Elizabethae Brown".

This was not what they were actually called by other people but simply how it was written in the records. In the 18th century, the Latin form of names became popular, but by this time almost all official registers were written in the English language.

Even after registers were no longer kept in Latin, some ministers used the language to write identifying or even uncomplimentary comments about their parishioners so that they would not understand what was written about them.

Archivists in Britain have to have a basic standard of Latin to get their qualifications, so they should be able

FURTHER HELP

McLaughlin, Eve *Simple Latin for Family Historians* (McLaughlin Guide)
Morris, Janet *A Latin Glossary for Family and Local Historians* (FFHS)

to help out with a phrase or very short passage. Dictionaries and glossaries will help to translate the more unusual occupations (the most common ones are given below). Sometimes the names of places were also entered in Latin, which might cause some confusion with proper names.

---

miles = soldier
mulier = (old) woman or wife
nauta = sailor
peregrinus/peregrini (m.)/ peregrina/peregrinae (f.) = traveller/of a traveller
Scotia/Scotius (m.)/Scotia (f.) = Scotland/ Scotsman/woman
senex = old man
virgo = (young) unmarried woman

Numerals
Numbers, especially sums of money, are often written in Roman numerals in documents that are otherwise in English.
i = 1
ii = 2
iii = 3
iv or iiii or iiij = 4
v = 5
vi or vj = 6
vii or vij = 7
viii or viij = 8
ix = 9
x = 10

xx = 20
xxx = 30
xl = 40
l = 50
lx = 60
lxx = 70
lxxx = 80
xc = 90
C = 100
D = 500
M = 1000

Dates
uno = 1st
duo = 2nd
tertius/tercius = 3rd
quartus = 4th
quintus = 5th
sextus = 6th
septimus = 7th
octavus = 8th
nonus = 9th
decimus = 10th
undecimus = 11th
duodecimus = 12th
tertius decimus = 13th
quartus decimus = 14th
quintus decimus = 15th
sextus decimus = 16th
septimus decimus = 17th

duodevicesimo = 18th
undevicesimo = 19th
vicesimo = 20th
unus et vicesimo = 21st
alter et vicesimo = 22nd
vicesimo tertio = 23rd
vicesimo quarto = 24th
vicesimo quinto = 25th
vicesimo sexto = 26th
vicesimo septimo = 27th
duodetricesimus or vicesimo octavo = 28th
undetricesimus or vicesimo nono = 29th
tricesimus = 30th
unus et tricesimus = 31st
The last day of the month, whatever its date, might also appear as "ultimo", sometimes abbreviated to "ult,". Since this means "the last", it may sometimes mean the previous month, e.g. where a child was baptized in the month following its birth and the clerk noted the dates of both the baptism and the birth.

Months
Januarius/Januarii = January/of January
Februarius/Februarii = February/of February
Martius/Martii = March/ of March
Aprilis/Aprilis = April/ of April
Maius/Maii = May/of May
Junius/Junii = June/of June
Julius/Julii = July/of July
Augustus/Augusti = August/of August
September/Septembris = September/of September
October/Octobris = October/of October
November/Novembris = November/of November
December/Decembris = December/of December

Days
dies domenicus = Sunday
dies lune = Monday
dies martis = Tuesday
dies mercurii = Wednesday
dies jovis = Thursday
dies veneris = Friday
dies sabbati = Saturday

Name changes and important dates

The county divisions in the British Isles have their roots in pre-Conquest times, but since then they have been changed to a degree. In 1888 and in 1974 changes were made and the boundaries reorganized.

ENGLISH COUNTY NAME CHANGES

A major reorganization of the English counties in 1974 means that some, but not all, were amalgamated or renamed. The ones which altered were as follows:

Cambridgeshire (enlarged to include Huntingdonshire)

Cumbria (previously the counties of Cumberland and Westmoreland)

Hereford & Worcester (previously the counties of Herefordshire and Worcestershire)

Humberside (created from parts of Yorkshire and Lincolnshire)

Leicestershire (enlarged to include Rutland)

Yorkshire was divided into North, West and South Yorkshire (previously North, East and West Ridings)

Six larger metropolitan counties were also created:

Greater Manchester
Merseyside
South Yorkshire
West Yorkshire
Tyne and Wear (including parts of Northumberland and Durham)
West Midlands
Greater London, which increased to absorb almost all of the old county of Middlesex as well as parts of Essex, Surrey, Kent and Hertfordshire, was also created.

SCOTLAND

The regions in Scotland, which resulted from changes made in 1973, are as follows:

Highland (Caithness-shire, Inner Hebrides, Morayshire [part], Nairn, Ross & Cromarty, Sutherland)

Grampian (Banffsire, Kincardineshire, Morayshire [part])

Tayside (Forfarsire, Perthshire [part])

Lothian (East Lothian, West Lothian, Nairn)

Borders (Berwickshire, Midlothian (part), Peebles-shire, Roxburghshire, Selkirkshire)

Central (Clackmannonshire, Fife, Kinross-shire, part of Perthshire, most of Stirlingshire, parts of West Lothian)

Strathclyde (Buteshire, Argyllshire [part], Ayrshire [part], Lanarkshire, Renfrewshire and Perthshire [part])

Dumfries & Galloway (Dumfriesshire, Kirkcudbrightshire, Wigtown)

IMPORTANT DATES

Because much of the information available to the family tree researcher is recorded by the Church, it is useful to be aware of the history of the established religious denominations in this country.

The history of Nonconformity

1570s Presbyterians and Independents founded.

1580 Separatists founded.

1604 Brownists founded.

1611 Anabaptists and Baptists founded. Anabaptists do not believe in baptism at all. Baptists, who believe that adults, not children, should be baptized, are further divided into General and Particular Baptists. The problems created for the family historian by people who do not baptize infants are obvious.

1624 The Religious Society of Friends, who became known as the Quakers, founded. They are unusual among early Nonconformists in keeping good records from the beginning.

1640 Independents and Congregationalists founded.

1649–1660 The Commonwealth Period. Seekers, Ranters, Fifth Monarchists, Muggletonians, etc. were tiny sects that never attracted a significant number of followers or established church buildings but lingered on after the Restoration (in the case of the Muggletonians to 1979).

1716 Unitarians split off from the Presbyterians.

1723 Moravian Church brought to England from Germany.

1730 Glasites founded by John Glas in Scotland. They did not believe in baptism. A follower, Robert Sandeman, came to London in 1760 and founded the Sandemanians. By 1870, they had died out in Britain but continued in America until 1890. (Registers were not surrendered in the 19th century.)

1740 Methodism founded.

1744 Hearers and Followers of the Apostles founded (disappeared before the end of the 18th century).

1753 Inghamites founded by Benjamin Ingham, formerly of the Moravian Church. United with the Scottish Daleite Society in 1814.

Welsh county name changes

Following an Act of 1972, the old Welsh counties were reorganized and renamed as follows:

Old name	New name (from 1972)
Brecknockshire	[Breconshire pref. spelling]
Montgomeryshire	no change
Radnorshire	Powys
Cardiganshire	no change
Carmarthenshire	no change
Pembrokeshire	Dyfed
Caernarvonshire	no change
Merionethshire	no change
Anglesey [plus part of Denbighshire]	Gwynedd
Denbighshire	no change
Flintshire [plus part of Merionethshire]	Clywd
Monmouthshire [plus part of Breconshire]	Gwent
Glamorgan	South Glamorgan West Glamorgan Mid-Glamorgan

1772 Ann Lee becomes leader of the Shakers, who went to America in 1774.

1779 The Countess of Huntingdon's Connexion split off from the Methodists.

1788 The New Church (Swedenborgians or New Jerusalemites) came to Britain.

1792 Universalists developed from the Unitarians.

1797 Methodist New Connexion founded.

1801 Primitive Methodists founded.

1806 Independent Methodists founded.

1815 Bible Christians split off from the Methodists.

1827 Plymouth Brethren founded. (They did not surrender their registers in the 19th century.)

1827 Catholic Apostolic Church (Irvingites) founded. They are not connected to the Roman Catholics but were ejected from the Scottish Presbyterian Church.

1836 Campbellites split off from Scottish Baptists.

1837 Church of Jesus Christ of Latter Day Saints (Mormons) first sent missionaries to Britain and encouraged converts to emigrate to the USA.

1857 United Methodist Free Churches founded. Those who decided against this union formed the Wesleyan Reform Union.

1865 Salvation Army founded.

1878 American Branch of the Salvation Army founded.

The history of British Catholicism

1661–5 A series of Acts were passed that were intended to enforce conformity to Anglicanism. Lists of Roman Catholics were often included in parish registers.

1661 The Corporation Act laid down that every elected official in local or national government had to take Holy Communion in a Church of England service. Those who did so were given a sacrament certificate, which was presented at Quarter Sessions for local government posts, or to one or other of the national courts, depending on the job involved. The former will now be in CROs and the latter in TNA.

1672 The Test Act widened the categories of the Corporation Act to include all officials, civil or military, who also had to take the oath of allegiance to the Crown and the oath of supremacy, which asserted the primacy of the Church of England. It was not until 1828 that a declaration was substituted for the sacrament certificate. This insistence on the Church of England meant that Nonconformists had difficulties taking the oath as well.

1676 Bishop Compton tried to discover how many Catholics there were in England. Only those over the age of 16 were recorded, mainly men. Surviving records are in the Diocesan Record Offices (DROs) in Canterbury, Winchester and Lichfield, with others in the Bodleian Library at Oxford University.

1696 The Solemn Association, an oath to support the (Protestant) succession, had to be taken by all office holders. Other groups of people were also encouraged to take it, and in some areas it seems that all men who had some status did so.

1702 The Security of Succession Act introduced an oath, which all officials had to take, denying the right of the exiled James II's son (Bonnie Prince Charlie) to succeed to the throne. As James and his son were both Roman Catholics, this created problems for some of their co-religionists.

1778 Catholics permitted to take the Oath of Allegiance, which was recorded on separate rolls from those used for Protestants.

1789 The Toleration of Catholics Act.

1829 The Catholic Emancipation Act.

Heraldry

In medieval times, when few people, including members of the aristocracy, could read, a pictorial representation was a useful way of distinguishing individuals. This might be on a seal to represent their signature, but it was especially important in battle, when the difficulty of telling one armour-clad warrior from another meant that the possibility of killing someone who was on the same side as you was high.

THE EVOLUTION OF ARMORIAL BEARINGS

Armorial bearings seem to have started out as devices embroidered on the surcoat, which went over the suit of armour (hence coat of arms), or painted on shields to identify knights. Knights also wore armour to compete in tournaments, where their supporters needed to identify whom they were cheering for or had bet on to win. Their followers or servants would wear a badge with the same design to show their allegiance. Out of this grew the art of heraldry, which seems to have arrived in England from France via Germany in about the middle of the 12th century, although there is evidence that warriors decorated their clothes and armour before that date.

ARMORIAL REGULATION

Heraldic matters are subject to strict regulation and administration, and there are various bodies to deal with them.

England, Wales and Northern Ireland

The College of Arms, which regulates armorial matters in England, Wales and Northern Ireland, was founded by Letters Patent granted by Richard III in 1484, but heralds were active in the business of armorial bearing before this date. The College consists of a number of officers who have jurisdiction over various parts of Britain and the Commonwealth, except for Scotland, which has its own regulatory system.

Between 1530 and 1687, heralds made visitations around Britain, during which they recorded the people using armorial bearings and investigated their right to them. This involved noting their pedigrees, which provide valuable information about ancestry before parish registers were kept.

Scotland and the Republic of Ireland

Although armorial practice is similar in Scotland, it is regulated there by the Lord Lyon King of Arms, whose powers are much greater than the College of Arms in England. The Lord Lyon can fine, or even imprison, people who falsely use armorial bearings. He, or she, also adjudicates on issues of genealogy and related matters.

Since 1943, the Republic of Ireland has had its own office supervising heraldic matters.

UNDERSTANDING ARMORIAL BEARINGS

The whole subject of heraldry is complicated. The following is a summary of the major points that the average family historian needs to understand. Heraldry's origins in the Middle Ages, when Norman French was the language of the court, is shown by the words still used to describe armorial bearings, often abbreviated to "arms". Arms were described in a way that made it possible to reproduce them from the words alone.

The entire armorial bearings are known as an "achievement". It consists of the most important part – the shield (also known as the escutcheon or scutcheon) – surrounded by a variety of devices and objects.

The shield

The shield is described in very particular heraldic language, called blazonry. The description of the shield starts

HERALDIC COLOURS AND THEIR HATCHING PATTERNS

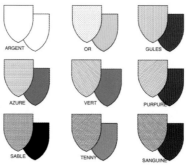

Argent (silver): plain
Or (gold): small dots
Gules (red): vertical lines
Azure (blue): horizontal lines
Vert (green): diagonal lines running from top left to bottom right
Purpure (purple): diagonal lines running from top right to bottom left
Sable (black): solid black, or grid of vertical and horizontal lines
Tenny (tawny orange): horizontal + diagonals from top right to bottom left
Brown (Gules + Vert): horizontal + diagonals from top left to bottom right

| VAIR | COUNTERVAIR | POTENT | COUNTERPOTENT |
| ERMINE | ERMINES | ERMINOIS | PEAN |

The heraldic backgrounds also have variations that are collectively called furs. Again their names are taken from the Norman French.

with the background, made up of certain "metals", colours or "furs".

The charge

On top of these backgrounds can be a variety of patterns and symbols. These symbols, called charges, often contain a play on words related to the family name: someone called Wood, for example, might have a tree.

Divisions

The shield can be divided into halves, quarters and eighths, horizontally, vertically or diagonally. All these have a specialized vocabulary to describe them. The description of the shield is from the point of view of the person carrying it, and so the dexter (Latin for "right") is actually on the left-hand side as you look at it. The other side, called the sinister (Latin for "left"), is on the right-hand side from the viewer's point of view.

The badge

The badge began as a picture on a flag so that soldiers would be able to rally around their lord or join up together after a battle. Followers and employees of a family would wear their badge. Today they survive as regimental and naval badges and, less obviously, in inn

signs – the White Hart, for example, was the badge of Richard II.

Devices and objects

The crest

This is the part above the shield and represents what the knight wore on his helmet. It often includes a helmet itself, but might contain other headwear, like a cardinal's hat. In the past, different members of a family might have different crests, but today the shield and crest are inherited together. It is possible to have a shield without a crest but not vice versa. Aristocrats usually have a coronet or crown instead of a helmet, and the design of it indicates their rank.

The torse

The torse, or wreath, lies between the shield and the crest. It represents either ribbons used to fasten the helmet together or, in tournaments, the favours of the lady for whom the knight was competing.

The mantling

The mantling, or lambrequin, is a stylized representation of the flap of material that hung down behind the helmet, covering the knight's neck.

Supporters

These are animals or figures standing on either side of the shield. The direction in which they are facing and their stances are carefully distinguished.

The motto

This usually appears on a ribbon at the base of the achievement.

Family relationships

Armorial bearings are granted on an individual basis. Although other members of a person's family can use them, there should be a small variation for each individual, and understanding these differences can be useful in working out relationships.

Only the head of the family and the male members can have a crest. Symbols denote where the man bearing the arms came in the family from first to ninth son; these are called marks of cadency.

When a man married, he might combine his arms with that of his wife on his shield. How this was done indicates whether or not she was an heiress. If he simply put his arms on the dexter side and hers on the sinister, this means that she was not an heiress, but if hers are placed in a small shield at the top of and in the centre of his, called a shield or escutcheon of pretence, it shows these two things:

1) her father is dead
2) she has no surviving brothers and they had no surviving children

Children would generally take just their father's arms, unless their mother was an heiress, in which case they would combine both. This also, incidentally, led to the practice of combining surnames to make sure that a family name survived, even after there were no sons to carry it on. Usually this is in the form of a double-barrelled name, but it might involve more than two names. The longest example on record in England is Major Leone Sextus Denys Oswolf Fraudati-filus Tollemache-Tollemache-de-Orellana-Plantagenet-Tollemache-Tollemache (1884–1917).

On their shield, men might also quarter the arms of wives who had died.

Women

Women's bearings appear on a lozenge (diamond-shaped) or elliptical shape. Women's arms never include a crest, although unmarried women might use a true lover's knot of blue ribbon in its place. In Scotland there are symbols showing their position in the family, but elsewhere there are no such marks of cadency. Widows continue to use their husbands' arms impaled with their own, unless they are heiresses, in which case hers appear in an escutcheon of pretence (see above) over his. In both cases, this is in a lozenge or ellipse.

Divorce and annulments of marriage

These were such rare events that no fixed way of dealing with them was laid down. In general, a woman who divorced her husband was considered entitled to continue to bear his arms, but if she were divorced by him she no longer had this right and should revert to using her father's arms but without a true lover's knot, which was the sign of an unmarried woman.

An annulment, which ruled that a marriage had never existed, was simpler to deal with: the man reverted to the arms he had used as a bachelor and the woman to the arms she had used as a spinster.

From all this, it follows that armorial bearings could change in the course of a person's lifetime. Careful reading of a succession of arms used by an individual at different times will

An example of "dimidiated" arms, the separate arms of Margaret of France and King Edward I of England are cut in half and combined to mark their marriage.

give clues to events that had happened between particular dates.

BOGUS COATS OF ARMS AND PEDIGREES

From very early days, people tried to give themselves and their families a spurious connection to nobility by creating and using their own heraldic devices. The Victorians were the worst offenders: men who had done well in life not only paid for genealogists to create a pedigree that "proved" they had noble descent, they also bought coats of arms.

Today there are a number of companies that will supply a reproduction of a coat of arms that, they claim, was borne by someone with the same name as the purchaser. They are careful not to say that the buyer is entitled to use the device, because who can and cannot is strictly regulated. The granting of arms is done on an individual basis, and it is the person who received them and his, or more rarely her, descendants who are entitled to use them, not everyone of that family name.

If you want to have your own coat of arms, you can apply to the College of Arms or the Lord Lyon King of Arms' court, but it's a long and expensive process.

RECORDS RELATING TO ARMORIAL BEARINGS

Some of the Heralds' Visitations are still held in the College of Arms. Others found their way into a variety of hands, including libraries like the British Library, the Bodleian and Queen's College Library in Oxford. A number of summaries of the holdings (though not the pedigrees themselves) have been published, and most CROs have copies of those relating to their county. The Society of Genealogists has a card index containing descriptions of many coats of arms.

In Scotland, the Lord Lyon King of Arms' court adjudicates on heraldic and genealogical matters, and you may find records of disputes that give useful information among its cases if you have Scottish ancestry.

RESEARCHING COATS OF ARMS

Organizations, as well as people, can be granted arms, so if you find a coat of arms on a family possession, such as a piece of china or a spoon, don't assume that it belongs to your family: it might be something presented to an ancestor by the company he worked for. Alternatively, it might have been bought or even stolen as a souvenir.

If you find you have a link to a family entitled to an armorial bearing, there should be a pedigree associated with it, which will in some cases allow you to trace the family back to the period before parish registers began. Mottos were usually chosen from a standard selection.

FURTHER HELP

Slater, Steven The Complete Book of Heraldry (Lorenz Books)
Swinnerton, Iain Identifying your World War I Soldier from Badges and Photographs (FFHS)

Dates, money and measurements

The first day of the year in England and Wales was 25th March (Lady Day) until 1752, when it was changed to 1st January, which it had been in Scotland for some time. This means that before 1752 dates between 1st January and 24th March would be given what looks to us now like the previous year. To prevent confusion, always write these dates in your notes as, for example, 27th February 1721/2. Although some people, notably the Mormons in their International Genealogical Index (IGI), "correct" the year, it is impossible to know whether it has been done or not, so it's best to write both years. You may find dates before 1752 annotated as "OS" for Old Style.

The year 1752 was also when the Julian Calendar was changed to the Gregorian. To make the adjustment, eleven days were lost: 2nd September was followed by 14th September.

Regnal years

In all very early documents and in legal documents until very recently, regnal years might be used instead of the calendar year. Regnal years are counted from the beginning of a monarch's reign, and since these started on different days of the year, the years have no link with the calendar. (Though Charles II dated his reign from 30th January 1648/9, when his father was executed, rather than 1660, when he was restored to the throne after the end of the Commonwealth.) An example of a regnal date is "on the twentieth day of May in the nineteenth year of our Sovereign King George the Second", which would refer to 20th May 1746, since George

II came to the throne on 11 June 1727.

Although there is usually a clue about the calendar year in the document (it might be dated next to the signature), you may need to use a chart of regnal years to check. This is especially true of a will that may have been written years before it was proved: the date of probate might be given as the regnal rather than calendar year.

MONEY

There is no easy way to translate sums of money into their modern equivalent. There are computer programs and sites on the internet to translate money into the modern equivalent in purchasing power, but these aren't entirely satisfactory because the comparative prices of goods have changed over the years. Food, for example, is relatively cheaper now than it was in the past, but housing is much more expensive. A very rough estimate can be made by taking the average wage as £1 a week. From that, you can work out how long the average person had to work to buy something.

There were also earlier coins. In Tudor times, the groat was a silver 4d piece. When a 4d piece was issued in 1836–56, it was usually called a groat. The angel, used between the reigns of Edward IV to Charles I, varied in value: when first issued, it was worth 6s 8d, but in the reign of Edward VI, it was 10s. In the medieval period, a mark was equal to 13s 4d (66p).

MEASUREMENTS

Land was measured in a number of ways. In the Domesday Book, hides and vergates are found, but later on:

Rood = 1,210 square yards

Acre = 4,840 square yards or 0.40468 hectares (= 4 roods)

Distance was measured by

Chain = 22 yards

Furlong = 220 yards (= 10 chains)

Mile = 1,760 yards or 1.6098 kilometres (= 8 furlongs)

Other measurements you might encounter include the gill (quarter of a pint) and the quart (2 pints), mainly used for liquids. The peck (= 2 gallons) and bushel (= 4 pecks, i.e. 8 gallons) were also measures of capacity and were usually used for dry goods, like grain. Thirty-six bushels = 1 chaldron.

Abbreviated coins

Before 1972, a currency of pounds, shillings and pence was used. £1, also written as 1l, = 20 shillings, abbreviated to s.
1s = 12 pence, abbreviated to d.
There were a number of coins:
A farthing = a quarter of a penny
A halfpenny = half a penny
A penny = 1d

A threepenny bit = 3d
A sixpence = 6d (2½p)
A shilling = 12d (5p)
A florin = 2s (10p)
A half-crown or half-a-crown = 2s 6d (12½p)
A crown = 5s (25p)
A guinea = 21 shillings (£1.05)
A sovereign was a gold £1 piece

Writing family history

At some stage, you need to consider writing up your findings in a way that other people can enjoy reading. This might be an article for a magazine, a booklet for your family or even a full-scale book. Family trees and their related notes will be fully understood only by genealogists, and they record only isolated events that happened to your ancestors, rather than giving a fuller idea of their lives. It is therefore much better to turn your work into a narrative. Remember that family history work never ends – there's always another discovery to be made, always a gap that might be filled – but don't put off writing it up "until it's finished". It never will be.

CORRELATING LIVES AND WIDER EVENTS

As you go along, you can keep notes that will help to prepare your complete family history, and work out a system of recording from the start. Use a loose-leaf or ring-backed binder filled with paper, and choose one branch of the family. For each opening, use the sheet on the left- or right-hand side for events in each ancestor's life and the opposite sheet for events in the world outside or their public lives.

Busy ancestors living in interesting times may need an entire sheet for everything that happened to them each year of their lives. Others may need just one sheet for the first ten years (which may be mainly taken up with the births of their siblings), half a sheet for each year of their apprenticeship or teenage years and then a sheet or half a sheet for the rest, depending on how much happened to them.

Photographs can tell a huge amount about the lives of people of the time.

RESEARCHING THE PERIOD

For those of us who are lucky enough to have ancestors who led action-packed lives there is little difficulty in producing a narrative. Most of our forebears will, however, have lived fairly humdrum existences, and this is where extra research into local and social history comes in. What was the place like where your forebears lived? What events – local, regional and national – would have affected their lives? Also, what would life at work have been like? Finding out all this information will help you to flesh out the bones of your family story.

Background information

Most places, however small, have had publications about their history written. Some are mainly architectural but others detail the main events that might have affected your ancestors.

You may have already looked through the parish records to find references to your ancestors, but it's worth going through them again to see what other events might have impinged on their lives. You may find epidemics of smallpox or measles in burial registers, or perhaps a mention of a neighbour dying of rabies. In the quarter sessions or manorial courts there may be complaints about the conditions of the roads. You may find that someone local kept a diary that has been deposited in a local record office or library or even published.

From the mid-19th century onwards much of the local history will come from newspapers. What were the big events in the town or village? When was gas or electric lighting introduced? What was happening in the cultural life of their town or village? Was there a theatre or, in the 20th century, a cinema, and, if so, what was being shown?

You will also find directories listing the inhabitants and tradespeople useful. They usually contain background information such as market day, fairs, the main industries in the area, schools, almshouses, etc. These may give clues as to who your ancestors socialized with if they were gentry, who their rivals were if they were tradespeople and where they were likely to have shopped or gone for a drink if they were working class.

You can illustrate your family history with old pictures, either photographs from record offices or postcards bought from shops or specialist fairs. If the family's home has not changed a great deal, you can take photographs yourself.

If your family lived in a village or town that hasn't changed much, it's a good idea to go there and get a sense of what it is like. What would they have seen as they walked along the High Street? Did they pass the churchyard or cemetery, and, if so, which of their ancestors were buried there? Was the pub in existence when they lived there?

Occupations

What was involved in the work that your ancestors did? You may find museums helpful here to see the type of tools and objects they would have used and what they would have produced with them. There are also many books about occupations in the past. If you have medical ancestors, for example, a history of medicine will tell you which drugs they were likely to have used, which treatments were in fashion when they were practising and which innovations came in during their working lives. For military and naval ancestors, you will find books that detail land and sea battles they were involved in.

In addition to what your ancestors did, you can find out what they would have been likely to earn. During the 19th century, social reformers collected information about the earnings of poorer people and how they were spent. Prices can be gleaned from newspaper advertisements and, in rural areas, from reports of how much agricultural produce was being sold for in the markets. When we read about old prices, we always marvel at how cheap things seem – only 50s (£2.50) for a Harris Tweed suit in 1912 – but this takes no account of how much people were earning. Try working out how long your ancestor had to work in order to afford something. In 1912, the average wage was

Family portraits should be used to illustrate your family narrative.

about £1 a week, so it would have cost two and a half week's wages to buy such a suit.

From all this, you can reconstruct a typical day for your ancestors. What time would they have got up? What would they have worn? What would they have eaten for breakfast? What route did they take to work?

WRITING UP YOUR RESEARCH

Once you've gathered enough material to start writing, you need to assemble everything into a narrative. This is news to your readers, so what you are essentially doing is reporting what happened, as a journalist does.

Journalists are taught that what they write should answer six fundamental questions: who, what, when, where, why and how. Bear this in mind as you write: who was involved, what happened to them, when did it happen, where did it happen, why and how? The last two usually require some speculation, because we rarely have concrete evidence about why an ancestor made a particular decision, though we can often guess. The most obvious example is moving from one place to another. This might be for economic reasons or for personal ones. If your ancestor moved away from his home town to his wife's, might that have been because her family needed support? Was her mother a widow, or did she die soon after, suggesting that she was ill? Were there employment opportunities where she came from?

All the research notes made in record offices need to be turned into stories, not only of events that happened but why they may have done so.

How something happened is likewise often a matter of speculation. On the subject of moving house, did the family go by coach, cart or walk? A guess can be made depending on a combination of distance, level of income and what was available. Directories usually give the times and routes of coaches and carriers, which you can incorporate into your narrative, for example, "In 1839, William and Elizabeth moved from Elstree to Shenley. They might have caught the coach that left from the Red Lion every evening at six o'clock, but he was a poor labourer and it was only a few miles. As young and healthy people, they probably chose to walk so that they could save the money to help furnish their new home."

You can also guess how your ancestors must have felt when some event befell them. We can all put ourselves into the shoes of a pregnant woman whose husband has just died leaving her to raise four children alone, but what if the death occurred during the

Civil War with a battle being fought 16km (10 miles) away? Her worries about the future would have been doubled: she would have felt not only grief for her personal misfortune and anxiety for her future but also fear about what would happen to her and her children if the soldiers reached their town.

Be careful to distinguish between fact (what you can corroborate by references to documents) and speculation (what might have happened). Generally speaking, it is reasonable to speculate about the implications of a factual event, but to speculate from the speculation is a step too far. For example, how a name is spelled in a document might lead you to suspect that your ancestor was French. That is a possibility, but then to speculate that this supposedly French ancestor came from a village in Provence where you once had a holiday and met an innkeeper with the same name is not justifiable. Beware of writing, or saying, "he or she must have" to fill a gap in

the facts. Either you can produce evidence or you must stick to "may have".

Writing style

Use active, not passive, verbs to describe something happening. Don't say "John was given a medal for good attendance at school", say "John won a medal for good attendance at school." It makes John sound a much more interesting person: he didn't just sit and wait to be given a medal, he went out and achieved something. A careful choice of verbs can give your writing a sense of activity and movement as well as bringing your ancestors to life.

Vary the length of your sentences and their structure. Avoid long lists of "Then... then... then..."

Many writers confuse writing in a convoluted and polysyllabic way with good style. "It was not long ere they knew a little stranger was on the way", is a facetious and unnecessarily elaborate way of saying, "Soon they were expecting a child."

Be sparing with exclamation marks! The reader finds it irritating to be constantly told what they should find important. You can make your point much better by your choice of words.

If you're not very confident about punctuation, there are a number of useful guides. Alternatively, you can get someone to proof-read your work. This has the further advantage of getting a second opinion on what you have written. You've been immersed in the research for so long that you will probably find it hard to realize what you need to explain to your readers. It may be clear in your mind, but will not be to them.

References and bibliography

As you write, put in references to where you found the information. This can be as footnotes at the bottom

During the 20th century, the two World Wars affected every family in the land. Finding out where and when a photo was taken will show what part an ancestor played in military or naval campaigns.

of the page or as endnotes at the end of each chapter or at the end of the book. Endnotes are less intrusive. Standard computer programs allow you to do this quite easily. The usual way of writing references from archives is to put the name of the archive first, then the document's reference number. Rather than endlessly writing out "The National Archives" or "Society of Genealogists", abbreviate them and put a list of the abbreviations at the beginning of the endnotes.

Books are referenced as author/editor, title (publisher/place of publication, date), page number, e.g. Silverthorne, Elizabeth (ed.) *Deposition Book of Richard Wyatt, J.P. 1767–1776* (Surrey Record Society 1978) p.15.

It is useful for future researchers to know which records you have already searched. If you have the space, it is helpful to list what you have consulted, even where nothing was found. Whether you decide to do this or not, you should list the books you read for background information, such as local histories, accounts of the development of an occupation or the history of a religious denomination.

PUBLISHING

There are a number of ways of getting your family history into print. You may find that you have enough material to make a full-length book, especially if you are writing up different branches of your family and they had eventful lives. Unless, however, you have exceptional ancestors, who had some effect on the times in which they lived, you will not find a commercial company that will pay to publish it. There are publishers whom you pay to produce books, but self-publishing is not an enterprise to be undertaken lightly: there are a lot of unscrupulous and expensive companies in this field.

The younger members of a wedding group may still be alive, and will have their memories of the day and of other people in the photograph.

Computer programs

There are desktop publishing (DTP) packages that will help you produce very professional-looking results, incorporating illustrations, which can be scanned in on your computer. You can do this from a very early stage in your research, perhaps sending out a newsletter to interested parties from time to time.

The simplest option, if you simply want to give copies to your relations, is to print out from your computer enough copies on both sides of the paper and put them into a binder bought from a stationery shop. If you want more copies than can be reasonably achieved like this, your local print shop will be able to photocopy and bind the pages, either with a plastic ring-binding, wire spiral binding or perfect-bound, where the pages are sealed along the edge with hot glue. Some will do this from a disc.

Somewhere between the two extremes of professionally produced hardback book and photocopied sheets lie the booklets produced by specialist printing companies. They manufacture short runs of stapled booklets from a computer disc and are worth considering if you want to make more than 25 copies, which is usually their minimum number. You may be able to get your family to contribute to the costs.

By whatever means you publish your family history, please be sure to deposit copies with the Society of Genealogists as well as your County or Local Record Office. If you produce a hardback book, the British Library and the other copyright libraries in the United Kingdom will also need copies, and you should get an ISBN number allocated for it.

FURTHER HELP

Titford, John *Writing and Publishing Your Family History* (FFHS)
Pascoe, L.C. (ed.) *Encyclopaedia of Dates and Events* (Headway/Hodder & Stoughton)

Timeline

Kings and Queens are shown in bold type. As well as knowing who was on the throne during your ancestors' lifetimes, it's useful to know what was happening in their worlds. Some of the more important, or interesting, events and inventions are given here but it should be remembered that they rarely had an immediate influence on people's lives. Additionally, inventions are seldom the result of one person's efforts but build on and incorporate previous achievements.

1066 William of Normandy (William the Conqueror) became King of England

The seal of William the Conqueror.

1067 Bayeux tapestry begun
1067 Tower of London begun
1073 Church courts no longer under Crown jurisdiction
1086 Domesday Book finished
1087 William II (William Rufus)
1096 First Crusade launched with the intention of bringing Jerusalem under Christian rule
1100 Henry I
1110 Miracle play in England first mentioned

1135 Stephen (nephew of Henry I)
1138 Matilda (daughter of Henry I) challenges Stephen for the throne, leading to civil war which lasts until 1147
1147 Second Crusade
1147 Geoffrey of Monmouth writes a history of Britain
1154 Henry II
1154 Nicholas Breakspear becomes first, and only, English Pope as Adrian IV (d. 1159)
1154 Anglo-Saxon Chronicle, account of events in England since 449, completed
1189 Richard I
1189 Third Crusade
1189 First mayor of London appointed
1199 John
1202 Fourth Crusade
1215 Magna Carta signed
1216 Henry III
1249 Roger Bacon wrote about explosives and may have invented gunpowder
1253 Linen manufactured in England
1272 Edward I
1300 Hallmarks used on silver assayed by the Goldsmiths' Company
1301 Edward (son of Edward I) created first English Prince of Wales
1303 Spectacles mentioned in a medical treatise
1307 Edward II
1327 Edward III
1348 Black Death (plague) entered Britain at Weymouth. Lasts until 1351: an estimated one-third of the population die of the disease

1361 Plague again appeared in Britain. There are recurrent outbreaks until the beginning of the 20th century
1362 *Piers Plowman*, ascribed to William Langland, one of the first works of literature written in English
1377 Richard II
1381 Peasants' Revolt in England, largely against the poll tax, defeated
1388 Chaucer's *Canterbury Tales* written, but never completed
1399 Henry IV: first King to address Parliament in English
1413 Henry V
1422 Henry VI
1461 Edward IV
1476 First printing press in Britain, brought from mainland Europe by William Caxton, produces Chaucer's *Canterbury Tales* and other works
1483 Edward V (reign lasted April–June)
1483 Richard III
1485 Henry VII
1488 Duke Humphrey's library, foundation of the Bodleian, established at Oxford
1493 Syphilis first described by the Italian Nicolo Leoniceno. Treatment, until the 20th century, was with mercury, whose side-effects were also hazardous
1508 First book printed in Scotland
1509 Henry VIII
1519 Cocoa beans brought from South America to Europe by Spanish explorers
1524 The use of hops in brewing beer introduced from Italy

Queen Elizabeth I's Great Seal of Ireland.

1535 First Bible in English printed in Germany

1546 First book printed in Welsh

1547 **Edward VI**

1549 The Book of Common Prayer issued

1553 **Jane (queen for nine days from proclamation to being deposed)**

1553 **Mary I**

1555 Persecution of Protestants, described in John Foxe's *Book of Martyrs* (published 1563), begins

1558 **Elizabeth I**

1563 The 39 Articles, foundation of the Anglican faith, formulated (revised 1571)

1564 The lead pencil invented in England

1576 First theatre in England opened in London by Richard Burbage. William Shakespeare (1564–1616) was among those who wrote for his company

1577 Francis Drake embarked on his round-the-world trip in the *Pelican* (renamed the *Golden Hind*). Returned 1581 bringing tobacco and potatoes

1590 First paper mill in England established at Dartford, Kent

1596 Water closets, designed by Sir John Harington, installed in the queen's palace. The idea didn't really catch on for the rest of the population until the 19th century

1603 **James I (James VI of Scotland)**

1605 The Gunpowder Plot to blow up Parliament discovered. Commemorated on 5th November every year since

1611 Authorized Version of the Bible published

1621 Slide rule invented by William Oughtred which, combined with Scotsman John Napier's logarithms, made mathematical calculation easier. Not superseded until the 20th century by electronic calculators

1625 **Charles I**

1628 William Harvey discovers the circulation of the blood

1649 **Commonwealth period. Oliver Cromwell Protector until 1658, succeeded by his son Richard Cromwell**

1659 Habeas Corpus Amendment Act required prisoners to be brought before a judge within a specified time period

1660 **Restoration of Charles II**

1665 Epidemic of plague in London

1666 Great Fire of London

1685 **James II**

1688 **William III and Mary II**

1696 First insurance company in England founded

1698 Thomas Savery constructed first practical engine to harness steam power

1701 Jethro Tull invented the first horse-drawn drill to sow seeds

1701 Act of Settlement introduced (among other measures) the paying of salaries to judges and the provision that they could only be removed with the agreement of both Houses of Parliament, making them more independent

1702 **Anne**

1707 Denis Papin of France constructed the first steamboat

1709 First piano built by the Italian Bartolomeo Cristofori

1709 Abraham Darby used coke to power blast furnaces, making the production of iron and steel more efficient, thus paving the way for the Industrial Revolution

1714 **George I**

1727 **George II**

1730 Viscount Townshend begins experiments on improving agricultural crops by using fertilization

1760 **George III**

1769 Paper patterns for dressmaking

London is consumed by flames in the Great Fire of 1666.

invented by the Frenchman F.A. de Garsault

1783 First balloon flight by the Montgolfier brothers in France

1786 Experiments on gas-lighting carried out

1796 Edward Jenner given the credit for discovering that inoculation with cowpox protected against smallpox (although its benefits had been recognized and used by non-medical men for some time)

Charles Darwin, 19th-century naturalist.

c.1800 Thomas Telford and John Macadam developed ways to improve the construction of roads

1803 New paper-making machine invented by Nicolas-Louis Robert of France allows paper to be produced ten times faster than the old handmade process

1805 Charles Stanhope, 3rd Earl Stanhope, develops method of stereotyping which allows printed material to be produced faster. Also improves the design of the printing press to increase efficiency

1814 Friedrich Konig harnesses steam power for printing

1820 **George IV**

1823 Charles Babbage devised a calculating machine that is the forerunner of computers

1825 Factory Act, first to regulate working conditions in factories

1826 Rev. Patrick Bell of Forfarshire produces a prototype of the first mechanical reaper

1830 **William IV**

1831 Cotton Mills Act introduces 12-hour working day for those under 18

1835 First photographic process to allow multiple copies invented by William Fox Talbot (although the principles of photography had been known since at least 1816)

1837 **Victoria**

1840 Rowland Hill introduces adhesive postage stamps in Britain

1843 Charles Goodyear of America invents vulcanization of rubber by adding sulphur to make it a stable material

1846 William Morton, the first person to use ether as an anaesthetic, extracted a tooth in Massachusetts, USA. Ether was soon used to perform surgical operations.

1859 Publication of Charles Darwin's *Origin of Species*, setting out his theories of evolution

1860 Cigarettes created by putting tobacco into paper tubes. Previously it was smoked in pipes

1865 Plastic invented by Alexander Parkes

1865 Joseph Lister recognized the importance of asepsis in medical treatment. Until now, although surgeons could perform invasive operations, patients frequently died of infections

1875 The first Public Health Act, which began the transfer of matters related to public health from national to local government

1876 Dr Charles Knowlton of America published *The Fruits of Philosophy*, the first book on contraception aimed at the general public, which caused great outrage. Although condoms were in use from at least the mid-17th century, they were mainly used to protect against venereal disease

1877 Thomas Edison invented the phonograph, forerunner of the gramophone

T. Edison, inventor of the phonograph.

1886 First linotype machine, employing hot metal to produce lines of type rather than using individual, pre-produced letters, used to print the *New York Tribune*

1888 Radio waves discovered by the German, Heinrich Hertz

1890s Sigmund Freud develops his theories of psychiatry in Germany

1895 The Lumiere brothers showed moving pictures in Paris

1895 Wilhelm Rontgen of Wurtzburg, Germany, discovered X-rays

1898 Pierre and Marie Curie discovered radium

1901 **Edward VII**

1901 The vacuum cleaner invented by Hubert Booth

1907 Introduction of probation for minor offences

1908 Creation of juvenile courts

1910 **George V**

1927 What is generally agreed to be the first talking picture, *The Jazz Singer*, made in America

1933 Gerhard Domagk of Germany discovers antibiotics

1936 **Edward VIII (from January–December)**

1936 **George VI**

1937 Work on modern computing begins in USA

1940 Radar developed for use in aerial warfare (heat was generated by the magentrons used and this realization contributed to the development of microwave ovens)

1947 Mobile phone developed in America

1947 Disposable nappy invented by Marion Donovan in America

1950 Credit card invented by Ralph Schneider of America

1952 **Elizabeth II**

1953 The structure of DNA discovered in Cambridge, England

1954 American Jonas Salk created a safe polio vaccine

1965 Abolition of the death penalty for murder in Britain

1967 First portable, electronic calculators made in America (though they wouldn't fit into anyone's pocket)

1969 The first internet, made possible by previous work done simultaneously in Britain and America, set up by the American Department of Defence

1975 Development of personal computers

1978 Louise Brown, the first baby to be produced by in vitro fertilization, born

ROYAL NAVY

England has always needed ships for defence, so the Navy's origins pre-date the Norman Conquest, and its history has a unique relevance.

1642 Permanent Navy structure established

1652 Creation of the post of "able" seaman, senior to and more experienced than the "ordinary" kind

1660 Samuel Pepys became Clerk of the Acts at the Navy Board. Between then and his resignation in 1689, by which time he had been promoted to Secretary of the Admiralty, he created an administrative system that lasted into the 19th century

1694 Foundation of Greenwich Hospital

1733 Royal Naval Academy founded (becomes Royal Naval College in 1806)

1755 Royal Marines transfer from Army to Navy control

1795 Issue of lemon juice to prevent scurvy introduced

1820 RN began surveying and mapping the seas

1824 First attempts to standardize uniforms

1825 Rum ration halved

1831 Beer ration abolished

1830 Gunnery School created

1835 Register of Seamen introduced

1840s Steam-powered ships introduced, requiring stokers to feed coal into the engines

1859 Royal Naval Reserve established

1871 Flogging in peacetime suspended (1879 suspended totally, but not actually abolished)

1873 Royal Naval College transferred to Greenwich

1880 Royal Naval Engineering College opened

1901 Submarines introduced

1903 Osborne section of the Royal Naval College opened on Isle of Wight

1918 Women's Royal Navy Service (WRNS) created

1937 Fleet Air Arm transferred from RAF to RN control

1963 First nuclear-powered submarine

1994 WRNS integrated into the RN

ROYAL AIR FORCE

With a much shorter timespan, the RAF still has its historical relevance to the family historian.

RAF records are well-kept and accessible.

1912 Royal Naval Air Service (RNAS) and Royal Flying Corps (RFC) established

1918 RNAS and RFC merged to form Royal Air Force (RAF)

1918 RAF Nursing Service created, becoming Princess Mary's RAF Nursing Service in 1923

1918 Women's Royal Air Force (WRAF) created, abolished 1920

1920 RAF College opened at Cranwell

1939 Women's Auxiliary Air Force (WAAF) created

1994 WAAF integrated into the RAF

Specialist museums and libraries

Museums and libraries can be a fruitful source of information for the family historian, either because they have information relating to an ancestor or because their holdings give information about his or her profession. The staff are usually very knowledgeable about people who have a particular interest in a subject or who are collecting biographical information.

MUSEUMS

Only the major museums have been mentioned throughout this book, but there are many other establishments, particularly local ones or those that recreate some aspect of the past, that might help family historians to understand more about their ancestors' lives.

The Rural History Centre

Until the mid-19th century, the majority of people lived in the countryside, and so most genealogists will have agricultural labourers among their ancestors. The Rural History Centre has a large collection of archives, photographs and objects where many organizations involved in agriculture have deposited their records. It contains material on Ireland as well as Britain, and has a museum. There are many other local museums that cover agriculture in their regions.

The Bank of England Museum

The Bank of England was founded by Royal Charter in 1694. Wills often mention money or stock held in the Bank of England, which you may be able to follow up in its archives. It also holds records relating to employees. It might also be worth investigating the archives of other old banks, such as Coutts or Hoares.

The National Portrait Gallery

In addition to its major collection of portraits and photographs of the famous, dating from medieval times to the present day, the National Portrait Gallery holds pictures of important Government officials.

LIBRARIES

Libraries may have more than books and documents in their collections, especially if they have been given family or estate papers, which might include portraits or photographs.

Copyright libraries

There are five copyright libraries to which a copy of each book published since 1911 in the British Isles must be sent. They also house historic collections of books. The libraries are:

Bodleian (Oxford)
British Library (London)
National Library of Scotland (Edinburgh)
National Library of Wales (Aberystwyth)
Trinity College (Dublin)

The British Library

The British Library holds a vast range of manuscripts and documents, including private papers deposited by families. It contains the Oriental and India Office Collection and the National Sound Archive. The Newspaper Library is a division based at Colindale in north-west London.

The Wellcome Institute for the History of Medicine Library

Although this is mainly an academic library covering medicine all over the world, the family historian may find forebears here, either because they wrote a book or article on some aspect of medicine or because they are mentioned in the papers of individuals or organizations held there. The library also has an extensive iconographic collection, although there are relatively few pictures of individual medical practitioners. A reader's ticket is necessary, but it can be issued there with proof of identity.

FURTHER HELP

Museumnet www.museums.co.uk is a website giving details of and links to museums all over the country.
Aslib, Staple Hall, Stone House Court, London ECD3 7PB www.aslib.co.uk This is the Association for Information Management. Its directory lists libraries, including those inside companies and other organizations.
Rural History Centre, University of Reading, Whiteknights, PO Box 229, Reading, Berkshire RG6 6AG

www.reading.ac.uk/Instits/im/index.html
Bank of England Museum, Threadneedle Street, London EC2R 8AH www.bankofengland.co.uk
National Portrait Gallery, St Martin's Place, London WC2H 0HE
Wellcome Institute for the History of Medicine Library, The Wellcome Building, 183 Euston Road, London NW1 2BE www.wellcome.ac.uk/library

Directories and ratebooks

Directories and ratebooks are particularly helpful to family historians researching people in cities (especially London) and towns because they help to locate an individual. County directories also provide information about those living in villages and rural areas. They were not official publications but were produced as commercial ventures by a number of different publishers.

DIRECTORIES

The first directories were produced for the City of London in the mid-17th century, and thereafter their numbers increased. The biggest growth was from the mid-19th century, when they included private residents, not just businesses. Not everyone living at an address is listed: only the main householder's name is given, and his or her tenants are not included. The best-known publishers were Kelly's Directories and Pigot & Co.

County directories

These were published from the mid-19th century. As well as Kelly's and Pigot & Co.'s publications, many local firms produced directories of their counties or areas. They have descriptions of the towns and villages in them, and list the gentry and tradesmen and women, giving the street in which they lived. The poor are not included. The information that the publishers gave about the towns and villages can also be useful in building up a picture of your ancestors' lives. Dates of fairs, for example, may be given, and the times that mail and other coaches left, with the route taken, are usually included.

A page taken from the 1893 edition of Kelly's Directory.

Trade directories

Trade associations have been producing yearbooks for their section of industry since the late 19th century. These list companies involved in a particular area of commerce and may also carry advertisements. They will also list the members of their associations.

Using directories

Directories are mainly of use to discover your ancestor's occupation. Using a directory with a map can help you to discover in which parish in which city or town your ancestor lived at a particular time, and this will help you to locate other records that may give further information.

RATEBOOKS

Rates were based on the value of a property. The parish and, later, local authorities decided how much money they needed to collect from each householder in order to provide their services, and set the rate accordingly as a proportion of the property's nominal value. This system lasted until the end of the 20th century. In the early period, separate rates were collected to pay for highway maintenance, supporting the poor, etc., but later a general rate to cover all services was collected. Surviving ratebooks will be found in CROs.

Using ratebooks

Combined with a map, ratebooks can make it possible to work out in which house your ancestor lived before the advent of house numbering. Numbers, when given, tend to follow the route taken by the person collecting the rates.

The amount collected will indicate the size of your ancestor's property and thus give an indication of his or her level of wealth.

The franchise (right to vote) was based on property: an ancestor who paid rates on a property valued above a certain level would be entitled to vote in local and national elections.

By checking ratebooks over a number of years, you can get an idea of when your ancestor either left a place or died, which will suggest further avenues of research.

FURTHER HELP

Facsimile editions of various directories have been published both as books and on CD-ROMs.

Books

In order to know more about how people in the past lived, family historians also need to have some knowledge of social, political and economic history. Novels can give some understanding of how people thought and behaved but fiction is usually about exceptional characters and events. Modern historical novels also tend to impose twentieth century beliefs and actions on the past, but this is to distort what really happened. Academic theses are less about what actually happened and more about interpretations of events, which, though interesting, rarely contain the kind of detail the family historian requires. The following books are of necessity a personal selection but they are a good starting point. Some of the older texts appear in editions published by more than one company. Note also that books may be published by different companies overseas.

If you have schoolchildren in your family, their textbooks can provide a handy introduction to political and social history. If not, any bookshop will have many general histories of Britain and of particular periods. It's just a question of browsing until you find one whose style of writing and choice of material is interesting and easy to read. You should also be able to find local histories in bookshops where your ancestors lived.

Diaries, letters and autobiographies give an insight into how people thought and organized their lives but they were mainly written by the literate and by those with time to write. *The Faber Book of Diaries*, edited by Simon Brett and published by Faber

& Faber, contains a list of diarists from the 17th to the 20th centuries that are worth following up. In the 1970s there was a fashion for accounts of the lives of the ordinary working classes, but most of these are now out of print. They are worth tracking down through libraries and second-hand bookshops. Alan Ereira's *The People's England* (Routledge & Kegan Paul) draws on autobiographical material.

GENERAL FAMILY HISTORY BOOKS

Bevan, Amanda *Tracing your ancestors in the Public Record Office* (TNA)

Bristow, Joy *The Local Historian's Glossary of Words & Terms* (Countryside Books)

Cox, Jane *New to Kew?: A First Time Guide for Family Historians at the Public Record Office* (TNA)

FitzHugh, Terrick V. H. *The Dictionary of Genealogy* (SoG)

EVERYDAY LIFE THROUGH THE CENTURIES

Black, Jeremy *Historical Atlas of Britain* (Sutton Publishing)

Burnett, John *A History of the Cost of Living* (Penguin)

Drummond, J.C. & Wilbraham, Anne *The Englishman's Food* (Pimlico)

Giroud, Mark *Life in the English Country House* (Yale University Press)

Laver, James *A Concise History of Costume* (Thames & Hudson)

Litton, Julian *The English Way of Death* (Robert Hale)

Nicholson, Graham & Fawcett, Jane *The Village in History* (Guild Publishing)

Porter, Roy & Hall, Lesley *The Facts of Life: the creation of sexual knowledge in Britain 1650–1950* (Yale University Press)

Trevelyan, G.M. *English Social History* (Longman)

19TH AND 20TH CENTURIES

Adburgham, Alison *Shops and Shopping 1800–1914* (Allen & Unwin)

Horn, Pamela *Pleasure and Pastimes in Victorian Britain* (Sutton Publishing)

Mingay, G.E. *Rural Life in Victorian England* (Sutton Publishing)

Reeves, Maud Pember *Round About a Pound a Week* (Virago) Originally published in 1912, this was a study of working class family life in London.

Stevenson, John *British Society 1914–45* (Penguin)

17TH AND 18TH CENTURIES

Hufton, Olwen *The Prospect Before Her: A History of Women in Western Europe 1500–1800* (Harper Collins)

Hunt, Tristram *The English Civil War at First Hand* (Weidenfeld & Nicholson)

Picard, Liza *Restoration London* and *Dr Johnson's London* (Weidenfeld & Nicholson)

TUDOR AND MEDIEVAL HISTORY

Coss, Peter *The Lady in Medieval England 1000–1500* and *The Knight in Medieval England 1000–1400* (Sutton Publishing)

Leyser, Henrietta *The Medieval Woman* (Phoenix)

Reeves, Compton *Pleasures and Pastimes in Medieval England* (Sutton Publishing)

Sim, Alison *Pleasures and Pastimes in Tudor England* (Sutton Publishing)

Ziegler, Philip *The Black Death* (Penguin)

OTHER COUNTRIES IN THE UNITED KINGDOM

Craig, Patricia (ed.) *The Oxford Book of Ireland* (Oxford University Press)

Cruikshank, Charles *The German Occupation of the Channel Islands* (Berlinn)

Daitches, David (ed.) *A Companion to Scottish Culture* (Edward Arnold)

Dodd, A.H. *A Short History of Wales* (Batsford)

Lempriere, Raoul *History of the Channel Islands* (Robert Hale)

Pakenham, Valerie *The Big House in Ireland* (Cassell)

Smout, T. Christopher *A History of the Scottish People 1560–1830* and *A Century of the Scottish People 1830–1950* (Collins)

Woodham Smith, Cecil *The Great Hunger: Ireland 1845–1849* (Penguin)

WORKING LIVES

The following books can be supplemented by histories of the development of individual professions or trades:

Horn, Pamela *The Rise and Fall of the Victorian Servant* (Sutton Publishing)

Mayhew, Henry *London Labour and the London Poor* (various editions)

Porter, Roy (ed.) *The Illustrated Cambridge History of Medicine* (Cambridge University Press)

Thompson, E.P. *The Making of the English Working Class* (Penguin)

Background reading will help you to obtain a picture of the period in which your ancestors were living.

CRIME AND PUNISHMENT

The Newgate Calendars (various editions) contain the stories of major criminals executed at Newgate

Chesney, Kellow *The Victorian Underworld* (Penguin)

Hughes, Robert *The Fatal Shore* (Harvill) is a history of transportation to Australia

Low, Donald A. *The Regency Underworld* (Sutton Publishing)

Priestley, Philip *Victorian Prison Lives* (Pimlico)

Rees, Siân *The Floating Brothel* (Headline) tells the story of a ship that transported a group of women convicts to Australia

Salgado, Gamini *The Elizabethan Underworld* (Sutton Publishing)

FOR CROWN AND COUNTRY

Boardman, Andrew W. *The Medieval Soldier* (Sutton Publishing)

Bowyer, Chas *The Royal Air Force 1939–1945* (Pen & Sword)

Chandler, David (ed.) *The Oxford Illustrated History of the British Army* (Oxford University Press)

Hill, J.R. (ed) *The Oxford Illustrated History of the British Navy* (Oxford University Press)

Holmes, Richard *Redcoat: The British Soldier in the Age of Horse and Musket* (HarperCollins)

Padfield, Peter *The Rule Britannia Victorian and Edwardian Navy* (Pimlico)

Rodger, N.A.M. *The Wooden World: An Anatomy of the Georgian Navy* (Collins)

Sharpe, Michael *The History of the Royal Air Force* (Parragon)

THE BRITISH OVERSEAS

Lawson, Philip *The East India Company: a history* (Longman)

Morris, Jan *The Pax Britannica trilogy* (Heaven's Command, Pax Britannica, Farewell the Trumpets) (Faber & Faber) describes the rise and fall of the British Empire

Trollope, Joanna *Britannia's Daughters: Women of the British Empire* (Hutchinson)

IMMIGRANTS

Endelman, Todd M. *The Jews of Britain 1650–2000* (California University Press)

Fryer, Peter *Staying Power* (Pluto Press)

Gwynn, Robin *Huguenot Heritage* (Sussex Academic Press)

Katz, David S. *The Jews in the History of England 1485–1850* (Oxford University Press)

Merriman, Nick (ed.) *The Peopling of London* (Museum of London)

Visram, Rosina *Asians in Britain: 400 years of history* (Pluto Press)

Addresses and websites

Unless otherwise stated, all places are in the United Kingdom.

Army Personnel Centre, Disclosure 2, Mailpoint 515, Kentigern House, 65 Brown Street, Glasgow G2 8EX www.veteransagency.mod.uk/servicerecs/army

Bodleian Library, Broad Street, Oxford OX1 3BG www.bodley.ox.ac.uk

Borthwick Institute of Historical Research, University of York, St Anthony's Hall, Peasholme Green, York, YO1 2PW www.york.ac.uk/inst/bihr

British Library, 96 Euston Road, London NW1 2DB www.bl.uk

British Library Newspaper Library, Colindale Avenue, London NW9 5HE www.bl.uk/collections/newspapers

Church of Jesus Christ of Latter-day Saints, Family History Library, 35 North West Temple Street, Salt Lake City, Utah, 84150-3400 www.familysearch.org

College of Arms, Queen Victoria Street, London EC4V 4BT www.college-of-arms.gov.uk

Family Record Centre, 1 Myddelton Street, London EC1R 1UW www.pro.gov.uk

Federation of Family History Societies, PO Box 8584, Shirley, Solihull B90 4JU www.fhs.org.uk

General Register Office for Scotland, New Register House, Edinburgh EH1 3YT www.open.gov.uk/gros/

General Register Office (Northern Ireland), Oxford House, 49–55 Chichester Street, Belfast BT1 4HL www.nics.gov.uk/nisra/gro/

The interior of a Family Record Centre.

General Register Office, Joyce House, 8–11 Lombard Street, Dublin 2, Republic of Ireland www.groireland.ie

Guildhall Library, Aldermanbury, London EC2P 2EJ www.ihrinfo.ac.uk/gh

House of Lords Record Office, London SW1A 0PW www.parliament.uk

Institute of Heraldic and Genealogical Studies, 79–82 Northgate, Canterbury CT1 1BA www.ihgs.ac.uk

Irish Manuscripts Commission, 73 Merrion Square, Dublin 2, Republic of Ireland www.irmss.i.e/

Ministry of Defence, CS(R)2, Bourne Avenue, Hayes, Middlesex UB3 1RF

National Archives of Ireland, Bishop Street, Dublin 8, Republic of Ireland www.nationalarchives.ie

National Archives of Scotland, HM General Register House, Edinburgh RH1 3YY www.nas.gov.uk

National Library of Wales, Aberystwyth, Ceredigion SY23 3BU www.llgc.org.uk

Oriental and India Office Collections, British Library, 96 Euston Road, London NW1 2DB www.bl.uk/collections/oriental

Public Record Office for Northern Ireland, 66 Balmoral Avenue, Belfast BT9 6NY www.proni.nics.gov.uk

Scottish Association of Family History Societies, 51/3 Mortonhall Road, Edinburgh EH9 2HN www.safhs.org.uk

Scottish Genealogy Society, 15 Victoria Terrace, Edinburgh EH1 2JL www.scotsgenealogy.com/

Society of Genealogists, 14 Charterhouse Buildings, Goswell Road, London EC1M 7BA www.sog.org.uk

The National Archives, Kew, Richmond, Surrey TW9 4DU

www.nationalarchives.gov.uk
This office was formed from the amalgamation of the Public Record Office and the Historical Manuscripts Commission.

If you need a researcher to do work for you, the following professional associations can supply lists of their members.

Association of Genealogists and Record Agents, 29 Badgers Close, Horsham, West Sussex RH12 5RU www.agra.org.uk/

Association of Scottish Genealogists and Records Agents, PO Box 174,

Edinburgh EH3 5QZ

Association of Professional Genealogists in Ireland, 30 Harlech Crescent, Clonskeagh, Dublin 4, Republic of Ireland http//indigo. ie/~apgi

Picture Acknowledgements

All photographs other than those listed below are copyrighted to Anness Publishing Ltd.

Reproduced by kind permission of:
(l = left, r = right, m = middle,
t = top, b = bottom)
AKG London: p3 m; p184; p191; p208 b; p211 b; p214 b; p218; p221 tl.
Hugh Alexander: p34; p38 t; p42 t; p58; p60 t; p 241 b; p252.
The Art Archive: p 202; p204 b; p208 t/Domenica del Corriere/Dagli Orti; p209 tr; p216 t; p222 t; p223 t/Geographical Society, Paris/Dagli Orti.
The Bridgeman Art Library: p21 br/Mallett & Son Antiques, UK; p31/Bristol City Museum and Art Gallery, UK; p49/Christie's Images, UK; p55/Private Collection; p67 b/Victoria & Albert Museum, UK; p72/Private Collection; p74/British Library; p76/Private Collection; p79 tr/Royal Geographical Society, London; p82 b/John Bethell; p104/Guildhall Library; p106/Private Collection; p114/Birmingham Museums and Art Gallery; p162 bl/Private Collection; p164/New Walk Museum, Leicester; p176 bl/Whitworth Art Gallery, br/Bradford Art Galleries and Museums; p199 t/Private Collection; p200; p210/Hudson Bay Company, Canada; p227/Fitzwilliam Museum, Cambridge.
The British Library: p60 b.
The Church of Jesus Christ of Latter-day Saints: p 40 t, bl, br, p41 t, p44
© 1999-2002 by Intellectual Reserve, Inc. Some material in this publication is reprinted by permission of The Church of Jesus Christ of Latter-day Saints. In granting this permission for the use of copyrighted material, the Church does not imply endorsement or authorization of this publication.
Corbis: p61 © Hulton-Deutsch Collection; p82 t; p83; p88; p91; p92 t; p152 © Burstein Collection; p193t © Christie's Images; p212 t © Hulton-Deutsch Collection, b; p213 © Hulton-Deutsch Collection; p214 t © Bettmann; p215 tr © Horace Bristol.
Mary Evans Picture Library: p4, p11 tr; p52; p63 t; p64 tr, tl; p73 b; p75 t; p92 b; p93; p120; p124; p131 bl, br; p142 b; p144 t; p163; p166; p190 t; p192; p204 t; p209 tl; p211 t; p216 b; p222 b.
Getty Images: p115.
Greater Manchester County Record Office: p 59 tl, tr; p229.
Robert Harding Picture Library Ltd: p26 t, b.
ISI: p1; p2 tr, mr, br; p3 r; p5; p6 l; p7 tl, tr, b; pp8/9; p11 tl, m, b; p13 tr, b; p14; p15 bl; p16 t; p17 t; p19 t; p23; p24; p35 t; p36 t, b; p37 t; p43 b; p54 t; pp56/57; p62; p63 b; p66; p67 t; p68 b; p69 t, b; p73 t; p75 b; p77; p78 bl; pp80/81; p89; p90; p94 t, b; pp96/97; p98 t, b; p99 t; p100 bl, br; p105, p108 tl, tr; p109 bl; p111 t, b; p112 t; p116; p118 t, b; p122; p123 t, b; p125; pp126/127; p128; p131 t; p134 t, b; p136; p137; p138; p140; p142 t; p146; pp148/149; p150 t, b; p151; p156 l, r; p157 t, b; p158; p159 l, r; p160; p162 br; p164; p165; p168 b; p169; p170; p171, p172, p174 t; p177; pp178/179; p182; p183; p186; p190 b; p193 t; p194; p195 tr; pp196/197; p198; p201 t, b; p205 t, b; p215 tl; p219 t, b; pp224/225; p226; p228; p240; p244; p245 t, b; p246 l, r.
Manx National Heritage Library: p95 t, b.
The National Archives Image Library: p2 tl, bl; p6 r; p10; p13 tl; p20; p21 bl; pp28/29; p30 t; p33, p35 b; p37 b; p38 b; p39; p48; p50; p54 br, bl; p68 t; p70; p71; p78 br; p79 tl; p102; p107; p109 br; p110 bl, br; p112 b; p113; p119; p121; p129 b; p141; p144 b; p145; p153; p154; p167; p168 t; p174 b; p175 t, m; p180; p181; p188 b; p195 tl; p199 b; p203; p217 t, b; p220; p221 tr, b; pp230/231; p249.
National Archives of Scotland: p 84; p85; p86; p87.
The National Library of Wales: p 223 b.
Office for National Statistics: p30 b/Crown ©/reproduced with the permission of the Controller of HMSO and Queen's Printer for Scotland.
Science and Society Picture Library: p129 t/Daily Herald Archive/NMPFT; p133/Kodak/NMPFT; p135/DHA/NMPFT; p143/Daily Herald Archive/NMPFT; p161/National Museum of Photography, Film & TV; p189 bl, br/DHA/NMPFT.
Wellcome Library, London: © p188 t.

Thanks to Mr and Mrs T J Sudell, Melanie Halton and Michael Morey for the use of their family photographs.
Web pages reproduced with the permission of: Origins.net, GENUKI, RootsWeb.com, Ancestry.com, GOONS, Society of Geneaologists. Familysearch.org © 1999-2002 by Intellectual Reserve, Inc.

Index

abbreviations in family charts 19
addresses of organizations 252
administrations 48, 49, 50–1
adoption 34, 73
Africa
  emigrants 218–19
  migrants 188–89
  slaves 162, 188, 212
Ancestral File 41
Ancient Order of Foresters 119
apothecaries 108
appeal courts 151, 152
apprenticeships 102–3, 139, 145, 146
Arab migrants 192
armed forces 128–130
armorial bearings 85, 228, 236–8
Army 34, 128, 131–3, 228
assizes 83, 157
attorneys 107
Australia
  emigrants 199, 214–15
  transportation of criminals 162, 163,
    198, 214

Bank of England Museum 248
bankruptcy 120–1
baptism records 62, 65
barristers 107
beginning a family history 10–13
birth brief 18
birth certificates 30–1, 32, 33, 82, 84, 88
black migrants 188–9, 192
books, background information 250–1
boroughs 116, 227
bravery awards 112
British Library 35, 61, 79, 113, 158, 229,
  243, 248, 252
  Newspaper Library 54, 55, 61
buildings in photographs 15
Bunhill Fields cemetery, London 76
burials 62, 63, 65

Canadian emigrants 199, 210–11
Caribbean 188
  emigrants 198, 212–13
  migrants 189
  slaves 162, 212, 213
censuses 33, 36–9, 90
Channel Islands 92–3, 184

charities 23
charts 16–19
China
  emigrants 199
  migrants 192–3
Church of England 23, 62, 74, 76, 226
  administrative structure 63
  clergymen 106–7
  courts 48, 150, 152–3
  role 66
  see also Diocesan Record Offices;
    parish
Church of Jesus Christ of Latter-day
  Saints (LDS) 24, 37, 40, 41, 46,
    84–5, 95, 165, 213, 252
City Record Offices (CROs) 60
class and social status 176
clergymen 106–7
clothes in photographs 14–15
Coastguard 175
Commonwealth War Graves
  Commission 129
company archives 112–13
computers 25, 243
concentric tree 19
conscientious objectors 128
convicts 159, 162–3, 214, 216
coroner 52, 53
county

directories 249
elections 117
name changes 234, 235
County Record Offices (CROs) 12, 13,
  55, 59, 71
Court of King's/Queen's Bench 151, 153,
  158–9, 165, 228
courts 150–1
  appeal 151, 152
  Church 48, 150, 152–3
  criminal 86, 156–60
  equity 164–5
  manorial 154–5
  Scotland 86
cousinship 17, 51
crime 23, 156–161, 176, 228
criminal courts 86, 151, 156–60
criminals, transportation of 162–3,
  198, 214
Customs and Excise 174–5

dates, changes and variations 239
day books 65
death certificates 31, 32, 33, 35, 82, 84, 88
death duties 51
decorative charts 19
dentists 109
Diocesan Record Offices (DROs) 13, 49,
  59, 65, 67, 78, 106, 109, 153, 227
directories 240, 249
District Record Offices 60
divorce 31, 34, 152, 153
dockyards, naval 140
Dr Barnardo's Homes 73, 200
Dr Williams's Library 75, 100
drop-line chart 16–17
Duchies 228
Dutch migrants 186, 187

East India Company 128, 192, 201,
  202, 203
education 98–101
elections 116–17
electoral registers 117
emigrants 198–223
equity law 164–5

Family History Societies (FHS) 38, 41,
  42–3, 47, 137

Family Record Centre (FRC) 12, 29, 32, 34–5, 38, 252
family tree, drawing up 16–19
Far Eastern emigrants 49, 198, 201–3, 221
Federation of Family History Societies (FFHS) 37, 42–3, 252
filing system 24–5
firefighters 112
Foundling Hospital, London 72–3
foundlings 72–3
France
    emigrants 222
    migrants 93, 184–5
franchise 116, 117
freemen 104, 105
Friendly Societies 118, 119

gaps in information 22
General Register Office (GRO) 30, 33, 252
Germany
    emigrants 222
    migrants 186–7
Gibson Guides 43
Greenwich Hospital 141
Guild of One-Name Studies (GOONS) 41
guilds 104–5, 145, 180, 227
    apprenticeships 102, 103, 145
Gypsies 194

handwriting styles 230–1
heraldry 236–8
Home Guard 137
hospitals 39, 109, 122–4
Huguenots 89, 92, 93, 180, 181, 184, 185, 187, 219

identification of ancestor system 24
illegitimacy 11, 31, 32, 64, 68, 70
illness 122–5
immigrants 180–93
income 176–7, 241
Independent Order of Oddfellows 119
India
    emigrants 49, 198, 201–3
    migrants 190–1
inheritance 82, 85, 86, 155, 169
inquests 52–3
Inquisitions Post Mortem 227
insolvency 121
Institute of Heraldic and Genealogical Studies (IHGS) 42
insurance 170
International Committee of the Red

Cross 129, 130
International Genealogical Index (IGI) 40–1, 43, 46, 95, 213, 239
internet 44–5
    genealogical sites 46–7
    publishing on 45
internment of civilians 129, 130
interviewing techniques 26–7
Ireland 184, 236
    records 47, 88–91
    surnames 21
Isle of Man 94–5, 129, 130, 142
Italian migrants 193
itinerants 115, 194–5

Jews 30, 76, 182–3, 220

land
    equity courts 164–5
    ownership 166–71, 226
    taxes 172–3
    tenure 155
    transfer 166–9
Latin, use of 232–3
law 23, 107, 150
    Ireland 89
    Latin documents 232–3
    Scotland 86
    see also courts
libraries 58, 60–1, 248
licences, occupations 114–15
life expectancy 146
lifeboats 145
lifetime, events in 146–7
lightermen 145

lighthouses 145
Lloyd's of London 143
local history centres 60
local studies libraries 60–1
London, research starting point 12–13
London Gazette 54, 121, 128, 169
London Metropolitan Archives (LMA) 73, 158, 183
lunatics 124–5, 160, 202

manorial records 154–5
maps 78–9
marriage 146
    certificates 31, 32, 33, 82, 84, 88
    invalid 153
    licences 65
    parish registers 62
    property 169
    regular and irregular 64
measurements 239
medical profession 108–9, 248
Mediterranean emigrants 220
mental illness 124–5
Merchant Navy 34, 35, 95, 142–3, 144
Methodists 55, 74, 75, 212
Middle East 192, 220
midwives 109
migrant ancestors 180–93
militia 136, 137
money 239, 248
    equity courts 164–5
    social status 171, 176
museums 248
myths in family history 11

names 20–1
    alternative first 32
    change of 169
    choice of to research 12
    county changes 234
    distribution of 228–9
    patterns 20
    Scottish family 84
    Welsh family 83
narrative indented tree 18
National Archives, The (TNA)
    see The National Archives
National Portrait Gallery 248
New Zealand emigrants 199, 216–17
newspapers 23, 54–55, 240
nicknames 21
Nonconformists 30, 41, 47, 63, 65, 74, 75, 76, 85, 87, 101, 107, 152, 212
    chronological history 234–5
nurses 109

occupations 110–13, 226, 240
licences 114–15
surnames 20
orphans 51, 66, 72–3
apprenticeships 103
emigrants 199–200

Pacific Islands 221
Palatinates 228
paleography 230–1
parish 62
officials 66
poor 66, 68–71
rates 67, 249
records 66–7, 240
registers 41, 47, 62–5, 233, 226;
Ireland 88, Scotland 84, Wales 82
tithes 67
Parliamentary elections 116–7
patronymics 21, 83
performers 194–5
periodicals 23, 43, 55
petty sessions 156–7
photographs 14–15
physicians 108
pilots, ships' 145
police 110–11
poll books 117
Poor law 68–71, 83, 86
apprenticeships 102, 103
Portugal 222–3
posse comitatis 136, 137
Post Office 112
pre-1538 research sources 226–9
Prerogative Court of Canterbury (PCC)
47, 50, 89, 203, 213, 227
Prerogative Court of York (PCY) 49
press gangs 140
prisoners of war 129
prisons 39, 121, 159, 160–1, 176
Probate Service 48, 49
property 164–71
Public Records Office (PRO)
see The National Archives
publications 42–3, 250–1
publishing your family history 243
punishments 152, 160

Quakers 30, 74, 76, 205
quarter sessions 78–9, 157
questioning techniques 26–7
railways 112
rates 67, 249
record-keeping 10, 22, 24–5, 240
Register General of Shipping and

Seamen 34
Religious Society of Friends see Quakers
research skills 12–13, 22, 58, 61, 240
Rhodesia 219
rich and poor 176, 177
Roman Catholicism 30, 62, 64, 74, 75,
77, 85, 87, 88, 100, 233
chronological history 235
Royal Air Force (RAF) 128, 134–5, 247
Royal Marines 138–9
Royal Navy 34, 128, 138–9, 144, 247
Rural History Centre 248
Russian emigrants 223

schools 98–100
Scotland 65, 145, 166, 184, 234
armorial bearings 85, 236, 238
names 21, 84
records 47, 84-7
servants 110
settlement and removal orders 68–70
ships 34, 138, 139, 142, 145, 151
slaves 162, 188, 189, 212, 213
Society of Genealogists (SoG) 12, 24, 42,
43, 47, 103, 121, 165, 200, 238
software packages 25, 243
solicitors 107
South Africa 163, 219
South American emigrants 199, 223
South Atlantic Islands 221
South Pacific Islands 215
suicide 53
Superintendent Registrars 33
surgeons 108

surnames 20–1, 32, 33, 41,
228, 229

Tasmania 163, 214
taxes 172–3, 226, 227, 228
telephone directories 23
tertiary education 100–1
The National Archives (TNA) 12, 42,
58–9
The Times 54–5, 121
timeline 244–7
tithes 67
maps 78
town record offices 60
trade unions 118–19
Trades Union Congress (TUC) 118–19
transportation of criminals 162–3,
198, 214
treasure-trove 53
Trinity House 144, 145

United States of America 50, 162,
163, 188
emigrants 198, 199, 204–9
migrants 192
universities 100–1
libraries 61

Vital Records Index 41
voluntary forces 136, 137
vote 116, 117

Wales 228
county name changes 235
parish registers 62
records 82–83
surnames 21
watermen, London 145
websites 44, 46–7, 252–3
Wellcome Institute for the History of
Medicine Library 124, 248
West Indies 162, 188
emigrants 198, 212–13
migrants 189
wills 47, 48–51, 82, 89, 150, 152, 155,
166, 213, 227, 248
workhouses 39, 69, 70, 72, 109, 119,
122, 124
World War I 34, 35, 93, 95, 128, 129,
132, 135, 139, 181, 186, 187, 189,
191, 192, 211
World War II 35, 92, 95, 128, 129, 130,
135, 137, 139, 145, 183, 189, 191,
192, 193, 211
writing up family history 240–3

NOTES

NOTES

NOTES

NOTES

NOTES

NOTES

NOTES